D0906074

Youth

and the
LABOR
MARKET

ANALYSES OF THE
NATIONAL LONGITUDINAL SURVEY

Michael E. Borus
Editor

Institute of Management
and Labor Relations
Rutgers University

1984

The W. E. Upjohn Institute for Employment Research

Library of Congress Cataloging in Publication Data

Main entry under title:

Youth and the labor market.

Includes bibliographical references.
1. Youth—Employment—United States—Longitudinal
studies. 2. High school graduates—Employment—United
States—Longitudinal studies. I. Borus, Michael E.
II. National Longitudinal Surveys of Labor Market
Experience (U.S.)
HD6273.Y648   1984   331.3'412'0973   84-2367
ISBN 0-88099-015-5
ISBN 0-88099-016-3 (pbk.)

THE INSTITUTE, a nonprofit research organization, was established
on July 1, 1945. It is an activity of the W. E. Upjohn Unemployment
Trustee Corporation, which was formed in 1932 to administer a fund set
aside by the late Dr. W. E. Upjohn for the purpose of carrying on
"research into the causes and effects of unemployment and measures for
the alleviation of unemployment."

iii

FOREWORD

Major issues confronting young people in the transition from home and school to the world of work are identified and analyzed in the papers presented in this volume. Changes in the labor market, educational choices, the quality of public and private schools, the effectiveness of academic and vocational education, and involvement in delinquency and the criminal justice system are highly relevant to the employment and unemployment experience of young people.

The National Longitudinal Surveys of Youth Labor Market Experience provide a uniquely rich data set for the analysis of these issues. Results of the analyses can add to the information available to policymakers who must deal with the labor market problems of youth.

Facts and observations expressed in the study are the sole responsibility of the authors. Their viewpoints do not necessarily represent positions of the W. E. Upjohn Institute for Employment Research.

Robert G. Spiegelman
Director

March 1984

AUTHORS

MICHAEL E. BORUS is professor of industrial relations and human resources in the Institute of Management and Labor Relations, Rutgers University. Between 1977 and 1983 he was director of the Center for Human Resource Research at The Ohio State University where he directed the National Longitudinal Surveys. Borus has been chairman of the National Council on Employment Policy on which he now serves and newsletter editor and executive board member of the Industrial Relations Research Association. He has served as a consultant on the evaluation of training programs for many foundations and government agencies; among his publications is *Measuring the Impact of Employment-Related Social Programs* published by the W. E. Upjohn Institute in 1979. Borus received his Ph.D. in economics from Yale University.

SUSAN A. CARPENTER received her MBA from The Ohio State University. Between 1978 and 1983 she was a research assistant working on the National Longitudinal Surveys at the Center for Human Resource Research, The Ohio State University.

JOAN E. CROWLEY received her Ph.D. in social psychology from the University of Michigan in 1978. She is currently employed as a senior research associate on the National Longitudinal Surveys of Labor Market Experience. Her previous research on the NLS includes evaluating the effectiveness of government employment and training programs and assessing the plans of young people for their future education and employment, as well as the relationship between employment and delinquency. At present, she is investigating the effects of life cycle transitions on alcohol use among young adults, and the effect of retirement on the life satisfaction of older men.

RONALD D'AMICO received his Ph.D. in 1978 from the Department of Social Relations at Johns Hopkins University. Since that time he has been employed on the research staff at the Center for Human Resource Research at The Ohio State University. In addition to time-use research, he has also investigated the causes and consequences of labor market structure, the interrelationship between husband's and wife's labor supply decisions, and the nature and consequences of high school employment for youth. He is currently continuing his analysis of labor market organization and is also involved in research on the problems in the school-to-work transition.

THOMAS DAYMONT received his Ph.D. from the University of Wisconsin and is currently assistant professor in the Department of Industrial Relations and Organizational Behavior at Temple University. Previously he was senior research associate at the Center for Human Resource Research at The Ohio State University. He has published on a variety of labor market topics including equal employment opportunity and the determinants of sex and race inequality. Other research interests include changes in productivity and labor market success over the career and the labor market behavior of older workers.

WILLIAM R. MORGAN has a Ph.D. in sociology from the University of Chicago. He has held academic positions at Indiana University, Bloomington, Bayero University, Nigeria, and The Ohio State University. His publications have appeared in the *American Sociological Review, American Journal of Sociology, Social Forces, Social Psychology Quarterly,* and *Sociology of Education.* As a research scientist at the Center for Human Resource Research, he has also served as associate director of the Center's Quality of Working Life research program. He is currently using the NLS data to study the labor market activity of high school dropouts and shifts in the supply of college students.

TOM K. POLLARD received a B.A. degree in economics from the University of Texas at Austin and a M.A. from the School of Labor and Industrial Relations at Michigan State University. After designing and administering manpower training projects for the Michigan Governor's Office of Manpower Planning during 1973 and 1974, he returned to the University of Texas at Austin, earning a Ph.D. in economics there in 1980. As a senior research associate at the Center for Human Resource Research at The Ohio State University he analyzed the National Longitudinal Survey. Tom is currently forecasting tax revenues, researching state labor market issues and constructing a regional econometric model for the Comptroller of Public Accounts of the State of Texas.

RUSSELL W. RUMBERGER is senior research associate and economist at the Institute for Research on Educational Finance and Governance, School of Education, Stanford University. He was formerly a senior research associate at the Center for Human Resource Research, The Ohio State University. Dr. Rumberger received his Ph.D. in the economics of education from Stanford University in 1978. His area of research includes education and work, the economics of education, labor economics, and education policy. He has published articles in scholarly journals of education, sociology, and economics. He has also published two books, *Overeducation in the U.S. Labor Market* (1981) and *A New Social Contract* (with Martin Carnoy and Derek Shearer, 1983).

ACKNOWLEDGMENTS

The National Longitudinal Surveys are sponsored primarily by the U.S. Department of Labor (DOL). We would like to thank Burt Barnow and Ellen Sehgal of the DOL Office of Research and Evaluation for their continuing support and encouragement. Chapter 2 was written at the invitation of Susan Sherman of the National Research Council; we thank her as well.

Our colleagues at the Center for Human Resource Research made many useful contributions to the analyses which appear here. Among them are Stephen Hills, Frank Mott, Gilbert Nestel, Herbert Parnes, Richard Santos, and Lois Shaw. We are also indebted to the many research assistants and computer programmers who worked on this volume; unfortunately, there are too many to identify by name. We also thank Phyllis Byard, Joyce Davenport, Sue Ellen Rumstay and Sherry Stoneman for typing the many drafts of the volume.

We are deeply in debt to Kezia Sproat and Anne Bertagnolli, whose editing changed government reports into an interesting book.

We want to thank Allan Hunt of the Upjohn Institute for his careful reading of this manuscript and advice on how to improve it.

Finally, this volume is dedicated to Patricia Shannon, whose death left all of us with a void that cannot be filled.

Contents

Chapter 1
Introduction and Summary
by Michael E. Borus

This volume contains analyses based on data from the 1979, 1980 and 1981 National Longitudinal Surveys of Youth Labor Market Experience. These data, collected for a nationally representative sample of 12,686 youth age 14-22 in 1979—of whom 12,141 and 12,195 were reinterviewed in 1980 and 1981, respectively—permit analysis of the changes in young peoples' lives as they move from an environment of family, home and school to a more independent life.[1] Early chapters show the employment situation of young people and how changes in the labor market may have affected employment and unemployment over the decade of the 1970s. The middle chapters discuss schooling decisions (in particular dropping out, returning to school and going to college), whether private or public schools are more effective, and whether vocational education is superior preparation for employment. Final chapters discuss how young people spend their time, which youth are involved in delinquency and the criminal justice system, and how such involvement may affect employment. The remainder of this chapter is a summary of all these findings.

Chapter 2 surveys the employment status in the Spring of 1981 of youth age 16 to 21. Multivariate analysis indicates that the incidence of unemployment, as shown by unemployment rates, is concentrated among certain groups of youth.

It was found for young women that the probability of being unemployed was higher for the young, for high school dropouts and graduates as compared with high school students, for black young women and those who resided in families where the income level was below the poverty line, those who had previously received government employment and training services and those living in their parental households. Unemployment was also higher in the Northeast, in urban areas, and in those areas where the unemployment rate was 12 percent or more. Among young men, the unemployment rate was higher among high school dropouts, among blacks and those in poverty, and among those youth living in their parental homes. However, unlike the case for females, male college students had lower probabilities of unemployment than high school students and very little difference in unemployment rates occurred by age. Young men in areas of unemployment between 9 and 11.9 percent had the highest rates of unemployment, as did those living in the North Central region, and for males receipt of government employment and training services was not associated with higher probabilities of being unemployed.

The majority of unemployed youth said that they were looking for work because they needed money. However, only 1 in 13 said they were looking for work to support themselves or to help with family expenses. The unemployed young people primarily made direct application to employers as their method of job search, although nearly a third checked local newspapers and between 10 and 20 percent used the public employment service, asked friends or relatives and placed or answered advertisements. About half were seeking full time work and a large proportion said that they would take any kind of work or could not identify a specific occupation. More than half of the youth said that they would take jobs at or below the minimum wage.

These data suggest questions about the seriousness of unemployment among many of these youth. To test this seriousness, we constructed an arbitrary definition of hard-core unemployed youth. This definition included 1 in 11 unemployed youth, or about 300,000. It was found that the hard-core unemployed tended to be older, more likely to have participated in training, to be married, to have children, to live in a central city of an SMSA, and to live in an area of high unemployment than was true of all unemployed youth.

In the Spring of 1981, approximately 56 percent of 16-to 21-year-olds were employed. The employment-to-population ratio rose with age, was lower for blacks than for Hispanics and whites, was considerably higher among high school graduates not enrolled in college than for college or high school students or high school dropouts and was considerably higher for men who had been married and lower for young women who were married and living with their husbands. The proportion of youth who were employed was highest in the West and Northeast and lowest in the South, and higher in urban than in rural areas. When a multivariate analysis was used, however, several differences appeared. Holding other factors constant, living in the South led to significantly more employment for males than those living in the North Central states. Residence in a rural area did not significantly influence the probability of employment, nor did living in the central city of an SMSA.

The jobs held by young people tended to be sex stereotyped. Young women were concentrated in clerical, service and sales jobs, while young men were employed in service jobs and as laborers, craftsmen and operatives. Of those young people who provided hourly rate of pay information, nearly one-fourth were working at jobs paying less than the minimum wage, and an additional 12 percent were working at the minimum wage. Over three-quarters of the jobs held by youth required educational levels below high school graduation and nearly half required no more than a short demonstration to learn. An additional one-fifth required less than 30 days on-the-job specific vocational training.

Chapter 3 investigates the relative employment positions of black and white young men in 1971 and 1979 who were out of school, 18-21 years old, and not in the military. The mean number of weeks of employment was dramatically lower for blacks in 1979 than in 1971. The proportions with no employment during the year or who worked 12 or less weeks increased much more for blacks than for whites. During 1971 the majority of blacks held multiple jobs, while the majority of whites held a single job; blacks showed relatively high turnover out of employment, with substantial periods of not working, but whites were more likely than blacks to hold a single job and to have less time between jobs if they did change employers. By 1979, however, blacks were more likely to have had but one employer, while among whites multiple job holding increased. Thus, over the decade employment declined somewhat among whites, apparently due to higher job turnover. On the other hand, the decline in black employment over the decade appears due to periods of lengthy joblessness among a growing subsample of the black population.

Multiple regression analysis was conducted in an attempt to explain these patterns. It was found that declines in marriage decreased the time that blacks were employed, and that shifts of blacks from the South to other parts of the country, and the growing number of blacks relative to whites living in SMSAs also contributed to lower black employment over the decade. On the other hand, changes in the distributions and effects of education and age between blacks and whites lessened the employment gap.

Most important, the regression analysis indicates that in 1971, lack of employment among blacks resulted from higher turnover and a stronger positive relationship between turnover and joblessness than existed for whites. In 1979, however, blacks had less turnover than whites and the relationship between number of employers and total employment was much weaker than in 1971. Thus, blacks did not gain from reduced turnover.

Further, as already noted, a substantial increase appeared in the number of blacks who had no employment during the year, along with a relative increase over the decade in the extent to which low employment in one year predicted low employment in the next year for blacks. Thus, one can conclude that the relative decline in employment was due to the relative concentration of joblessness among a group of black youth over the decade of the 1970s and not due to increased turnover and job search.

Three schooling decisions are studied in chapter 4: the decision to drop out of school without finishing the 12th grade, the decision to return to school after having dropped out, and the decision to go directly on to college after completing 12th grade. Black and Hispanic youth have higher dropout rates and lower probabilities of moving from high school directly to college than do whites, but these differences are not due to race and ethnicity; when family background, attitude and schooling variables are taken into account, minorities are no more likely than whites to drop out of school or not to continue on to college.

Coming from a poverty household and being unemployed while in school tend to raise the probability of dropping out, other factors held constant. The effects of these two variables are not large, however, and a reduction of less than one percentage point in the national dropout rate would result if there were no poverty and all youth were employed or not in the labor force. Although on average youth from poor families were less likely to attend college immediately following the 12th grade, this, too, was probably due to family background variables; when these were controlled, the differences between poor and nonpoor youth were not statistically significant.

School segregation did not affect either the dropout or college attendance probabilities significantly when other factors were controlled. This finding appears to indicate that integration efforts will not affect these two variables directly.

Participation in a college preparatory program is associated with lower dropout rates and higher college attendance. It is not possible, however, to say if placement of more students in college preparatory tracks would lead to reduced numbers of dropouts because self-selection may be involved.

Other school characteristics appear to have only limited influence on dropout and college attendance rates. The dropout rate was somewhat higher in schools with higher student-teacher ratios and less local government funds. Although lowering student-teacher ratios and increasing government expenditures on education would lead to some reduction in dropouts, the data suggest that the impact of these policies would not be very great.

Pregnancy is one of the major reasons teenagers drop out of school. Obviously, to the extent that childbearing is delayed until schooling is completed, educational attainment will be increased as will these young peoples' subsequent labor market success, which is correlated with high school graduation.

In 1981 Coleman, Hoffer and Kilgore published a study which concluded that public secondary schools provide an inferior education relative to private schools. Chapter 5 uses the NLS data, with its larger sample of schools, to test this conclusion. Two outcomes were measured: score on the Armed Forces Qualifications Test and educational expectations, using multivariate analyses to account for family background and other variables which might be correlated with choice of type of secondary school.

The results indicate that students in nonpublic schools were much more likely to be enrolled in college preparatory curricula and less likely to participate in vocational training, and it is the choice of curriculum that is crucial in determining the youths' achievement scores, not the type of school. Also, while there was a slight increase in expected education among students in Catholic schools, this was not the case for other private schools when curriculum was taken into account. Thus, the clear conclusion is that being in the college preparatory curriculum in either public or private secondary schools is much more critical than the type of school for maximizing the two educational outcomes.

Although taking college preparatory courses increased achievement and educational expectations equally for all three racial-ethnic groups, analyses conducted separately by race and ethnic background show some differences between public and private school students. Hispanics had higher achievement levels when in a private school, particularly in their scores on word knowledge and paragraph comprehension.

There are some nonachievement benefits to be derived from private school enrollment. Estimates of some quality of school life variables were higher for private school students: i.e., quality of class instruction, strictness of discipline, and, to a lesser extent, personal safety and friendship opportunities at school. Private school students, however, rated lower than public school students in their degree of learning freedom and opportunities for job counseling. Thus, except for Hispanics, beliefs about the superiority of private education should be restricted to the quality areas. Learning is not better in private schools.

Chapter 6 investigates the effects of high school curriculum on the labor market experience of young men and women who do not go on to college. For young women, an additional half year of academic or vocational courses increases hourly earnings by 3 percent, reduces unemployment by 1.5 weeks per year and increases annual hours worked by 150 hours. For young men, academic and vocational training do not affect hourly earnings, but both types of training reduce the number of weeks unemployed, and vocational training increases the number of hours worked annually. Apparently both academic and vocational curricula have a significant positive impact on labor market success.

Vocational training taken in conjunction with a planned program has a greater impact on labor market outcomes of high school graduates than does a random series of vocational courses taken in unrelated areas. The payoff for vocational training is also higher for persons employed in jobs where their training can be used, and the strongest vocational training effects are associated with office occupations. No difference appears between disadvantaged and not disadvantaged youth in the effects of vocational and academic training on weeks unemployed or hours worked, but vocational training has stronger effects on hourly earnings of youth who are not disadvantaged. The effect of vocational training on hourly earnings also appears smaller for blacks than for whites.

How young people spend their time is the subject of chapter 7. The data refer to an average week in the Spring of 1981. Among youth who work, the length of the average workweek shows only modest variance across race and sex groups. White females work the shortest week, 28 hours, while Hispanic males are employed for the longest period, 35 hours. Generally, women work two to four hours less per week than do men. On the job, females spend about twice as much time as males reading and writing and considerably more time dealing with people. However, both men and women spend about three-quarters of their time working with their hands.

Those enrolled in school spend between 25 and 30 hours a week at school; 18-22 of these hours are spent in class. The students spend from 7-9 hours per week studying away from school. American youth also spend a substantial part of their week watching TV, with females averaging about 2.3 hours a day and males 1.8 hours. In contrast to their leisure time spent watching TV, there is strikingly little time spent reading during the week—less than three-quarters of an hour per day. Finally, the youth spend between 8 and 19 hours a week on household chores, with women spending approximately twice as much time on these activities as young men.

When the time-use of youth is examined by their socio-economic status (SES), it is found that those from high SES households spend two to three less hours per week at work if employed and approximately one and one-half hours per week more in reading and four to six hours less watching TV than do youth from low socio-economic households. This finding may reflect in part the fact that those youth from high SES backgrounds are much more likely to be enrolled as full-time students. Finally, the youth from low socio-economic backgrounds are more likely to be in jobs where they spend time working with their hands than is true of the youth from higher socio-economic backgrounds.

When the time-use of nonstudents who are unemployed is examined, it is found that relatively few are involved in any kind of training program—3 to 4 percent. Quite surprisingly, the number of hours spent by the unemployed looking for work is very small—roughly 3.5 hours per week for young women and 5.5 hours per week for young men.

Chapter 8 treats delinquent behavior among youth, and by any measure criminal or disruptive behavior is widespread. Substantially over half of the respondents report some level of illegal behavior, and one-third of the males report some form of police contact. A substantial minority of youth, one-fifth of males and one-tenth of females, report that at least part of their financial support is derived from illegal activities. Marijuana and its derivatives had been used at least once in the previous year by almost half of the sample, and older respondents reported more prevalent use. Illegal behavior other than drug use is reported more frequently by youth under the age of 18 than by adults.

As expected, males report much more frequent illegal behavior than females. Besides gender, the other major variable associated with the distribution of delinquency is school enrollment status: dropouts are much more likely to participate in virtually every category of illegal behavior, and the association between illegal behavior and social class, measured by race and poverty status, is much weaker than the association with education. Among males it is the non-poor who are more delinquent, particularly in drinking and drug use, although males from nonpoor families are also more likely to report vandalism, shoplifting, assault and fraud. Likewise, more affluent women are more likely to report alcohol and drug use than are poor women, although poor women report more involvement with offenses involving personal violence. Few major differences appear by race, although drug use and drinking are more common among whites than among Hispanics and blacks.

The results for reports of police contacts parallel the results for illegal activities. Males and dropouts have substantially more contacts with police than do females and other enrollment status groups. There is no difference by income in frequency of young males being stopped by police without further processing, and poor females are actually somewhat less likely than affluent females to be simply stopped by police. However, poor youth are consistently more likely to be formally charged, convicted, put on probation or incarcerated than are nonpoor youth.

The link between employment and crime was tested using a model based on both sociological and economic accounts of the causation of delinquency. Contrary to the hypothesis that crime substitutes for employment as a source of income, employed high school students were actually more likely to participate in illegal activities, particularly drug use. This relationship probably reflects the greater discretionary income and freedom from adult control among youth who are working. Among noncollege youth 18-23 years old, however, there did seem to be a tendency for youth who reported higher levels of illegal income to report more weeks unemployed.

The picture of the youth labor market presented here derives from statistical analyses of data collected from young Americans during three years in the late twentieth century. Our findings are not intended to suggest that what has happened to large proportions of NLS respondents might happen in the life of any specific individual in the future. It is hoped instead that the studies presented here will suggest routes to improvements in the youth labor market.

NOTE

1. More detailed information on the surveys appears in Center for Human Resource Research (1983).

REFERENCE

Center for Human Resource Research. 1983. *NLS Handbook, 1983.* Columbus: The Ohio State University.

Chapter 2
A Description of Employed and Unemployed Youth in 1981*
by Michael E. Borus

The problems of youth unemployment have occupied the attention of policymakers and social scientists for many years. Particular emphasis has been given to this subject for the last half dozen years because unemployment among youth has grown both in absolute numbers, relative to the population of youth (as measured by the unemployment rate of youth) and as a proportion of total unemployment. A number of hypotheses have been suggested to explain this increase. These hypotheses are tested elsewhere in this volume and in other studies.[1]

This chapter describes the magnitude of the youth unemployment problem. In addition to presenting information on unemployed youth, we also describe the characteristics of discouraged workers, i.e., youth who are no longer looking for work because they believe that no jobs are available. In an expanding economy, these young people will soon begin job search again and thus shift to the

*A longer, somewhat different version of this paper was commissioned by and prepared for the Committee on Vocational Education and Economic Development in Depressed Areas (Commission on Behavioral and Social Sciences and Education, National Research Council). Tables from that paper appear in Appendix A of the committee's final report, *Education for Tomorrow's Jobs,* published by the National Academy Press, 1983.

category of the unemployed. Finally, employed youth serve as a useful reference group for the unemployed because the types of jobs they have may also be available for unemployed youth.

Data from the National Longitudinal Surveys of Youth Labor Market Experience gathered in the Spring of 1981 will be used to describe the characteristics of employed and unemployed youth as of that time. Most analyses are limited to youth who were age 16 to 21 at that interview.[2]

I. Description of Unemployed Youth Age 16 - 21

One can piece together a picture of unemployed youth by examining their various characteristics as of the Spring of 1981. Overall, approximately three and a half million youth were unemployed and the unemployment rate for youth age 16-21 was 20 percent, according to the NLS.[3]

Approximately 400,000 more young men than young women were unemployed and the unemployment rate among the males—16 percent—was three percentage points higher than for the women (table 2.1). With the exception of 21-year-olds, the male unemployment rates were higher than or equal to the rates for women of the same age. Unemployment rates were higher for females than for males in a few subgroups of youth: blacks, high school dropouts, those youth with less than high school educations, those who were or had been married, persons who had children in their household and youth in the Northeast.

The unemployment rate declined substantially as the youth aged (table 2.1). The rate was 31 percent among 16-year-olds but only 13 percent among those who were 21 years old. The decline was steady for both males and females with the exception of 21-year-old females, who had a higher unemployment rate than 20-year-olds.

Table 2.1
Distribution of Youth Age 16-21 by Sex,
Employment Status and Age, Spring 1981[a]

Age in 1981		Employed	Unemployed	Out of labor force	Unemployment rate (%)
		Females			
16	No. (000s)	581	245	710	30
	Percent	38	16	46	
17	No. (000s)	893	353	830	28
	Percent	43	17	40	
18	No. (000s)	1,034	303	650	23
	Percent	52	15	33	
19	No. (000s)	1,225	214	610	15
	Percent	60	11	30	
20	No. (000s)	1,244	140	633	10
	Percent	62	7	31	
21	No. (000s)	1,242	210	597	15
	Percent	61	10	29	
Total	No. (000s)	6,218	1,466	4,030	19
	Percent	53	12	34	
		Males			
16	No. (000s)	620	296	729	32
	Percent	38	18	44	
17	No. (000s)	1,071	463	612	30
	Percent	50	22	29	
18	No. (000s)	1,096	323	492	23
	Percent	57	17	26	
19	No. (000s)	1,232	285	413	19
	Percent	64	15	21	
20	No. (000s)	1,244	291	402	19
	Percent	64	15	21	
21	No. (000s)	1,474	192	325	12
	Percent	84	10	16	
Total	No. (000s)	6,736	1,849	2,973	22
	Percent	58	16	26	

(continued)

Table 2.1 (continued)

Age in 1981		Employed	Unemployed	Total Out of labor force	Unemployment rate (%)
16	No. (000s)	1,201	541	1,439	31
	Percent	38	18	45	
17	No. (000s)	1,965	816	1,442	29
	Percent	47	19	34	
18	No. (000s)	2,129	625	1,142	23
	Percent	55	16	23	
19	No. (000s)	2,457	500	1,023	17
	Percent	62	13	26	
20	No. (000s)	2,487	431	1,035	15
	Percent	63	11	26	
21	No. (000s)	2,715	402	922	13
	Percent	67	10	23	
Total	No. (000s)	12,954	3,315	7,002	20
	Percent	56	14	30	

a. Persons 16 years of age born in 1965, i.e., those having their birthday between January 1, 1981 and the interview date, are not included. This reduces the number of 16-year-olds by approximately 21 percent.

Unemployment among minority youth was particularly high (table 2.2). The rate among blacks was 37 percent, compared to 24 percent for Hispanics and 18 percent for whites. Although blacks accounted for 14 percent of the youth population, they made up 23 percent of the unemployed. More than one million black and Hispanic youth were unemployed in the Spring of 1981.

As would be expected, table 2.3 shows high school dropouts suffered the highest unemployment rates—37 percent for females and 29 percent for males. Only slightly lower were the unemployment rates for high school students—27 percent overall, 26 percent for females and 29 percent for males. These two groups—high school dropouts and high school students—representing slightly less than half of the youth population, accounted for nearly 63 percent of the unemployed. The reasons for their unemployment, however, are different: dropouts are viewed as lacking skills and motivation while high school students are restricted in the hours of employment that they are willing and able to work.

Table 2.2
Distribution of Youth Age 16-21 by Sex,
Employment Status and Race, Spring 1981[a]

	Race		Females		
		Employed	Unemployed	Out of labor force	Unemployment rate (%)
Black	No. (000s)	582	364	715	38
	Percent	35	22	43	
Hispanic	No. (000s)	341	90	298	21
	Percent	47	12	41	
White	No. (000s)	5,296	1,011	3,018	16
	Percent	57	11	32	
Total	No. (000s)	6,218	1,466	4,030	19
	Percent	53	12	34	

	Race		Males		
		Employed	Unemployed	Out of labor force	Unemployment rate (%)
Black	No. (000s)	714	383	495	35
	Percent	45	24	31	
Hispanic	No. (000s)	422	151	168	26
	Percent	57	20	23	
White	No. (000s)	5,601	1,315	2,310	23
	Percent	61	14	25	
Total	No. (000s)	6,736	1,849	2,973	22
	Percent	58	16	26	

(continued)

Table 2.2 (continued)

Race		Employed	Unemployed	Out of labor force	Unemployment rate (%)
				Total	
Black	No. (000s)	1,296	747	1,209	37
	Percent	40	23	37	
Hispanic	No. (000s)	762	242	466	24
	Percent	52	16	32	
White	No. (000s)	10,896	2,326	5,328	18
	Percent	59	12	29	
Total	No. (000s)	12,954	3,315	7,002	20
	Percent	56	14	30	

a. Persons 16 years of age born in 1965, i.e., those having their birthday between January 1, 1981 and the interview date, are not included. This reduces the number of 16-year-olds by approximately 21 percent.

Table 2.3
Distribution of Youth Age 16-21 by Sex, Employment Status and Enrollment Status, Spring 1981[a]

Enrollment status as of 1981 interview		Employed	Unemployed	Out of labor force	Unemployment rate (%)
				Females	
High school dropout	No. (000s)	522	309	730	37
	Percent	33	20	47	
Enrolled in high school	No. (000s)	1,615	555	1,583	26
	Percent	43	15	42	
Enrolled in college	No. (000s)	1,295	153	1,064	11
	Percent	52	6	42	
High school graduate, not enrolled	No. (000s)	2,781	448	646	14
	Percent	72	12	17	
Total[b]	No. (000s)	6,218	1,466	4,030	19
	Percent	53	12	34	

(continued)

Table 2.3 (continued)

Enrollment status as of 1981 interview		Males			
		Employed	Unemployed	Out of labor force	Unemploy- ment rate (%)
High school dropout	No. (000s)	1,082	447	269	29
	Percent	60	25	15	
Enrolled in high school	No. (000s)	1,871	767	1,518	29
	Percent	45	18	36	
Enrolled in college	No. (000s)	1,232	150	972	11
	Percent	52	6	41	
High school graduate, not enrolled	No. (000s)	2,551	479	212	16
	Percent	79	15	6	
Total[b]	No. (000s)	6,736	1,849	2,973	22
	Percent	58	16	26	

Enrollment status as of 1981 interview		Total			
		Employed	Unemployed	Out of labor force	Unemploy- ment rate (%)
High school dropout	No. (000s)	1,603	756	1,000	32
	Percent	48	22	30	
Enrolled in high school	No. (000s)	3,486	1,322	3,101	27
	Percent	44	17	39	
Enrolled in college	No. (000s)	2,527	303	2,037	11
	Percent	52	6	42	
High school graduate, not enrolled	No. (000s)	5,332	928	859	15
	Percent	75	13	12	
Total[b]	No. (000s)	12,954	3,315	7,002	20
	Percent	56	14	30	

a. Persons 16 years of age born in 1965, i.e., those having their birthday between January 1, 1981 and the interview date, are not included. This reduces the number of 16-year-olds by approximately 21 percent.

b. School enrollment status information was not available for 17,500 youth.

Unemployment rates are directly related to lack of education (table 2.4). The unemployment rate for those with less than one year of high school completed was an extremely high 40 percent; for those who had completed some high school but not the 12th grade it declined to 28 percent, and for those who had completed college (a relatively small number in this age group) it fell to only 3 percent.

Nearly 24 percent of the youth had participated in a government-sponsored employment or training program. The unemployment rate was 27 percent for those individuals who had participated in a program (but were no longer participating) as compared with 19 percent of those who had never participated. The fact that the poor and minorities are primarily the individuals eligible for government employment and training programs may partly explain why participating youth continue to have higher than average unemployment rates.

On the other hand, if one looks at those who had training other than in regular school and government programs, one finds somewhat lower unemployment rates than among those who did not—17 percent compared to 21 percent. These observed lower rates for those who had received primarily post-secondary vocational training may reflect the benefits of receiving such training or the somewhat older age of persons who participate. In either case, the declines in the unemployment rate were not dramatic.

Only one in seven youth age 16-21 had ever been married, although nearly 20 percent of the young women had. Young men who had married had much lower unemployment rates than did those who never married. Married and single young women had the same rate, however, and women who were divorced or separated had an unemployment rate nearly half again as high as those who never married or who were married and living with their spouse.

About 15 percent of the women and 4 percent of the men—10 percent of all youth—had children of their own living with them. Again we find different patterns for men and women. Young women with children had much higher unemployment rates than those without children—31 percent as compared to 18 percent. Among males, the unemployment rates were 18 percent and 22 percent, respectively.

Two-thirds of all youth lived with their parents, but nearly 80 percent of the unemployed lived in their parents' homes—84 percent of the males and 73 percent of the females (table 2.5). The higher rate of unemployment among those living with their parents may be a function of the younger age of youth with this living arrangement.

In 1981 there were slightly higher youth unemployment rates in the North Central and Southern regions than in the Northeast and West, although the differences were not dramatic. Males had a 27 percent unemployment rate in the North Central states, the highest rate of the four regions. In contrast, the female unemployment rate of 17 percent in that region was the lowest of the four parts of the country. This difference may reflect the substantial layoffs in manufacturing and construction in this section of the country which affected males more than females.

Youth living in counties which were 50 percent or more rural had identical unemployment rates with those living in counties that were 50 percent or more urban. There were slight differences based on location in or out of an SMSA. Those not in an SMSA had an unemployment rate of 21 percent, which was slightly lower than the 24 percent for those living in the central city of an SMSA and slightly higher than the 18 percent unemployment rate of those living in an SMSA but not in the central city. These figures contradict the commonly held belief that youth unemployment is highly concentrated in the central cities of SMSAs.

Table 2.4
Distribution of Youth Age 16-21 by Sex,
Employment Status and Educational Attainment, Spring 1981[a]

Highest grade completed as of 1981 interview		Females			
		Employed	Unemployed	Out of labor force	Unemployment rate (%)
No schooling	No. (000s)	71	74	199	51
through	Percent	20	22	58	
8 years					
Some	No. (000s)	2,065	790	2,114	28
high school	Percent	42	16	42	
12th grade	No. (000s)	2,702	488	984	15
	Percent	65	12	24	
One through	No. (000s)	1,356	113	727	8
three years	Percent	62	5	33	
college					
Four years	No. (000s)	18	1	0	5
college	Percent	96	4	0	
Graduate	No. (000s)	0	0	0	0
school	Percent	0	0	0	
Total[b]	No. (000s)	6,218	1,466	4,030	19
	Percent	53	12	34	

Highest grade completed as of 1981 interview		Males			
		Employed	Unemployed	Out of labor force	Unemployment rate (%)
No schooling	No. (000s)	224	119	116	35
through	Percent	49	26	25	
8 years					
Some	No. (000s)	2,729	1,095	1,671	29
high school	Percent	50	20	30	
12th grade	No. (000s)	2,797	521	573	16
	Percent	72	13	15	
One through	No. (000s)	972	108	611	10
three years	Percent	58	6	36	
college					
Four years	No. (000s)	13	0	1	0
college	Percent	92	0	8	

(continued)

Table 2.4 (continued)

Highest grade completed as of 1981 interview		Males			
		Employed	Unemployed	Out of labor force	Unemployment rate (%)
Graduate	No. (000s)	1	0	0	0
school	Percent	100	0	0	
Total[b]	No. (000s)	6,736	1,849	2,973	22
	Percent	58	16	26	

Highest grade completed as of 1981 interview		Total			
		Employed	Unemployed	Out of labor force	Unemployment rate (%)
No schooling through 8 years	No. (000s)	294	194	315	40
	Percent	37	24	39	
Some high school	No. (000s)	4,795	1,885	3,785	28
	Percent	46	18	36	
12th grade	No. (000s)	5,499	1,008	1,557	15
	Percent	68	12	19	
One through three years college	No. (000s)	2,328	222	1,338	9
	Percent	60	6	34	
Four years college	No. (000s)	31	1	1	3
	Percent	94	2	3	
Graduate school	No. (000s)	1	0	0	0
	Percent	100	0	0	
Total[b]	No. (000s)	12,954	3,315	7,002	20
	Percent	56	14	30	

a. Persons 16 years of age born in 1965, i.e., those having their birthday between January 1, 1981 and the interview date, are not included. This reduces the number of 16-year-olds by approximately 21 percent.

b. School enrollment status information was not available for 17,500 youth.

Youth unemployment followed a pattern of general unemployment in that the rates were higher in local areas which had high overall unemployment rates. The youth unemployment rate was 18 percent in areas with less than 6 percent unemployment, 20 percent in those that had between 6 and 9 percent unemployment, and about 26 percent in those areas having 9 percent or higher unemployment rates.

Table 2.5
Distribution of Youth Age 16-21 by Sex,
Employment Status and Living Arrangements
at Time of 1981 Interview, Spring 1981[a]

Living arrange- ments at time of 1981 interview		Females			
		Employed	Unemployed	Out of labor force	Unemploy- ment rate (%)
Living with parents	No. (000s)	4,007	1,071	2,292	21
	Percent	54	14	31	
Away from household in college or military	No. (000s)	398	34	580	8
	Percent	39	3	57	
Living in own household	No. (000s)	1,813	360	1,158	17
	Percent	54	11	35	
Total	No. (000s)	6,218	1,466	4,030	19
	Percent	53	12	34	

Living arrange- ments at time of 1981 interview		Males			
		Employed	Unemployed	Out of labor force	Unemploy- ment rate (%)
Living with parents	No. (000s)	4,888	1,556	2,120	24
	Percent	57	18	25	
Away from household in college or military	No. (000s)	365	70	630	16
	Percent	34	7	59	
Living in own household	No. (000s)	1,484	222	223	13
	Percent	77	12	12	
Total	No. (000s)	6,736	1,849	2,973	22
	Percent	58	16	26	(continued)

Table 2.5 (continued)

Living arrange- ments at time of 1981 interview		Total			
		Employed	Unemployed	Out of labor force	Unemploy- ment rate (%)
Living with	No. (000s)	8,891	2,628	4,412	23
parents	Percent	56	16	28	
Away from	No. (000s)	763	104	1,210	12
household in	Percent	37	5	58	
college or military					
Living in own	No. (000s)	3,296	583	1,381	15
household	Percent	63	11	26	
Total	No. (000s)	12,949	3,315	7,002	20
	Percent	56	14	30	

a. Persons 16 years of age born in 1965, i.e., those having their birthday between January 1, 1981 and the interview date, are not included. This reduces the number of 16-year-olds by approximately 21 percent.

When asked why they were looking for work, a majority of the unemployed who provided a reason, said that they were doing so because they needed money (table 2.6). Another fifth had either lost or quit their previous job. On the other hand, only about 1 in 13 said that they were looking for work to support themselves or help with family expenses.

Unemployed young people, like adults, relied most heavily on direct applications to employers in their search for employment; 58 percent of the unemployed made direct application to employers. The next most popular method of job search was checking local newspapers, used by 31 percent of the youth. Approximately 1 in 6 used the public employment service and a similar percentage asked friends or relatives about employment. Placing or answering advertisements was used by about 12 percent of the sample. The type of job search did not vary appreciably by sex, although females were more likely to look in the newspaper and place or answer ads while males were slightly more likely to use friends and relatives. It should be noted that school employment services were used by only 6 percent of the youth and private employment agencies by 4 percent.

Table 2.6
Distribution of Reasons for Looking for Work
Among Unemployed Youth Age 16-21, by Sex, Spring 1981[a]

Reason looking for work		Females	Males	Total
Need money	No. (000s)	737	879	1,616
	Percent	50	48	49
Lost job	No. (000s)	125	228	353
	Percent	8	12	11
Quit job	No. (000s)	151	151	302
	Percent	10	8	9
Family expenses	No. (000s)	71	50	121
	Percent	5	3	4
Support self	No. (000s)	40	56	96
	Percent	3	3	3
Left school	No. (000s)	32	69	100
	Percent	2	4	3
Enjoy working	No. (000s)	67	29	96
	Percent	5	2	3
Other	No. (000s)	168	206	374
	Percent	11	11	11
No reason given	No. (000s)	76	180	256
	Percent	5	10	8
Total	No. (000s)	1,466	1,849	3,315
	Percent	100	100	100

a. Persons 16 years of age born in 1965, i.e., those having their birthday between January 1, 1981 and the interview date, are not included. This reduces the number of 16-year-olds by approximately 21 percent.

Approximately half of the unemployed youth, 48 percent, sought full time employment. The remaining youth (who were primarily younger and in school) wanted only part-time employment. When asked what kind of work they were seeking, 40 percent of the males and 27 percent of the females said either that they would take any kind of work or could not identify an occupation. Of the others, the females were primarily searching for clerical (28 percent of the unemployed), service (20 percent of the unemployed) and sales jobs (12 percent of the unemployed). None of the other occupational categories were sought by even as many as 5 percent of the young female unemployed. Among males, 14 percent sought jobs as laborers, 12 percent in service jobs and 12 percent in jobs in the crafts.

When asked the wage rate necessary to induce them to take the jobs they were seeking (the reservation wage), the largest group responded with the federal minimum wage of $3.35 (38 percent of those who gave a reservation wage). See table 2.7. It should be noted that 21 percent of those who provided a reservation wage said that they would take jobs at less than the minimum wage, although the vast majority of these set a reservation wage between $3.00 and $3.34. It is also true that females were more likely to accept sub-minimum wages than were males.

The Hard-Core Unemployed Age 16-21

The previous section has described all of the youth who were unemployed. It is possible to argue that the need for employment among many of these youth is not great; they are in school, they live in their parents' homes, they seek only part-time employment, and they may have been unemployed for only a short period of time. Therefore, it may be useful to examine the characteristics of those youth who were truly among the hard-core unemployed, although

Table 2.7
Minimum Wage Necessary to Induce Unemployed Youth Age 16-21
to Accept a Job for Which They Were Looking, by Sex, Spring 1981[a]

Reservation wage		Females	Males	Total
Less than $2.50	No. (000s)	32	24	57
	Percent	2	1	2
$2.50 - $2.99	No. (000s)	17	28	44
	Percent	1	2	1
$3.00 - $3.24	No. (000s)	160	148	309
	Percent	11	8	9
$3.25 - $3.34	No. (000s)	118	123	241
	Percent	8	7	7
$3.35	No. (000s)	561	616	1,176
	Percent	38	33	36
$3.36 - $3.49	No. (000s)	58	40	98
	Percent	4	2	3
$3.50 - $3.99	No. (000s)	200	212	412
	Percent	14	12	12
$4.00 - $4.49	No. (000s)	110	241	350
	Percent	8	13	11
$4.50 - $4.99	No. (000s)	27	58	84
	Percent	2	3	2
$5.00 - $5.49	No. (000s)	50	117	166
	Percent	3	6	5
$5.50 or more	No. (000s)	42	127	169
	Percent	3	7	5
Data not available	No. (000s)	91	116	207
	Percent	6	6	6
Total	No. (000s)	1,466	1,849	3,315
	Percent	100	100	100

a. Persons 16 years of age born in 1965, i.e., those having their birthday between January 1, 1981 and the interview date, are not included. This reduces the number of 16-year-olds by approximately 21 percent.

obviously, the definition of who they are must be arbitrary. For the purposes of this paper the following definition will be used: youth who are out of school; who reside either in their own or their parents' household where the family income is below the poverty level; and who have been unemployed at least ten weeks. Using this definition about 300,000, or 1 in 11, unemployed youth were hard-core unemployed in the Spring of 1981.

The hard-core unemployed were almost equally divided between males and females. Very few were less than 18 years of age and they were distributed about equally among 18-, 19-, 20- and 21-year-olds. According to our definition, the proportion of unemployed youth who were hard-core did not vary substantially by race—it was 11 percent of the unemployed blacks, 10 percent of the Hispanics, and 8 percent of the whites. Contrary to what might be expected, the proportion of the unemployed who were hard-core also did not vary depending on whether one was a high school dropout or graduate. Eighteen percent of unemployed high school dropouts were hard-core, as were 16 percent of unemployed high school graduates who were not enrolled. The proportion did vary, however, with educational attainment. Twenty-one percent of the unemployed who had no schooling through eight years of education were hard-core, as compared to 5 percent of the unemployed who had some high school, and 14 percent of those who had completed the 12th grade.[4] Of those unemployed youth who received government training prior to the 1981 interview, 13 percent could be labeled hard-core, while only 7 percent of those who had never received government employment or training were classified in this way. Similarly, 11 percent of the unemployed who had received training other than in regular schools and government programs were hard-core as compared to 8 percent of those who had not participated in such programs.

The nature of the definition of hard-core unemployed leads to strikingly different proportions based on family living circumstances. Six percent of those unemployed youth who had never married fell into the category of hard-core unemployed as opposed to 25 percent of those who were married and living with their spouse and 31 percent of the youth in other marital situations; 27 percent of the respondents who had a child in their household were categorized as hard-core unemployed as compared with only 7 percent of those respondents who did not have their own children in their household; and 29 percent of those living in their own households met the hard-core definition while only 5 percent of those living with their parents did so.

On a regional basis, the proportions of the unemployed who were hard-core were very similar except in the West, where 14 percent of the unemployed met the definition. The proportion who were hard-core did not vary with rural or urban residence, although youth identified as living in the central city of an SMSA had a slightly larger proportion who were hard-core, 13 percent, as compared to those in an SMSA who were not in the central city, 6 percent, and those not in an SMSA, 8 percent. Finally, the proportion of unemployed youth who were hard-core increased from 6 percent in areas with less than 6 percent unemployment to 9 percent in areas with 6.0 to 8.9 percent unemployment to 15 percent in areas of 9.0 to 11.9 percent unemployment, but then fell to 7 percent among those living in areas where the unemployment rate exceeded 12 percent.

To summarize: using an arbitrary definition, we find that the hard-core unemployed tended to be older, more likely to have participated in training, to be married, to have children, to live in the central city of an SMSA, and to live in an area of high unemployment than was true of all unemployed youth.

Multivariate Analysis of the Unemployed

Because many of the characteristics associated with being unemployed are correlated, a multivariate analysis was undertaken. A probit equation was estimated to calculate the independent influence of various characteristics when others were taken into account. Separate equations estimated for females and males appear in tables 2.8 and 2.9.

For young women, the probability of being unemployed was higher among high school dropouts and graduates than among high school students, and this probability declined with age. Black young women had a higher probability of being unemployed, as did those who resided in families whose income was below the poverty line. The probability of unemployment was higher among those who had previously received government employment and training services and who lived in their parental household. Finally, unemployment was significantly higher in the Northeast than in the South or North Central states, in urban areas and in those areas with unemployment rates of 12 percent or more.

Among the young men, many of the same factors were associated with unemployment. The unemployment rate was higher for high school dropouts than for high school students, among blacks and those in poverty, and among those youth living in their parents' households. Unlike the females, however, college students had significantly lower probabilities of unemployment than high school students, and only among 21-year-olds was there a significantly lower probability of unemployment than was true of 16-year-olds. Youth unemployment was highest in areas with 9.0 to 11.9 percent aggregate unemployment and in the North Central region. Finally, unlike the findings for females, for males the receipt of government employment and training services was not associated with significantly higher probabilities of being unemployed.

Table 2.8
Probit Estimates of the Probability
of Unemployment Among Females Age 16-21, Spring 1981[a]

	Coefficient	t-Value	Partial derivative evaluated at mean
Age			
16	--	--	--
17	-0.024	-0.26	-0.005
18	-0.080	-0.74	-0.017
19	-0.282	-2.28*	-0.059
20	-0.424	-3.30**	-0.089
21	-0.244	-1.87+	-0.051
Race			
Black	0.302	4.45**	0.064
Hispanic	-0.115	-1.39	-0.024
White	--	--	--
Poverty Status			
In poverty	0.124	2.03*	0.026
Not in poverty	--	--	--
Enrollment Status			
High school dropout	0.367	3.90**	0.077
High school student	--	--	--
College student	-0.157	-1.39	-0.033
Nonenrolled graduate	0.215	2.16*	0.045
Received Government Employment or Training			
Yes	0.152	2.53*	0.032
No	--	--	--
Received Other Training			
Yes	-0.039	-0.55	-0.008
No	--	--	--
Living in Parental Household			
Yes	0.039	4.56**	0.071
No	--	--	--
Marital Status			
Never married	--	--	--
Other	0.075	0.81	0.016
Has Children in Household			
Yes	0.073	0.93	0.015
No	--	--	--

(continued)

Table 2.8 (continued)

	Coefficient	t-Value	Partial derivative evaluated at mean
Region			
Northeast	0.203	2.58**	0.043
North Central	-0.077	-1.00	-0.016
South	--	--	--
West	0.091	1.12	0.019
Rural Residence			
Yes	--	--	--
No	0.136	1.86+	0.029
Central City of an SMSA			
Yes	-0.226	-0.33	-0.005
No	--	--	--
Local Unemployment Rate			
Less than 6 percent	-0.020	-0.32	-0.004
6.0 percent to 8.9 percent	--	--	--
9.0 percent to 11.9 percent	0.090	1.02	0.019
12.0 percent or more	0.312	2.67**	0.066
Constant	-1.585	-12.72**	-0.333

N = 3801

2*Log likelihood ratio   182.08

a. Persons 16 years of age born in 1965, i.e., those having their birthday between January 1, 1981 and the interview date, are not included. This reduces the number of 16-year-olds by approximately 21 percent.

+ Significant at $P \le .10$

*Significant at $P \le .05$

**Significant at $P \le .01$

Table 2.9
Probit Estimates of the Probability
of Unemployment Among Males Age 16-21, Spring 1981[a]

	Coefficient	t-Value	Partial derivative evaluated at mean
Age			
16	--	--	--
17	0.088	1.06	0.022
18	0.018	0.19	0.005
19	-0.077	-0.69	-0.020
20	-0.064	-0.55	-0.016
21	-0.251	-2.03*	-0.064
Race			
Black	0.223	3.40**	0.057
Hispanic	0.064	0.83	0.016
White	--	--	--
Poverty Status			
In poverty	0.244	4.19**	0.062
Not in poverty	--	--	--
Enrollment Status			
High school dropout	0.374	4.64**	0.096
High school student	--	--	--
College student	-0.329	-2.97**	-0.084
Nonenrolled graduate	0.086	0.93	0.022
Received Government Employment or Training			
Yes	0.051	0.92	0.013
No	--	--	--
Received Other Training			
Yes	0.102	1.55	0.026
No	--	--	--
Living in Parental Household			
Yes	0.360	4.47**	0.092
No	--	--	--
Marital Status			
Never married	--	--	--
Other	-0.152	-1.09	0.039
Has Children in Household			
Yes	0.261	1.67+	0.067
No	--	--	--

(continued)

Table 2.9 (continued)

	Coefficient	t-Value	Partial derivative evaluated at mean
Region			
Northeast	0.048	0.63	0.012
North Central	0.354	5.07**	0.091
South	--	--	--
West	0.084	1.06	0.021
Rural Residence			
Yes	--	--	--
No	0.106	1.56	0.027
Central City of an SMSA			
Yes	0.001	0.02	0.003
No	--	--	--
Local Unemployment Rate			
Less than 6 percent	-0.053	-0.90	-0.014
6.0 percent to 8.9 percent	--	--	--
9.0 percent to 11.9 percent	0.144	1.70 +	0.037
12.0 percent or more	0.062	0.60	0.016
Constant	-1.590	-12.99**	-0.407

N = 3711

2*Log likelihood ratio   244.67

a. Persons 16 years of age born in 1965, i.e., those having their birthday between January 1, 1981 and the interview date, are not included. This reduces the number of 16-year-olds by approximately 21 percent.

+ Significant at $P \leq .10$

*Significant at $P \leq .05$

**Significant at $P \leq .01$

In summary, the multivariate analysis revealed only a few changes from the bivariate analysis. The decline with age in the probability of being unemployed was not so dramatic among males. High school students were less likely to be unemployed when other factors were taken into account than was evidenced in the bivariate tables. Participation in a government employment or training program was only significantly associated with unemployment among females, and receipt of training other than in school or government programs neither increased nor decreased the probability of unemployment significantly. Marital status and having children in the household did not make a difference in the multivariate framework, although they did in the cross-tabular analysis. The other factors found to be associated with higher unemployment in the bivariate tables were also significant in the multivariate analyses.

II. Description of Discouraged Workers Age 16 - 21

Among the over seven million youth age 16-21 who were not in the labor force in the Spring of 1981 were approximately 200,000 young people who were not looking for work because they believed no jobs were available. Presumably, most of these youth would seek work if employment opportunities were more readily available.

The characteristics of the discouraged workers differed somewhat from those of the unemployed. The discouraged workers were more concentrated among 16- and 21-year-olds than was true of the unemployed. Blacks made up 34 percent of the discouraged youth but only 23 percent of the unemployed. More of the discouraged workers were dropouts and fewer of them were high school graduates than was true among the unemployed. The discouraged workers had a higher proportion with less than 12 years of education or with some college than was true for the unemployed, whereas the unemployed had a much higher proportion who had completed just 12 years of schooling. In percentage terms, more of the discouraged workers than the unemployed had never been married, although somewhat more of the discouraged workers had children living in their households. The discouraged workers were particularly concentrated in the South, where almost half lived, although less than one-third of the unemployed were in the South. More of the discouraged workers also lived in rural areas and outside of SMSAs. They were also more concentrated in local areas with high unemployment rates, particularly those with unemployment rates above 9 percent (30 percent of the discouraged workers lived in these areas as compared to 20 percent of the unemployed). The two groups did not differ appreciably by gender, nor in other areas, such as receipt of various types of training and the proportion living with their parents.

III. Description of Employed Youth

The NLS found that over 13 million people age 16-21 were employed in the Spring of 1981. They represented 56 percent of the population in this age group. Employed youth as a percentage of the total population (the employment-to-population ratio) was higher for the young men (58 percent) than for the young women (53 percent).

The numbers and proportions employed increased markedly with age (table 2.1). Among 16-year-olds, 38 percent were employed, compared to two-thirds of the 21-year-olds. Slightly different patterns were found for men and women: women 19, 20 and 21 years of age all had approximately the same employment-to-population ratio while young men showed a substantial increase from 64 percent for 19- and 20-year-olds to 74 percent for 21-year-olds.

As might be expected, the employment-to-population ratios were much lower for blacks, 40 percent, than for Hispanics, 52 percent, and whites, 59 percent (table 2.2). The differences between young men and women were also more marked among minorities. The employment-to-population ratios for women were 10 percentage points below those of men among both blacks and Hispanics, whereas the difference among whites was only 4 percentage points. This race and gender difference was due in part to the fact that higher percentages of minority women were out of the labor force. The most notable difference appeared among Hispanics, where 41 percent of the females and 23 percent of the males were not participating in the labor force; the gender differential for whites, in contrast, was only 7 percentage points. Among males, the lower employment-to-population ratios for blacks resulted from both substantially higher unemployment and lower labor force participation. Twenty-four percent of the blacks as opposed to 14 percent of whites were unemployed, and 31 percent of blacks as compared to 25 percent of whites were not participants in the labor force. To reiterate the most important finding, however, white youth had an almost 50 percent higher proportion employed in the Spring of 1981 than was true of blacks.

As table 2.3 shows, the employment-to-population ratio for high school graduates not enrolled in college was considerably higher than the ratios for college students, high school dropouts and high school students (75 percent, 52 percent, 48 percent and 44 percent, respectively). Sex differences occurred primarily among the high school dropouts and nonenrolled high school graduates. Seventy-nine percent of the male graduates and 72 percent of the female graduates were employed. On the other hand, among dropouts, 60 percent of the males and only 33 percent of the females were working. A much higher percentage of the females, 47 percent, as opposed to 15 percent of males were not participating in the labor force. It is likely that many of the female dropouts had left school in order to marry or have children.

This pattern is also evident when one examines educational attainment (table 2.4). The proportion of women with less than 12th grade educations who were employed was substantially less than for males, but the proportion who were out of the labor force was substantially higher. On the other hand, among those with some college education, females had higher employment-to-population ratios than did males, although the numbers and differences were relatively small. There was a slight drop in the employment-to-population ratios among youth who had completed one to three years of college as compared to those who had completed only the 12th grade. This difference probably appears because those with 13-15 years of school completed are more likely to still be enrolled in post-secondary school.

The proportion employed of youth who participated in a government employment or training program prior to the 1981 interview was not very different from the proportion who had never received government training or participated in a government work program. Overall, 53 percent of the former and 56 percent of the latter were employed in the Spring of 1981. Those who received training outside of the regular school system or a government program, however, had substantially higher employment-to-population ratios than those who had not participated in such training, 67 percent and 53 percent, respectively. Again, since most of these nongovernment training programs follow secondary schooling, the age of their participants is probably higher and this age advantage may account for the difference in employment levels.

The employment-to-population ratios were considerably higher for men who had been married as opposed to those who were never married, 85 percent and 56 percent, respectively. Among young women, however, those who were married and living with their husbands had a somewhat lower percentage employed than those who had never married (48 percent and 54 percent, respectively). As one would expect, these same relationships exist for youth who had children; among males, substantially more were employed and among females the proportion who had children and were working was considerably lower.

There was no difference in the employment-to-population ratio for females who lived with their parents as opposed to those who lived in their own households (table 2.5). Fifty-four percent of both groups were employed. Among males, however, 77 percent of those living in their own households were employed, but only 57 percent of those living with their parents were working in the Spring of 1981.

The proportion of youth who were employed was highest in the West and Northeast and lowest in the South for both young men and young women. For females, the employment-to-population ratio was 59 percent in the West and only 46 percent in the South. For males it was 65 percent in the West and 55 percent in the South. Similarly, employment-to-population ratios were higher in urban than in rural areas, with differences of 6 percentage points for both men and women. Within SMSAs, those living in the central city had somewhat lower employment-to-population ratios than those who lived in other parts of the SMSA.

Interestingly, the employment-to-population ratio did not move with the area unemployment rate, particularly among men. The proportion who were working was highest, at 62 percent, in areas where the unemployment rate was 12 percent or higher, followed by areas of low unemployment rate (i.e., less than 6 percent), and lowest among those areas where unemployment was 9.0 to 11.9 percent. Among females, the employment-to-population ratio was highest in the areas of low unemployment but was greater in areas with over 12 percent unemployment than in those areas with 9.0 to 11.9 percent unemployment.

Jobs held by youth in the Spring of 1981 varied by sex. Young women tended to be concentrated in clerical jobs (37 percent), service jobs (30 percent) and sales jobs (10 percent). Young men on the other hand were employed in service jobs (22 percent), as laborers (18 percent), as craftsmen (14 percent) and as operatives (13 percent). The industrial structure of employment also varied by sex. The largest group of both young men and women were in retail trade, where 34 percent of the men and 38 percent of the women found employment. Women, however, were more likely to be in professions (22 percent as opposed to 10 percent for young men) while the young men were more likely to be in manufacturing (19 percent as opposed to 11 percent) and construction (8 percent as opposed to less than 1 percent).

Some differences also appeared in the hours worked by young men and women employees. The percentage of young women working less than 20 hours a week was somewhat higher than for young men (31 and 24 percent, respectively) while the proportion of young men working for more than a 40 hour week was considerably higher—16 percent as compared to 5 percent. Overall, more than half of the employed youth worked less than full time (35 hours a week). Nearly half of both men and women worked on the day shift, one-sixth the evening shift and about 1 in 14 worked the night shift. As might be expected, given the combination of work with schooling by many of the youth, a quarter of them worked varying hours. There were not substantial differences between the sexes.

Of those youth providing an hourly rate of pay, nearly one-fourth (24 percent) worked at jobs paying less than the federal minimum wage of $3.35 an hour (table 2.10). An additional 12 percent worked at the federal minimum wage. Young women as compared to young men were more likely to work at jobs paying less than $3.00 an hour—17 and 10 percent, respectively. Young women were also more likely to be earning between $3.35 and $4.00 an hour than were young men—38 percent versus 30 percent. On the other hand, more young men were earning salaries of $5.00 or more—31 percent as compared to 15 percent.

The amount of education and training required for the jobs held by the youth varies. Using a scheme developed by Eckhaus (1964), we find that 28 percent of the jobs required only an elementary school education. Fifty-one percent required less than high school graduation, 14 percent required a high school diploma and the remaining 7 percent required at least 13 years of education. In terms of the specific training required to do the jobs, nearly half (46 percent) required no more than a short demonstration and an additional 22 percent required less than 30 days of on-the-job specific vocational preparation. An additional 19 percent required no more than three months of specific vocational training. Thus 87 percent of the jobs could be learned with less than three months training. Examination of the educational and training requirements by sex indicate that the jobs held by young men were more likely to require only an elementary education. However, more of the jobs held by females could be learned within the period of 30 days to three months while more of the jobs held by young men required between three and six months of specific training. Thus, employed male youth were more likely to be in jobs requiring little formal education but slightly more specific training than was true for young women.

Table 2.10
Distribution of Hourly Rates of Pay
for Employed Youth Age 16-21, by Sex, Spring 1981[a]

Hourly rates of pay		Females	Males	Total
Less than $2.50	No. (000s)	676	335	1,011
	Percent	11	5	8
$2.50 - $2.99	No. (000s)	334	323	657
	Percent	5	5	5
$3.00 - $3.24	No. (000s)	402	410	813
	Percent	6	6	6
$3.25 - $3.34	No. (000s)	231	252	483
	Percent	4	4	4
$3.35	No. (000s)	820	662	1,482
	Percent	13	10	11
$3.36 - $3.49	No. (000s)	368	255	623
	Percent	6	4	5
$3.50 - $3.99	No. (000s)	1,037	1,021	2,058
	Percent	17	15	16
$4.00 - $4.49	No. (000s)	771	802	1,573
	Percent	12	12	12
$5.00 - $5.49	No. (000s)	374	510	884
	Percent	6	8	7
$5.50 or more	No. (000s)	1,488	926	2,414
	Percent	22	15	19
Data not available	No. (000s)	274	241	515
	Percent	4	4	4
Total	No. (000s)	6,218	6,736	12,954
	Percent	100	100	100

a. Persons 16 years of age born in 1965, i.e., those having their birthday between January 1, 1981 and the interview date, are not included. This reduces the number of 16-year-olds by approximately 21 percent.

Multivariate Analysis of Employment

To determine the independent effects of various characteristics, the probability of being employed was estimated using probit analysis. Separate equations were used for males and females and are presented in tables 2.11 and 2.12. As was true in the bivariate analysis, the probability of employment increased with age and was significantly lower for black females and black and Hispanic males than for whites. There was not a significant difference for Hispanic females, however. Nonenrolled high school graduates of both sexes had substantially higher probabilities of being employed than did high school students. College students of both sexes and female high school dropouts did not differ significantly from high school students, although male high school dropouts had significantly higher proportions employed. As in the bivariate analyses, women who had never married had significantly higher probabilities of being employed, while men who had never been married were significantly less likely to be employed. Similarly, those males who had children in their households were more likely to be working while the young women with children were significantly less likely to. Youth of both sexes whose family incomes were below the poverty line had significantly lower probabilities of being employed.

The bivariate analysis and multivariate analyses showed that receipt of government employment or training services did not affect the probability of being employed, but unlike the bivariate analysis, the multivariate showed that receipt of training other than regular schooling or government-sponsored employment and training programs was not significant. Living in the parental household was associated with a marginal increase in the probability of being employed for males but did not significantly affect females. When the South is used as a base for comparison, males in the North Central states were significantly less likely to be employed while females in the North Central and Western states were significantly more likely to be. Residence in a rural area and in the central city of an SMSA did not significantly influence the probability of employment. These findings differ somewhat from the bivariate analyses, which showed that the proportion of youth employed was highest in the West and Northeast, higher in urban than rural areas, and somewhat lower for residents of central cities. The association of employment with local unemployment rates, however, was the same as in the bivariate analysis. Youth of both sexes residing in areas where the unemployment rate was less than 6 percent had significantly higher probabilities of employment than those residing in areas with 6.0 to 8.9 percent unemployment rates, and the probability decreased significantly for those in areas of 9.0 to 11.9 percent unemployment.

Table 2.11
Probit Estimates of the Probability
of Employment Among Females Age 16-21, Spring 1981[a]

	Coefficient	t-Value	Partial derivative evaluated at mean
Age			
16	--	--	--
17	0.161	1.96+	0.064
18	0.371	3.94**	0.148
19	0.453	4.22**	0.180
20	0.591	5.39**	0.235
21	0.604	5.33**	0.241
Race			
Black	-0.365	-6.24**	-0.145
Hispanic	-0.046	-0.69	-0.018
White	--	--	--
Poverty Status			
In poverty	-0.411	-7.75**	-0.164
Not in poverty	--	--	--
Enrollment Status			
High school dropout	-0.005	-0.05	-0.002
High school student	--	--	--
College student	0.086	0.94	0.034
Nonenrolled graduate	0.598	6.91**	0.238
Received Government Employment or Training			
Yes	0.020	0.39	0.008
No	--	--	--
Received Other Training			
Yes	0.085	1.49	0.034
No	--	--	--
Living in Parental Household			
Yes	0.090	1.53	0.036
No	--	--	--
Marital Status			
Never married	--	--	--
Other	-0.212	-2.81**	-0.085
Has Children in Household			
Yes	-0.502	-7.29**	-0.200
No	--	--	--

(continued)

Table 2.11 (continued)

	Coefficient	t-Value	Partial derivative evaluated at mean
Region			
Northeast	0.027	0.40	0.011
North Central	0.133	2.18*	0.053
South	--	--	--
West	0.165	2.47	0.066
Rural Residence			
Yes	--	--	--
No	0.067	1.15	0.027
Central City of an SMSA			
Yes	-0.034	-0.60	-0.013
No	--	--	--
Local Unemployment Rate			
Less than 6 percent	0.178	3.57**	0.071
6.0 percent to 8.9 percent	--	--	--
9.0 percent to 11.9 percent	-0.211	-2.85**	-0.084
12.0 percent or more	-0.133	-1.30	-0.053
Constant	-0.502	-4.90**	-0.200

N = 3801

2*Log likelihood ratio   662.95

a. Persons 16 years of age born in 1965, i.e., those having their birthday between January 1, 1981 and the interview date, are not included. This reduces the number of 16-year-olds by approximately 21 percent.

+ Significant at $P \leq .10$

*Significant at $P \leq .05$

**Significant at $P \leq .01$

Table 2.12
Probit Estimates of the Probability
of Employment Among Males Age 16-21, Spring 1981[a]

	Coefficient	t-Value	Partial derivative evaluated at mean
Age			
16	--	--	--
17	0.252	3.34**	0.099
18	0.370	4.28**	0.146
19	0.465	4.66**	0.183
20	0.421	4.04**	0.166
21	0.556	5.13**	0.219
Race			
Black	-0.231	-3.98**	-0.091
Hispanic	-0.043	-0.63	-0.017
White	--	--	--
Poverty Status			
In poverty	-0.451	-8.49**	-0.178
Not in poverty	--	--	--
Enrollment Status			
High school dropout	0.205	2.76**	0.081
High school student	--	--	--
College student	-0.011	-0.12	-0.004
Nonenrolled graduate	0.557	6.64**	0.220
Received Government Employment or Training			
Yes	-0.008	-0.17	-0.003
No	--	--	--
Received Other Training			
Yes	0.054	0.92	0.021
No	--	--	--
Living in Parental Household			
Yes	0.115	1.81+	0.045
No	--	--	--
Marital Status			
Never married	--	--	--
Other	0.569	4.64**	0.225
Has Children in Household			
Yes	-0.090	-0.62	-0.035
No	--	--	--

(continued)

Table 2.12 (continued)

	Coefficient	t-Value	Partial derivative evaluated at mean
Region			
Northeast	0.006	0.10	0.003
North Central	-0.137	-2.23*	-0.054
South	--	--	--
West	0.105	1.54	0.041
Rural Residence			
Yes	--	--	--
No	0.049	0.83	0.019
Central City of an SMSA			
Yes	-0.055	-0.98	-0.022
No	--	--	--
Local Unemployment Rate			
Less than 6 percent	0.107	2.12*	0.042
6.0 percent to 8.9 percent	--	--	--
9.0 percent to 11.9 percent	-0.136	-1.78 +	-0.054
12.0 percent or more	0.151	1.56	0.060
Constant	-0.382	-3.76**	-0.151

N = 3711

2*Log likelihood ratio   494.67

a. Persons 16 years of age born in 1965, i.e., those having their birthday between January 1, 1981 and the interview date, are not included. This reduces the number of 16-year-olds by approximately 21 percent.

+ Significant at P ≤ .10

*Significant at P ≤ .05

**Significant at P ≤ .01

IV. Summary and Policy Implications

The preceding analyses have shown that youth unemployment may constitute a national problem. Substantial proportions of the youth population are unemployed. Perhaps more important, unemployment is concentrated among certain groups of young people.

The highest unemployment rates occurred for the youngest group, the 16- and 17-year-olds. The unemployment rate declined with age, particularly among females, even when a number of other characteristics were controlled in a multivariate framework. The seriousness of unemployment among 16- and 17-year-olds is subject to question. When constraints were established that the unemployed were out of school, living in their own households or in parental households with incomes below the poverty line and had been unemployed for at least 10 weeks, almost all of the 16- and 17-year-old unemployed were excluded. On the other hand, 45 percent of the youth and 58 percent of the 16- and 17-year-olds claimed to have been affected by problems of age discrimination.[5] Thus, to the youth themselves, unemployment may be perceived as a major problem, even though they are still in school, living in their parents' households and seeking jobs for spending money rather than to support themselves or their families. The policy issue revolves around the allocation of relatively scarce resources. Should the government allocate its employment and training funds to this group who may be less in need than older youth or should it concentrate on the approximately 300,000 "hard-core unemployed?"

The unemployment problems associated with racial discrimination are much more clear-cut. Black youth suffer disproportionately high unemployment rates and have significantly higher unemployment rates than whites even when a variety of characteristics are taken into account in a multivariate analysis. The fact that 21 percent of blacks perceived that they had been discriminated against on the basis of their race may truly reflect discrimination against them. The reservation wages of young black males did not differ appreciably from those of young whites with similar characteristics, but the market appeared to offer them lower wages. Further, the finding that lower proportions of blacks were holding more than one job during a year indicated that "job shopping" was not the cause of their higher unemployment rates.[6] If the decision were made to concentrate government programs on the hard-core unemployed, these programs would disproportionately aid blacks because 29 percent of the hard-core unemployed were black.

School enrollment status was found to be strongly associated with unemployment. Although overall, high school students were found to have very high unemployment rates, when age and living in the parental household were taken into account, high school students did not appear to be as disadvantaged.[7] The major problem group appears to be high school dropouts, who in the bivariate analysis had unemployment rates more than twice as high as high school graduates and who made up 48 percent of the hard-core unemployed. Further, this lack of education was perceived as a barrier to employment by 21 percent of the high school dropouts. Whether their problems arise from the lack of credentials, their lack of knowledge, or from other characteristics which led them to drop out of school is not clear. Obviously further research is necessary to determine which of these factors is dominant in leading to the higher unemployment rate for dropouts, since the policy recommendations would differ with each cause. (Chapter 4 in this volume identifies some of the factors affecting the decision to drop out of high school.)

Persons receiving government employment and training services had somewhat higher unemployment rates, and this difference was significant for females in the multivariate analysis. It is doubtful that the unemployment rates were caused by the training, however; persons eligible for these programs already have substantial unemployment histories. In fact, 47 percent of the hard-core unemployed had participated in a government employment or training program prior to their current unemployment.

Participation in programs other than regular schooling or government-sponsored employment and training did not significantly reduce the level of unemployment for youth. This finding should not, however, be interpreted as demonstrating that these programs have no effect on unemployment because the outcomes of vocational training may not appear for some time after the courses are completed.[8]

Surprisingly little variation appeared in unemployment rates based on residence. Residence in the central city of an SMSA and in a rural area were not significantly related to unemployment in the multivariate analysis. Although the probability of being unemployed was significantly higher in areas with high local unemployment rates, the pattern was not clear-cut. Thus, it would appear that targeting employment and training programs for youth in specific local areas may have little impact on the distribution of unemployment.

Although employment is not the reverse of unemployment, when the characteristics of the employed were examined, they tended to confirm the finding and implications discussed above. Blacks had significantly lower proportions employed; employment increased substantially with age; high school graduates were substantially better off than high school dropouts; training programs and residence in a central city or a rural area produced no effect on the employment rate; and although employment was higher in areas with low unemployment rates, the relationship was not linear.

When the jobs sought by the unemployed youth are compared with jobs held by employed youth, the unemployed did not seem to be unrealistic in their aspirations. One-third said that they would take any type of job, and the distribution of the remaining group by occupation was similar to that of youth who were working.

There were some differences (tables 2.7 and 2.10) in the wage rates at which the youth would be willing to accept a job and the hourly rates of pay for the employed. Many more of the unemployed listed the minimum wage of $3.35 as their reservation wage—36 percent as compared to 11 percent of employed youth who actually earn this wage. On the other hand, while 23 percent of the employed youth earned less than the minimum wage, 19 percent of unemployed youth were willing to accept subminimum wages. At the other end of the spectrum, a smaller proportion of the unemployed youth, 10 percent, sought wages at $5.00 or more, while 26 percent of employed youth were actually earning this amount.

These gross comparisons, however, do not take account of the differences in the characteristics of the employed and unemployed youth. As noted above, the employed youth tended to be older, have more education, and to include more whites, factors which would lead to higher wage rates.

Finally, the education and training requirements for jobs held by youth appear to be quite low. Only 6 percent required more than a high school education and about 80 percent required less than 12 years of schooling. Further, only 4 percent of the jobs required six months or more of specific training and almost one-half could be learned without anything more than a short demonstration. Thus, although

14 percent of the youth cited lack of experience as having led to difficulty in getting a good job, lack of training per se does not appear to be a major cause of youth unemployment.

NOTES

1. See, for example, chapters 3 and 6 in this volume; Anderson and Sawhill (1980); and Freeman and Wise (1982).

2. The NLS sample contains youth born in the years 1957 through 1964. Since the interviews were conducted in the Spring of 1981, some youth born in 1965 had their 16th birthday prior to the interview and these youth are excluded from the NLS. As a result the data presented here underrepresent 16-year-olds, including only those whose birthdays fell after the Spring. The approximately 800,000 youngest 16-year-olds are missing. This will bias slightly the employment-to-population ratios (upward) and the unemployment rates (downward).

3. The National Longitudinal Surveys have historically found higher rates of labor force participation, employment and unemployment than has the Current Population Survey (CPS). See Santos (1981).

4. Only 5 percent of the unemployed who had attained only some school met our definition of hard-core unemployed because many unemployed in this attainment group were still enrolled in school.

5. Information on the barriers to employment discussed in this section are from Borus et al. (1983).

6. See chapter 3.

7. There may be problems of multicollinearity between these variables, however.

8. The reader should see chapter 6 for further discussion of this point.

REFERENCES

Anderson, Bernard E. and Isabel V. Sawhill. 1980. *Youth Employment and Public Policy.* Englewood Cliffs, NJ: Prentice-Hall, Inc.

Borus, Michael E. 1982. "Willingness to Work Among Youth." *Journal of Human Resources.* Vol. 17, No. 4 (Fall), pp. 581-93.

Borus, Michael E., Choongsoo Kim, Richard Santos and David Shapiro. 1983. "Youth Looking for Work," in *Tomorrow's Workers.* Michael E. Borus, ed. Lexington, MA: D.C. Heath, pp. 59-102.

Eckhaus, Richard S. 1964. "Economic Criteria for Education and Training," *Review of Economics and Statistics.* Vol. 46 (May), pp. 181-90.

Freeman, Richard B. and David A. Wise, eds. 1982. *The Youth Labor Market Problem: Its Nature, Causes and Consequences.* Chicago: University of Chicago Press.

National Longitudinal Surveys Handbook. 1982. Columbus: Center for Human Resource Research, The Ohio State University.

Santos, Richard. 1981. "Measuring the Employment Status of Youth— A Comparison of the Current Population Survey and the National Longitudinal Survey," *Proceedings of the Thirty-Third Annual Meetings.* Madison: Industrial Relations Research Association, pp. 62-68.

Chapter 3
Changes Over the 1970s in the Employment Patterns of Black and White Young Men

by Tom K. Pollard

Over the decade of the 1970s, the labor market clearly slackened more for young black men than for young white men. This deterioration is most often illustrated by the relative fall in the black employment-to-population ratio and the relative increase in the black unemployment rate.[1]

The divergence in the black and white employment-to-population ratios has been associated with radical change in the distribution of unemployment among the black youth population. In the early 1970s, employment was distributed fairly evenly over both the black and white youth populations, with the vast majority of youths only briefly unemployed during the year. By the end of the decade, however, blacks had become overrepresented among those experiencing high total unemployment during any given year, and whites tended toward less annual unemployment.[2]

The gravity of this situation is debatable, however. The private and social costs of the increase in the black-white differential in aggregate employment are dependent on the specific underlying individual patterns of employment. Two broad opposing views of the individual patterns emerge from

57

a study of the literature. Some analysts see unemployment as the result of labor market dynamics; the flow of individual workers between jobs causes unemployment as they engage in job search.[3] These analysts hold that lower annual employment among black youth comes from their higher turnover out of employment and their consequent more numerous periods of job search. The opposing view is that unemployment is caused, in general, not by the turbulence of the labor market, but by stagnation.[4] This latter explanation is based on the idea that black youth in certain submarkets or with certain characteristics experience chronic, long term unemployment. They may, therefore, have long periods of unemployment at times when persons in other submarkets or with other characteristics are experiencing little unemployment. For these black youth, unemployment results from low movement into employment rather than high turnover out of employment.

Viewed from an efficiency standpoint, high turnover unemployment is often a necessary, if not beneficial, characteristic of the early labor market experiences among youth reflecting their instability and the imperfection of job/worker matching processes. If this theory is correct, policies to lower unemployment should be directed not toward the problems of specific workers, but toward improving the workings of the market in general. Stagnation with chronic, long term unemployment, on the other hand, is far more serious and suggests that some groups are being systematically excluded from employment. For youth, such exclusion is particularly serious because very limited employment early in one's career may likely limit future success. If unemployment is associated with stagnation for certain groups of workers, policies to decrease unemployment must address the problems specific to those workers experiencing it. Here we examine whether the turnover or the chronic unemployment model accurately portrays black and white youth unemployment and, therefore, with what urgency and with which policies the worsening position of blacks relative to whites should be addressed.

Due to restrictions imposed by the data set, employment (time employed) will be used instead of unemployment (time not employed while in the labor force) as the labor market indicator for purposes of this study.[5] In general, unemployment may be the theoretically superior measure because it takes into account labor force participation decisions, but the significance of the labor force/not-in-the-labor force distinction may be limited by the sample selection rules used which limit the comparisons to out of school youth who are not in the military—the vast majority of whom are in the labor force. This limitation enhances the credibility of the employment measure and aids interpretation of our results by reducing the effects of two demographic trends that have certainly contributed to the divergence in black/white employment-to-population ratios and unemployment rates over the decade—increased military enlistment and school enrollment among black relative to white youth.[6] The NLS Survey of Young Men provides the data on men age 18-21 for the early part of the decade (1970-71); the NLS Youth Survey provides data on males of the same age at the end of the decade (1979-80).

The years chosen for observation also definitely bear on the interpretation of our results. The unemployment rates among white prime-age males were similar in 1970-71 and in 1979-80.[7] Although the earlier observation was made at a trough in the business cycle and the later at a peak, the similarity of the white male labor market in the two periods indicates that our choice of these years for observation controls to some extent for labor market conditions.

Over the 1970s, black and white youth have experienced reduced aggregate employment rates and a skewing of the employment distributions toward lower total annual employment. Further, individual employment patterns have indeed changed for both black and white youth, the change having been much more drastic for blacks. Not working in the early part of the decade was associated with high turnover for both blacks and whites, but a similar reduction in employment rates for blacks and whites over the decade was accompanied by blacks moving, much more than whites, toward reduced employment characterized by stagnation.

I. Change Over the 1970s
in Employment Means and Distributions

The percentage of the population employed during the survey week decreased by 18 percent for black and 9 percent for white males over the decade (see table 3.1).[8] The percentage of blacks employed was 86 percent of that for whites in 1971 and only 78 percent in 1980.

Associated with this decrease in the survey week employment ratio was an increase in the proportion of the black and white young men employed all year (with no periods out of work). In both years, however, a larger portion of the whites than the blacks was employed all of the preceding year (in 1971, 48 percent for whites versus 34 percent for blacks and in 1980, 54 percent for whites and 38 percent for blacks).

Even though for both blacks and whites the proportion employed all year increased, the average weeks worked by employed young men decreased. The decrease in average weeks worked was modest for whites, decreasing from 45 weeks in 1970-71 to 44 weeks in 1979-80, but more substantial for blacks, falling from 41 weeks to 38 weeks. (Table 3.2)

The decrease in average annual weeks of employment over the decade was distributed fairly evenly over the white sample, but for blacks it became more concentrated among those persons who were out of work for a large portion of the year.

Table 3.1
Employment Status During Survey Week by Year of Survey and Race

	1971								1980							
	Black		White		Total				Black		White		Total			
	#	%	#	%	#	%			#	%	#	%	#	%		
Working	221	77.6	1,395	89.9	1,616	88.0			217	63.6	1,676	81.2	1,893	78.7		
Unemployed	39	13.8	117	7.6	157	8.6			88	25.8	293	14.2	381	15.8		
OLF	24	8.6	39	2.5	63	3.4			36	10.6	94	4.6	131	5.5		
Population (weighted) 000s	285	100	1,551	100	1,836	100			341	100	2,064	100	2,405	100		

UNIVERSE: Civilian males, ages 18-21 who were not enrolled in school as of the 1970 survey for the 1971 observation and the 1979 survey for the 1980 observation.

Table 3.2

Employment Experience During the Preceding Year by Year of Survey and Race

| | Population characteristics | | | |
| | 1971 | | 1980 | |
	Black	White	Black	White
Persons employed during the year	267	1,502	296	1,955
Average weeks employed per person employed during the year	41.3	44.8	37.9	43.7
Persons with periods not working during the survey year	188	807	212	946
Average weeks not employed per person with periods not employed during the survey year	17.6	14.4	24.5	15.4
Total population - weighted - 000s	285	1,551	341	2,064
Total population - unweighted	209	397	197	450

UNIVERSE: Males, ages 18-21 as of the beginning of the survey year, who were not enrolled in school and not in the military during the survey year.

In 1970-71, the distribution of weeks worked was similar among blacks and whites. Eighty percent of the black and 89 percent of the white youth were employed more than 26 weeks (table 3.3); but by 1979-80, the distribution of employment among blacks had undergone a fundamental change while the distribution for whites changes relatively little. Twenty percent of the blacks worked less than 13 weeks during 1979-80 compared to 11 percent of the blacks in 1970-71. For whites, only 4 percent worked less than 13 weeks in 1979-1980, a decline in this category from the 1970-71 level of 6 percent (table 3.3). These trends in the white distribution indicate a relatively small decrease in employment among a large portion of the white sample, while the decreasing equality of the black distribution indicates a significant relative decrease in employment among a relatively small subsample of blacks.

Table 3.3
Distribution of Total Weeks Employed
During the Survey Year
for Total Sample by Year of Survey and Race

Weeks employed	1971		1980	
	Black	White	Black	White
52	29.3	44.8	35.0	52.8
48-51	20.7	21.3	13.6	13.3
38-47	16.1	13.9	12.3	14.4
26-37	13.7	8.7	10.5	10.1
13-25	9.0	5.1	9.2	5.2
0-12	11.2	6.2	19.5	4.2
Population (000s)	285	1,551	341	2,064

Finally, despite the rough nature of the breakdowns, the distribution of employed persons across number of employers and total weeks employed categories indicates that the relative decline in average annual employment and growing concentration of periods of not working among blacks have been accompanied by a relative decrease in turnover among blacks (table 3.4). Here we use the number of employers as a proxy for job turnover: the larger the number of employers the greater the presumed level of job turnover during the year.[9]

Table 3.4
Percentage Distribution of Weeks Worked
and Number of Jobs Held for Those Employed
During the Year by Survey Year and Race

Total number	1971		1980	
of Weeks/Jobs	Black	White	Black	White
No. of weeks				
1-38	31.2	18.1	40.8	22.6
39+	68.8	81.9	59.2	77.4
No. of Jobs				
1	47.4	61.4	60.5	52.8
2 +	52.6	38.6	39.5	47.2
No. of weeks/jobs				
1-38 1	3.8	5.8	20.9	8.9
2+	27.4	12.2	20.0	13.7
39+ 1	43.6	55.6	39.6	43.9
2+	25.2	26.4	19.5	33.5
Total employed (000s)	267	1,503	296	1955

UNIVERSE: Males, ages 18-21 as of the beginning of the survey year, who were not enrolled in school, not in the military, and who were employed at least one week during the survey year.

During 1970-71, more blacks held multiple jobs while the majority of whites held a single job. When we consider the number of weeks employed along with the number of employers, we find that more than half of blacks who held multiple jobs had less than 39 weeks of total employment while less than one-third of multiple jobholding whites worked less than 39 weeks. We can therefore characterize the 1970-71 patterns of blacks as showing relatively high turnover out of employment with substantial periods of not working. Whites, on the other hand, were more likely than blacks to hold a single job, and when an employer change did occur it was associated with more weeks of annual employment than was the case for blacks.

The 1979-80 figures show whites more likely than they were in 1970-71 to hold multiple jobs. Blacks show a major reversal of their earlier pattern, being more likely in 1979-80 to have one employer rather than multiple employers during the year. Most of the increase in single jobholding among blacks is in jobs lasting for fewer than 39 weeks (21 percent of blacks held one job for fewer than 39 weeks in 1979-80 compared to 4 percent in 1970-71). Whites show a more modest increase over the decade in the likelihood of having a single job lasting less than 39 weeks (9 percent of whites held one job for fewer than 39 weeks in 1979-80 compared to 6 percent in 1970-71). The increase over the decade in multiple jobholding among whites appears almost totally in the 39 + weeks-of-employment category, indicating that the increased turnover among whites was accompanied by relatively short spells of not working. In summary, although employment did decline somewhat among whites over the decade, higher job turnover seems to be the major force operating. On the other hand the decline in black employment over the decade appears to be associated more with increased instances of lengthy periods of joblessness among a growing subsample of the black population.

Over the decade, the annual number of weeks without work has thus become concentrated among a smaller proportion of black and white male youth. Blacks moved toward lower annual employment, both absolutely and relative to whites. Further, black employment changed from a phenomenon characterized by high turnover out of employment to one characterized by low movement into employment.

II. Individual Regressions

Using multiple regression techniques, we can examine further the relationship between turnover and employment, identify some causes for the decrease in employment over the decade, and look at the persistence of employment from one year to the next among blacks and whites. In order to portray changes in employment over the decade more accurately, we estimated regression equations for black and white youths separately in each year. The dependent variable for each of these four equations is the proportion of a given year that a person was employed (the 1970-71 survey year for the earlier sample and calendar year 1979 for the later sample). The explanatory variables used were marital status, educational attainment, age, South/non-South residence, SMSA/non-SMSA residence, number of employers during the year, and weeks employed in the previous year (see table 3.5 for definitions of the variables used). Three well-documented trends, decreasing marriage and residence in the South and increased residence in SMSAs among blacks relative to whites, were expected to contribute to the divergence in black and white employment.[10] Although age and educational attainment were expected to affect employment positively, relative trends in these variables and their effects are not as well understood.

Table 3.5
Variable List for Employment Regressions

WKEMPR$_t$ Proportion of year t employed (for earlier observation t = survey year 1970-71; for later observation t = calendar year 1979).

MARRIED   Equals 1, if respondent was married on both surveys considered (1970 and 1971, for the earlier observation; 1979 and 1980, for the later observation); 0 otherwise.

AGE   Equals 1 if respondent was 20 or 21; 0 otherwise.

SOUTH   Equals 1 if respondent was living in the South on both survey dates considered (1970 and 1971 for earlier observation and 1979 and 1980 for the later observation); 0 otherwise.

EM1   Equals 1, if the respondent had 1 employer during year t; 0 otherwise.

EM2   Equals 1, if the respondent had 2 employers during year t; 0 otherwise.

EM3   Equals 1, if the respondent had 3+ employers during year t; 0 otherwise.

ATTAIN   Equals 1, if the respondent had completed 12+ years of schooling; 0 otherwise.

SMSA   Equals 1, if the respondent resided in an SMSA on both survey dates considered (1970 and 1971, for the earlier observation; 1979 and 1980, for the later observation); 0 otherwise.

We focus mainly on the relationship between number of employers and total employment, which serves as our test of the turnover hypothesis: a negative relationship indicates that reduced employment results from employer changes and the higher the number of employers, the lower employment is likely to be. The alternative to the turnover hypothesis is that the lack of employment among blacks stems more from severe stagnation among a subsample of blacks. In this case, employment will not be related to turnover. Further levels of employment may be highly correlated from one year to the next, so we add lagged employment to test for a difference between blacks and whites in the persistence of employment from one year to the next.

The sample means in table 3.6 show that the members of the white sample were employed an average of 86 percent of the 1970-71 survey year, and the members of the black sample were employed an average of 77 percent.[11] Sample means in table 3.7 reveal that for calendar 1979 the white sample was on average employed 88 percent of the time, i.e., more than in 1970-71, while the figure for the black sample had fallen to an average of 70 percent of the year. Changes in the sample means of the predictor variables and their effects may partially explain this divergence in black and white male employment.[12]

The large relative decline over the decade in the proportion of the black sample who were married contributed to the divergence in employment. The married portion of the white sample fell from 41 percent in 1970-71 to 21 percent in 1979; for blacks the figure declined from 29 percent in 1970-71 to 6 percent in 1979. The effect of marital status on employment is positive and substantial for both blacks and whites in 1970-71, and this effect increased by about the same percentage for both groups over the decade.

The movement of blacks from the South also contributed to a divergence in black and white employment over the decade. The proportion of blacks living in the South declined over the decade relative to whites. The positive effect on employment for blacks of living in the South increased also relative to that for whites over the decade. Thus, although blacks in the South had higher employment in both 1970-71 and 1979, the increased effect of living in the South and the decline in the proportion of blacks living there contributed to the divergence in employment over the decade.

Although in 1979 blacks were still substantially less likely than whites to finish high school, the proportion of those who did rose over the decade. The estimated effect of high school graduation on employment is generally positive (although it is statistically insignificant for blacks) and converges for blacks and whites over the decade. Thus, changes in the distribution and effects of education, if anything, contributed to a convergence in black and white employment.

The black sample, younger on average than the white sample in 1970-71, had the same average age in 1979. In 1970-71, the effect of age on employment was positive for whites and insignificant for blacks. In 1979, it was more strongly positive for blacks than for whites. These findings indicate that over the decade, the trends in both the age distribution and age effects acted to decrease the employment difference between blacks and whites.

The growing representation of blacks relative to whites in SMSAs contributed marginally to the divergence in employment over the decade. The proportion of both samples living in SMSAs fell over the decade, but the fall was greater for whites, yielding a slight decrease in the relative representation of blacks. In both 1970-71 and 1979 residence in an SMSA had a positive effect on employment for whites and a negative effect on employment for blacks; further, the effects increased slightly over the decade.

Turnover, as measured by the number of employers during the year, decreased markedly over the decade among blacks but remained relatively unchanged among whites. The percentage of blacks not working at all during the year rose from 4 percent in 1970-71 to 11 percent in 1979. Only 1 percent of whites did not work at all in 1970-71, and that low figure also prevailed in 1979. Multiple job holding increased slightly over the decade among whites (from 38 percent of the white sample in 1970-71 to 43 percent in 1979) and

Table 3.6
Employment Regressions for White and Black Males, 1970-71

	Blacks			Whites		
	Sample means	Estimated coefficients (t-stats. in parentheses)		Sample means	Estimated coefficients (t-stats. in parentheses)	
		Regression I	Regression II		Regression I	Regression II
Dependent variable: $WKEMPR_t$	.77	—	—	.86	—	—
Explanatory variables:						
AGE	.59	-.008 (-.24)	-.002 (-.06)	.66	.062 (2.56)	.031 (1.36)
ATTAINMENT	.37	.001 (.03)	-.015 (-.48)	.70	.045 (1.80)	.023 (.98)
EM1	.45	.893 (10.25)	.684 (7.89)	.61	.872 (9.6)	.622 (7.02)
EM2	.28	.624 (6.99)	.490 (5.77)	.25	.782 (8.48)	.564 (6.36)
EM3	.23	.702 (7.75)	.512 (5.77)	.13	.680 (7.22)	.459 (5.08)
MARRIED	.29	.110 (3.02)	.077 (2.26)	.41	.061 (2.59)	.031 (1.4)

SMSA	.69	-.027 (-.67)	-.058 (-1.57)	.64	.005 (.22)	.004 (.19)
SOUTH	.61	.074 (1.95)	.037 (1.04)	.32	.060 (2.36)	.051 (2.21)
WKEMPR$_{t-1}$	.77	—	-.340 (-6.06)	.87	—	-.404 (-8.11)
Constant term	—	-1.02	-.713	—	-1.07	-.730
	n = 195	$R^2 = .45$	$R^2 = .54$	n = 341	$R^2 = .33$	$R^2 = .44$
		F = 19.8	F = 24.4		F = 20.8	F = 29.4

UNIVERSE: Males, 18-21 as of the survey in 1969, who were neither enrolled in school nor in the military between the survey in 1969 and the survey in 1971.

Table 3.7
Employment Regressions for White and Black Males, Calendar 1979

	Blacks			Whites		
	Sample means	Estimated coefficients (t-stats. in parentheses)		Sample means	Estimated coefficients (t-stats. in parentheses)	
		Regression I	Regression II		Regression I	Regression II
Dependent variable: WKEMPR$_t$	.70	—	—	.88	—	—
Explanatory variables: AGE	.69	.093 (1.82)	.037 (.82)	.69	.027 (1.27)	.018 (.94)
ATTAINMENT	.51	.075 (1.59)	.0002 (.006)	.72	.086 (3.73)	.031 (1.40)
EM1	.57	.681 (8.62)	.629 (9.08)	.56	.843 (11.49)	.626 (8.69)
EM2	.24	.661 (7.77)	.614 (8.23)	.31	.818 (11.08)	.610 (8.46)
EM3	.08	.728 (6.83)	.635 (6.75)	.12	.792 (10.28)	.592 (7.95)
MARRIED	.06	.166 (1.70)	.088 (1.02)	.21	.068 (2.78)	.046 (2.06)

SMSA	.68 (-.25)	-.014 (-.56)	-.026	.59 (1.47)	.030 (2.01)	.038
SOUTH	.53	.056 (1.05)	-.009 (-.20)	.29	.067 (2.99)	.057 (2.81)
$WKEMPR_{t-1}$	.64	—	-.395 (-6.94)	.86	—	-.351 (-8.54)
Constant term	—	-1.04	-.721	—	-1.07	-.763
	n=161	R^2 = .45	R^2 = .58	n=386	R^2 = .34	R^2 = .44
		F = 15.4	F = 23.3		F = 23.9	F = 33.4

UNIVERSE: Males, 18-21 as of January 1, 1978, who were neither enrolled in school nor in the military between January 1, 1978 and December 31, 1979.

decreased substantially among blacks (from 51 percent of the black sample in 1970-71 to 32 percent in 1979).

The regression results for 1970-71 reveal for whites a statistically significant negative relationship between the number of employers and employment (based on pairwise t-tests of the difference between the estimated coefficients on EM1, EM2, and EM3). White workers who had two employers during the year were employed five weeks less on average than those with a single employer during the year, and those with three or more employers were working 13 weeks less on average than those with two employers. Although the relationship among blacks is not as striking, it is definitely negative. Annual employment among blacks with one employer and those with three or more employers was almost identical to that of whites. Blacks with two employers had much less employment than whites in the same category. Blacks with two employers experienced 13 less weeks of employment and those with three or more employers 10 weeks less employment than those with a single employer. These results indicate that in 1970-71 the lower number of weeks of employment among blacks resulted from: (1) their somewhat greater representation among those with no employment during the year and, (2) higher average turnover among the employed together with a stronger negative relationship between turnover and employment.

In the 1979 estimates, the positions of blacks and whites with regard to turnover are reversed. Blacks move to a position of less turnover than whites, and the proportion of blacks not working during the year increases greatly relative to whites. In addition, the relationship between number of employers and total employment is only weakly negative among whites and totally absent for blacks, black workers with three or more employers experiencing slightly more time employed than those with fewer employers. In 1979, therefore, the reduced employment among blacks results from a much larger proportion of the black than the white sample having had no job during the year, blacks having fewer employers on average and less employment among those with just one or two employers during the year.

As a crude test of whether employment levels are more persistent among blacks or whites, we added employment in the previous year, $WKEMPR_{t-1}$, to the regression equation, and the results are shown as Regression II in tables 3.6 and 3.7. The size of the estimated coefficient on this variable indicates the extent of the relationship between levels of employment in subsequent years. In 1970-71 the coefficient is smaller for whites than for blacks, but in 1979 the opposite is true. Although the differences are not statistically significant in either case, they indicate a change in the relative size of the measures. Thus, as the employment distribution during the year for blacks has become more bimodal, the persistence in these levels from year to year has increased for blacks relative to whites.

III. Conclusion

This paper addressed the question of whether the relative decline in employment and the relative concentration of joblessness among black youth during the 1970s was associated with a relative increase in movement out of employment or, alternatively, with a relative decrease in turnover out of unemployment, which would indicate increasing stagnation. We found support for the latter.

Average annual employment among blacks is increasingly being determined by a subgroup with little or no employment experience. Observing a sample of civilian males age 18-21 who were not enrolled in school in 1971, and a similar sample in 1979, we found that as annual employment decreased over the decade for blacks, job mobility also decreased drastically. And while lower employment experienced in 1970-71 was positively related to the number of employers the individual had during the year (an indication of turnover), this relationship was much weaker for whites and totally absent for blacks in 1979. Further, there was a relative increase over the decade for blacks in the extent to which high or low employment in one year predicts high or low employment in the next year.

It was beyond the scope of this study to consider specific policies to address the deterioration in black employment patterns over the 1970s. We have shown, however, that the growth in joblessness among young black males, both absolutely and relative to that for young white males, must not be treated as an aggregate, or market, phenomenon for purposes of policy formulation. Rather, the problems are specific to that growing subgroup of blacks being chronically excluded from employment. If the plight of these young black males is to be improved, the problems must be identified and addressed directly.

NOTES

1. For a review of the literature on the divergence in black and white unemployment rates over the last three decades see Mare and Winship (1980). Other examples of empirical work on the divergence in unemployment rates over the 1970s are: Iden (1980), pp. 10-15; Bowers (1979), pp. 4-19; Newman (1979), pp. 19-27.

2. For excellent studies of the differing and changing distributions of unemployment for blacks and whites, see Clark and Summers (1979); Lerman, Barnow, and Moss (1979); and Levy (1980).

3. For an example of this view, see the comments by Robert Hall following Clark and Summers (1979); Hall (1970); and Hall (1972).

4. See: Clark and Summers (1979) and Levy (1980) for examples of this view.

5. There are a large number of missing values in the NLS youth data on those variables used to designate periods in an individual's work history as either unemployed or out-of-labor force time. Further, the missing values are concentrated among those persons with relatively long periods out of work. The situation is serious enough to bias downward an unemployment measure based on the work history. For this reason the labor force determination is ignored and time of employment is used.

6. It is possible that the relative increase in military enlistment and school enrollment among blacks has to a growing extent over the decade removed the most able persons from the black labor force and from our sample of blacks. This would lead to a decrease in the employability of our sample over the decade relative to the entire black population and relative to the white sample and, thereby, bias our results. The comparison of sample and population characteristics indicates that this effect on our results is minor.

7. The CPS unemployment rates for white males 25-54 in the modal month for the NLS surveys were 3.7 percent in 1971 and 4.3 percent in 1980. The average monthly CPS unemployment rates for the months covered by the work history data were 3.5 percent in 1970-71 and 3.6 percent in 1979-80.

8. Among the *entire* youth population there has been a definite divergence in the employment of blacks and whites. It is due in large part to a relative increase in black school enrollment and military enlistment. However, any trends we find are net of the effects of increasing enrollment and enlistment since we have sampled only nonenrolled, civilian males.

9. We recognize the number of employers is certainly not a perfect measure of turnover; it considers only movements in and out of employment and measures these movements with substantial variance since persons with one employer during the year could have had from zero (if they held the job for the entire year) to two transitions (if they found and lost the job during the course of the year). These problems notwithstanding, the number of employers does indicate the number of periods of job search during the year.

10. There are certainly other factors which might well have contributed to the divergence in employment over the decade; among the most important is the availability of unearned income and central city residence. Preliminary regressions using these variables did not yield significant results. The employment patterns of blacks in central cities were not significantly different from those of noncentral city residents of SMSAs,

although the concentration of blacks in central cities increased over the decade. Although positive trends in unearned income have been put forth as important explanations of declining black employment, we found no evidence of this in preliminary regressions. However, the large number of missing values on this variable reduced the sample sizes greatly and prevented generalization from our results.

11. The assessment of the impact of the predictors on the black/white employment differential will center on Regression I of tables 3.6 and 3.7. Table 3.6 includes the regression results for 1970-71 for the white and black samples, respectively, and table 3.7 presents the results for whites and blacks in 1979. Regression II on these tables includes $WKEMPR_{t-1}$ as an explanatory variable. This variable is certainly correlated with some if not all of the other regressors since to some extent factors predicting high (low) employment in one year will predict high (low) employment the next year; thus its inclusion would complicate our discussion of the trends in the effects of the other regressors.

12. To determine the contribution of a given variable to the divergence in black and white employment over the decade we use a variant of the procedure used to decompose the difference in sample means into the portion due to (1) the difference in intercept terms, (2) the difference in sample distributions across values for the explanatory variables, (3) differences in the effects of the explanatory variables, and (4) the interaction of differences in effects and differences in distributions. For an explanation of this procedure see: Althauser and Wigler (1972), and, a companion piece, Iams and Thornton (1975). However, instead of summing across all variables to get the total contribution of (1) - (4) to the difference in sample means, we sum across the effects above to get the total contribution of each variable to the difference in sample means of the dependent variable.

REFERENCES

Althauser, R.P. and Wigler, M. 1972. "Standardization and Component Analysis." *Sociological Methods and Research* I, 1: 97-135.

Bowers, N. 1979. "Young and Marginal: An Overview of Youth Employment." *Monthly Labor Review* 102, 10 (October): 4-18.

Clark, K.B. and Summers, L.H. 1979. "Labor Market Dynamics and Unemployment: A Reconsideration." *Brookings Papers on Economic Activity* 1: 13-60. Washington, DC: The Brookings Institution.

Hall, R.E. 1970. "Why is the Unemployment Rate so High at Full Employment." *Brookings Papers on Economic Activity* 3: 369-402. Washington, DC: The Brookings Institution.

_____ . 1972. "Turnover in the Labor Force." *Brookings Papers on Economic Activity* 3: 709-756. Washington, DC: The Brookings Institution.

Iams, H.M. and Thornton, A. 1975. "Decomposition of Differences: A Cautionary Note." *Sociological Methods and Research* 3, 3: 341-352.

Iden, G. 1980. "The Labor Force Experience of Black Youth: A Review." *Monthly Labor Review* 103, 8 (August): 10-16.

Lerman, R.; Barnow, B.; and Moss, P. 1979. *Concepts and Measures of Structural Unemployment.* Technical Analysis Paper No. 64 (March). Office of the Assistant Secretary for Policy, Evaluation, and Research. U.S. Department of Labor.

Levy, F. 1980. *Labor Force Dynamics and the Distribution of Employability.* Working Paper; 1269-02 (January). Washington, DC: The Urban Institute.

Mare, R.D. and Winship, C. 1980. *Changes in the Relative Labor Force Status of Black and White Youths: A Review of the Literature .* Madison: University of Wisconsin, Institute for Research on Poverty.

Newman, M.J. 1979. "The Labor Market Experience of Black Youth, 1954-1978." *Monthly Labor Review* 102, 10 (October): 19-27.

Chapter 4
Choices in Education

Michael E. Borus
and
Susan A. Carpenter

As high school students advance through the educational system, they must make a variety of important decisions which will affect the rest of their lives. Among these decisions are (1) to drop out of school without completing the 12th grade, (2) to reenter and try to complete high school if they have dropped out, and (3) to go directly from the 12th grade on to college. Here we will study all three decisions and the factors that seem to influence these decisions. All of these decisions can radically influence the student's future occupation, earning ability, and even social class. For this reason, inequality in education today may lead to continuing inequality in the labor market for years to come. To the extent that this country sets equal opportunity in the labor market as a goal, it must first make equal quantity and quality of education a priority.

National statistics show that as a group, blacks and Hispanics complete fewer years of schooling than whites. Many government programs, such as income transfers, aid to education, and tax laws can affect the quantity and quality of schooling youth get. In order to estimate the effects of such programs, however, we must first determine whether current inequalities are due to race and ethnicity per se, or due to other characteristics which are correlated with race and ethnicity. Such characteristics may include parental education, being in poverty, living with a single parent, and such schooling characteristics as the student-teacher ratio. Any of these characteristics, alone or in combination, can influence the number of years of schooling completed. We will examine all of these characteristics, and many more, to determine how to most effectively attack the problem of educational inequality.

The decisions to drop out or go on to college have been studied extensively elsewhere, while returning to school has received relatively little attention. This study, however, differs from previous ones by drawing on the 1979 and 1980 NLS data. These longitudinal data permit measurement of attitudes and other characteristics prior to the decision in order to predict subsequent behavior. Cross-sectional analyses cannot permit this type of prior measurement. This study also makes use of information gathered directly from the schools attended by the respondents, and thus it takes into account both the school environment variables and the individual characteristics of students, whereas most previous examinations of dropping out and going on to college have had only one or the other of these. This data set is national, permitting more general conclusions to be drawn, as opposed to many previous studies which are at the state, city or even individual school level. Fourth, school, background and attitudinal variables not previously available to researchers are contained in this very large data set. Finally, these data are also quite recent, which is important because aggregate statistics indicate an increase in dropout rates nationwide and increasing college enrollment by women and minorities which would not be reflected in earlier studies.

I. Dropping Out[1]

Between the Spring of 1979 and the Spring of 1980, approximately 820,000 youth born from 1957 to 1964 left school without completing the 12th grade.[2] They represent 5.1 percent of all young people in this age group who were enrolled below the college level. The first column of table 4.1 indicates the dropout rates during this year's period[3] for various groups of the 16,230,000 young people enrolled in Spring 1979. Substantially above average dropout rates are found for the following groups: Hispanics; youth who had a child during the year; youth from households with low parental education; youth who lived in single parent households when they were 14 years old; youth who were unemployed at the 1979 interview; youth who did not expect to go on to college; youth who could not state a curriculum; those who were dissatisfied with school and young people below grade level by two years or more.

A number of factors have been found to be related to dropping out of school.[4] Minorities and males have higher dropout rates in the aggregate data.[5] Other characteristics found to be associated with increased dropping out are: increased age (Watson 1976); lower socioeconomic status, as measured by parental education (Masters 1969, Rumberger 1981, Watson 1976) and a measure of reading material in the home (McNally 1977, Rumberger 1981); living in the South (Nam, Rhodes and Herriott 1968); living in a rural area (Conlisk 1969); living in a single parent household (Bachman, Green and Wirtanen 1971, Shaw 1979); having a larger number of siblings (Bachman, Green and Wirtanen 1971, Rumberger 1981, Shaw 1979, Watson 1976); and being non-Catholic (Nam, Rhodes and Herriott 1968). Also, Rumberger (1981) found that less knowledge of the world of work (an intelligence proxy), educational expectations, being married, living in an SMSA, and a lower local unemploy-

Table 4.1
Factors Influencing Dropping Out of School
Before Completing 12th Grade During 1979-80 (Probit Results)

Characteristic[a]	Mean Dropout Rate	Maximum Likelihood Estimate	t-value	Partial Derivative Evaluated at Means
Age		0.130	4.85**	0.009
Race				
Black	5.9	-0.345	-4.12**	-0.025
Hispanic	9.0	-0.065	-0.77	-0.005
White	4.6	—	—	—
Had Child Between Interviews				
Yes	28.0	0.832	5.80**	0.059
No	4.9	—	—	—
Father's Education				
0-11 years	9.4	0.399	3.29**	0.028
12 years	3.3	0.137	1.08	0.010
More than 12 years	1.4	—	—	—
Education not available	10.8	0.442	2.76**	0.032
Poverty Status of Family in 1978				
Above poverty	4.3	—	—	—
Below poverty	10.5	0.200	2.64**	0.014
Income not available	4.9	0.125	1.45	0.009
Mother in Home at Age 14				
Yes	4.7	—	—	—
No	14.8	0.323	2.76**	0.023

Father in Home at Age 14				
Yes	4.3	--	--	--
No	9.2	0.139	1.89+	0.010
Frequency of Religious Attendance		-0.004	-3.94**	-0.0003
Knowledge of the World of Work Score		-0.053	-3.04**	-0.004
Intend to Work at Age 35				
Yes	4.3	-0.227	-2.63**	-0.016
No	3.6	--	--	--
Not Available	11.3	-0.017	-0.14	-0.001
Intend to Join Military				
Yes	10.5	0.241	2.31*	0.017
No	4.9	--	--	--
Intend to Marry Within 5 Years - Female				
Yes	8.2	0.180	2.24*	0.013
No	3.0	--	--	--
Intend to Marry Within 5 Years - Male				
Yes	7.8	0.212	2.52**	0.015
No	6.0	--	--	--
Residence in an SMSA				
Yes	5.2	0.127	1.78+	0.009
No	4.8	--	--	--

Table 4.1 (continued)

Characteristic[a]	Mean Dropout Rate	Maximum Likelihood Estimate	t-value	Partial Derivative Evaluated at Means
Employment Status at 1979 Interview				
Employed	4.4	0.013	0.17	0.001
Unemployed	9.1	0.261	3.31**	0.019
Out of labor force	4.5	--	--	--
Expects to Attend College				
Yes	1.7	-0.480	-6.39**	-0.034
No	9.4	--	--	--
High School Curriculum				
General	6.5	--	--	--
College preparatory	1.2	-0.353	-3.55**	-0.025
Vocational	5.5	-0.109	-1.25	-0.008
Curriculum not available	19.4	0.384	3.29**	0.027
School Satisfaction				
Satisfied	4.4	-0.339	-4.42**	-0.024
Unsatisfied	9.8	--	--	--
Two or More Years Behind Modal Grade				
Yes	16.8	0.286	3.56**	0.020
No	4.0	--	--	--

Student-Teacher Ratio				
Less than 15	2.7	--	--	--
15	3.5	0.130	0.52	0.009
16	4.4	0.338	1.55	0.024
17	3.2	-0.014	-0.06	-0.001
18	3.3	0.258	1.35	0.018
19	5.8	0.398	2.20*	0.028
20	6.3	0.452	2.36*	0.032
21	4.3	0.392	2.18*	0.028
22	8.2	0.582	3.03**	0.042
23	6.3	0.475	2.30*	0.034
24 or more	7.7	0.530	2.99**	0.038
Not available	5.4	0.419	2.66**	0.030
Mean	5.1			
Constant		-3.676	-7.54**	-0.263
2 times log likelihood ratio		565.518		
N		5165		

UNIVERSE: Respondents age 14-21 on January 1, 1979 who were enrolled in primary or secondary school at survey date 1979 or May 1, 1979, whichever was earlier.

a. The values entering the intercept were being white, not having a child between interviews, father's educational attainment more than 12 years, family income in 1978 above poverty level, mother and father in home at age 14, not intending to work at age 35, not intending to join the military, not intending to marry within five years, living outside of an SMSA, being out of the labor market at the time of the 1979 interview, not expecting to attend college, enrolled in general high school curriculum in 1979, dissatisfied with school, not being two or more years behind grade level, and being enrolled in a school with a student/teacher ratio of less than 16.

+Significant at $P = .10$
*Significant at $P = .05$
**Significant at $P = .01$

ment rate (which may reflect the opportunity costs of remaining in school) increase the probability of dropping out. Bachman, Green and Wirtanen (1971) and Rumberger (1981) both found that individuals who were more internal (felt they had control over their own affairs) had lower dropout rates than those who felt their lives were externally controlled. Finally, McNally (1977) found lower dropout rates for those youth who were employed.

Attitudes toward school were related to the probability of leaving in Bachman, Green and Wirtanen (1971).[6] They also found that students behind grade level and blacks attending segregated schools had higher probabilities of dropping out. McNally (1977) found a positive relationship between student-teacher ratios and dropping out for blacks and between the dropout rate and being behind grade level in school. Curriculum might also be expected to affect dropout rates: those students having specific goals as evidenced by participation in vocational or college preparatory programs might be less likely to drop out, although McNally (1977) did not find a significant relationship when looking only at participation in vocational education.

In addition, the NLS provides school, background and attitudinal variables which can be hypothesized to affect the probability of dropping out of school and which are not contained in other studies. Receipt of remedial English or mathematics training could be expected to indicate a problem in school and consequently to be associated with higher dropout rates among those students who have received these services. Students in smaller schools, private schools and those from areas where greater expenditures on education were made from government funds were hypothesized to have lower dropout rates because of the additional attention and resources which would be provided to them. Those young persons who had moved in the preceding year were thought to be more prone to dropping out because they lacked roots in their new schools. Second generation Americans possibly lack the home support for staying in school although the pressures to "Americanize" may counteract this. Those who attend religious services more frequently were expected to stay in school. Students who do not view the labor force as their prime goal (i.e., said they would not be working at age 35), those intending to join the military, and those who are married or intend to marry within five years, all were felt to be more likely to drop out of high school. Finally, those students whose 1979 family income was below the poverty level, as defined in the Current Population Survey, can be expected to have higher dropout rates due to their greater financial need.

Findings

The dependent variable for analysis was defined as whether or not youth who were 14-22 and enrolled below the college level when interviewed in 1979 had dropped out of school without completing the 12th grade when interviewed in 1980. All of the independent variables discussed above were included in the model, using their values as of Spring 1979 unless otherwise noted. The data were run using both ordinary least squares and probit analysis and the results are presented in table 4.1.[7]

Many of the variables previously found to lead to dropping out were significant in this analysis too. Exceptions were number of siblings, parental nativity, availability of reading materials in the home at age 14, religion, extent of internality/externality, region of the country, residence in a rural area, the local unemployment rate, local government spending per student, and the degree of segregation in the school.[8]

After controlling for the other variables, it is found that black youth have an approximately 2.5 percentage point lower probability of dropping out of school.[9] Each additional year of age increases the dropout probability by about

1 percentage point and those youth who have had a child be-tween the interviews have a dropout probability 6 percentage points higher than those who did not. Family background is important, in that coming from a household where the father did not complete the 12th grade[10] increases the dropout probability by nearly 3 percentage points. Those whose family incomes in 1978 were below the poverty line had a 1 percentage point higher probability of dropping out of school and those whose mothers were not in the household at age 14 had about a 2 percentage point higher probability of leaving school. Those youth with more regular religious attendance were less likely to be dropouts. Also, youth having less knowledge of the labor market (a partial proxy for ability—see Parnes and Kohen 1975) had higher probabilities of dropping out by up to 4 percentage points.

Intentions for the future are also important correlates of dropping out of school. Those who intend to work at age 35 are about 1.5 percentage points more likely to stay in school, as are those who do not intend to join the military. Similar increases in the probability of remaining in school occurred among those youth who did not intend to marry within five years. A substantially lower dropout rate (a reduction of nearly 3.5 percentage points) was found for those who expected to attend college. Similarly, dropout rates about 2 percentage points lower were found for students enrolled in college preparatory curricula as opposed to general curricula, for students who were satisfied with school, and for those who were not two or more years behind modal grade. Students in schools with higher student-teacher ratios were more likely to be dropouts than those in schools with student-teacher ratios less than 15, although the relationship was not linear. Finally, those youth who were unemployed at the time of the 1979 interview had higher dropout rates than those who were out of the labor force or employed.[11]

II. Dropouts Returning to School[12]

Between Spring 1979 and 1980, approximately 8 percent, or about 280,000, of the 14-22-year-olds who had dropped out of high school returned. One would hypothesize that the same variables which lead to dropping out of school would influence the decision to return to school, but that the signs on the variables would be in the opposite direction. For instance, students with high educational expectations after dropping out would be more likely to return to school.[13] Thus, the independent variables used in the analysis included all those in the equations for dropping out of school.[14] The dependent variable was whether or not nonenrolled youth age 14-22, who had not received a high school diploma or GED when interviewed in 1979, were enrolled when interviewed in 1980. Again, ordinary least squares and probit analyses were conducted.

Findings

Only a few factors influence the return to school (table 4.2). Older youth were less likely to return: each additional year of age decreased the probability by 2 percentage points. Those youth expecting to attend college were more likely to return—this increased the probability by 6 percentage points—as were never married youth, 3 points. Finally, youth living in counties where local government expenditures per student were over $975 were more likely to return than youth from schools where less was spent on the schools.

Table 4.2
Factors Influencing Returning to School by High School Dropouts
14-22 Years Old During 1979-1980 (Probit Results)

Characteristic	Mean Rate of Returning to School	Maximum Likelihood Estimate	t-value	Partial Derivative Evaluated at Means
Age		-0.290	-6.43**	-0.020
Ever Married				
Yes	2.4	-0.394	-2.26*	-0.027
No	10.6	–	–	–
Poverty Status of Family in 1978				
Above poverty	8.8	–	–	–
Below poverty	7.4	-0.223	-1.60	-0.015
Income not available	6.5	-0.236	-1.40	-0.016
Intend to Join Military				
Yes	13.6	0.135	0.75	0.009
No	7.4	–	–	–
Local Unemployment Rate				
Less than 3 percent	5.2	–	–	–
3-6 percent	8.1	0.039	0.10	0.003
6-9 percent	7.0	-0.026	-0.07	-0.002
9-12 percent	15.9	0.397	0.90	0.027
More than 12 percent	8.0	-0.495	-0.87	-0.034
Expects to Attend College				
Yes	23.0	0.894	5.55**	0.061
No	6.0	–	–	–

High School Curriculum				
General	8.2	--	--	--
College preparatory	1.1	-0.064	-0.24	0.004
Vocational	13.0	0.299	1.75	0.020
Curriculum not available	2.6	-0.662	-3.00**	-0.045
Two or More Years Behind Modal Grade				
Yes	20.4	-0.107	-0.66	-0.007
No	6.0	--	--	--
Student-Teacher Ratio				
Less than 15	11.0	--	--	--
15	8.7	-0.659	1.15	-0.045
16	2.8	-0.639	-1.50	-0.044
17	5.1	-0.716	-1.86†	-0.049
18	3.5	-0.544	-1.57	-0.037
19	14.7	-0.019	0.06	0.001
20	9.1	-0.524	-1.48	-0.036
21	6.7	-0.474	-1.37	-0.032
22	5.2	-0.608	-1.71†	-0.042
23	8.7	-0.733	-1.76†	-0.053
24 or more	9.7	-0.267	-0.85	-0.018
Not available	8.1	-0.433	-1.68†	-0.030

Table 4.2 (continued)

Characteristic	Mean Rate of Returning to School	Maximum Likelihood Estimate	t-value	Partial Derivative Evaluated at Means
Local Government Spending on Education per Student in County				
$1 - $749	3.5	--	--	--
$750 - $974	3.3	0.123	0.53	0.008
$975 - $1149	9.6	0.629	3.16**	0.043
$1150 - $1249	9.2	0.490	2.21*	0.034
$1250 or more	16.8	0.812	3.78**	0.056
Not available	8.3	0.537	1.55	0.037
Constant		4.208	4.64**	0.288
Mean	7.9			
2 times log likelihood ratio	170.585			
N	1337			

UNIVERSE: Respondents age 14-21 on January 1, 1979 who were not enrolled in primary or secondary school at survey date 1979 or May 1, 1979, whichever was earlier.

a. The values entering the intercept were being never married, family income in 1978 above poverty level, not intending to join the military, local unemployment rate less than 3 percent, not expecting to attend college, enrolled in general high school curriculum when dropped; out of school, not being two or more years behind grade level, having been enrolled in a school with a student/teacher ratio of less than 15, and living in a county where less than $750 of local government funds is spent on education per student.

†Significant at P = .10
*Significant at P = .05
**Significant at P = .01

III. Going Directly to College

Of the 3,190,000 youth enrolled in the 12th grade in the Spring of 1979, 48 percent were enrolled in college a year later. The same variables which influence dropping out of high school apparently also influence the decision to go directly to college. Race (Kolstad 1979), sex (Robertshaw and Wolfle 1980) and age (Rumberger 1981) have been found to be important variables. Parental education has been found to be positively correlated with college attendance in almost all studies (Bachman, Green, and Wirtanen 1971; Christensen, Melder and Weisbrod 1975). Likewise, Kolstad (1979), Robertshaw and Wolfle (1980), and Rumberger (1981) all found that number of siblings, educational expectations and a measure of academic ability influence enrollment in college. Kolstad (1979) also found that high school curriculum was important. Robertshaw and Wolfle (1980) found a rural background to lead to lower enrollment and Rumberger (1981) found a positive correlation with the reading materials index, living in the South, local unemployment rates, marital status, having a child, and, for Hispanics, living in a central city. Bachman, Green and Wirtanen (1971) found lower college attendance among those youth who had failed one or more times in school, had negative attitudes toward school, came from broken homes, were non-Jews, or were blacks in racially segregated schools.

In addition to including all the above variables, we hypothesize that the other variables used in the previous analyses will also apply to college decisionmaking. For example, the student-teacher ratio in high school should be a predictor on the basis that those students coming from high schools with lower student-teacher ratios are more likely to be academically prepared to go on to college. Receipt of remedial English or mathematics training could be expected to indicate poor academic preparation and, therefore, lower the rate of college attendance. Coming from a household in poverty during 1978 should indicate financial hardship which limits college attendance. Finally, youth who are not in the labor force, who plan to work at age 35 and who do not plan to join the military (those presumably more committed to school than work) would be expected to have higher percentages going directly to college than would other youth.

Findings

Our analysis of the determinants of moving directly from the 12th grade on to college showed that most of the variables were significant (see table 4.3). Much higher probabilities of moving from the 12th grade to college were found for older students (about 10 percentage points with each year of age); for those whose fathers attended college (19 to 26 points higher); and for females (8 to 11 points). Those students who thought they had more control over their environments, those who did not intend to marry within five years as compared with those with such intentions, and those who attended religious services more often also were more likely to move directly to college.[15]

Also more likely to go on directly to college were more able students, where ability is shown by knowledge of the labor market (up to 25 points); those not two or more years behind modal grade (33 points) and not having taken remedial education (18 points); those in college preparatory curricula (28 points above those in general programs and 38 points above those in vocational curricula); those from schools with 1,000-1,749 students, and of course those youth who said they expectd to attend college when in the 12th grade. Finally, we found that minorities who attend predominately white schools (i.e., less than 10 percent minority student bodies) were substantially less likely to attend college during the following year.

Table 4.3
Factors Influencing Going from 12th Grade to College
During 1979-1980 (Probit Results)

Characteristic[a]	Mean Rate of Going to College	Maximum Likelihood Estimate	t-value	Partial Derivative Evaluated at Means
Age		0.275	2.80**	0.104
Sex				
Female	51.0	--	--	--
Male	44.1	-0.301	-2.04*	-0.114
Father's Education				
0-11 years	28.0	-0.680	-4.60**	-0.258
12 years	39.5	-0.505	-3.63**	-0.192
More than 12 years	72.6	--	--	--
Education not available	22.2	-0.565	-2.16*	-0.215
Poverty Status of Family in 1978				
Above poverty	50.2	--	--	--
Below poverty	28.9	0.062	0.40	0.023
Income not available	45.2	-0.288	-2.08*	-0.110
Mother Born Outside the United States				
Yes	56.0	0.449	1.87†	0.171
No	46.7	--	--	--

Table 4.3 (continued)

Characteristic[a]	Mean Rate of Going to College	Maximum Likelihood Estimate	t-value	Partial Derivative Evaluated at Means
Father Born Outside the United States				
Yes	60.3	0.163	0.60	0.062
No	46.9	--	--	--
Frequency of Religious Attendance		0.006	3.46**	0.002
Knowledge of the World of Work Score		0.067	2.28*	0.025
Rotter Score		-0.091	-3.43**	-0.035
Intend to Work at Age 35				
Yes	49.3	0.258	1.67†	0.098
No	40.8	--	--	--
Not available	40.3	0.103	0.40	0.039
Intend to Marry Within 5 Years - Female				
Yes	43.9	-0.383	-2.68**	-0.146
No	48.9	--	--	--
Intend to Marry Within 5 years - Male				
Yes	31.4	-0.307	-1.89†	-0.117
No	51.4	--	--	--

Variable	%			
Expects to Attend College				
Yes	68.7	1.446	11.27**	0.550
No	8.2	—	—	—
High School Curriculum				
General	49.6	—	—	—
College preparatory	81.4	0.741	6.19**	0.282
Vocational	13.7	−1.39	−0.253	−1.56 −0.096
Curriculum not available	18.4	−0.670	−2.31*	−0.255
Two or More Years Behind Modal Grade				
Yes	14.4	−0.875	−3.10**	−0.333
No	49.7	—	—	—
Remedial Education Received				
Yes	24.0	−0.465	−2.95**	−0.177
No	52.5	—	—	—
Not available	46.7	−0.052	−0.36	−0.020
Student-Teacher Ratio				
Less than 15	41.9	—	—	—
15	40.9	−0.504	−1.54	−0.192
16	43.9	−0.511	−1.66†	−0.194
17	52.0	−0.199	−0.72	−0.076
18	57.2	−0.086	−0.32	−0.033
19	42.0	−0.425	−1.71†	−0.161
20	54.9	−0.357	−1.26	−0.136
21	50.6	−0.409	−1.56	−0.156
22	52.0	−0.346	−1.14	−0.131
23	44.2	−0.491	−1.61	−0.187
24 or more	46.4	0.022	0.09	0.009
Not available	44.2	0.131	0.38	0.050

Table 4.3 (continued)

Characteristic[a]	Mean Rate of Going to College	Maximum Likelihood Estimate	t-value	Partial Derivative Evaluated at Means
School Size				
1-999 students	41.6	-0.012	-0.08	-0.005
1000-1749 students	54.4	0.358	2.42*	0.136
More than 1750 students	50.2	--	--	--
Not available	43.8	-0.441	-1.33	-0.168
Minority Status of Respondent and Percentage of Minority Students in School				
Minority respondent, school less than 10 percent minorities	29.0	--	--	--
Minority respondent, school 10-50 percent minorities	46.2	1.285	3.17**	0.488
Minority respondent, school more than 50 percent minorities	45.3	0.900	2.23*	0.342
White respondent, school less than 10 percent minorities	45.7	0.795	2.02*	0.302

White respondent, school more than 10 percent minorities	52.1	0.803	2.01*	0.305
Not available	47.4	0.948	2.32*	0.360
Constant		-5.206	-2.87**	-1.987
Mean	47.5			
2 Times Log Likelihood Ratio		536.339		
N		971		

UNIVERSE: Respondents age 14-21 on January 1, 1979 who were enrolled in primary or secondary school at survey date 1979, or May 1, 1979, whichever was earlier.

a. The values entering the intercept were being female, mother and father born in the U.S., father's educational attainment more than 12 years, family income in 1978 above poverty level, not intending to marry within five years, not expecting to attend college, enrolled in general high school curriculum in 1979, not being two or more years behind grade level, did not receive remedial education, and being enrolled in a school with a student/teacher ratio of less than 15.

†Significant at P = .10
*Significant at P = .05
**Significant at P = .01

Several variables which were not statistically significant were: race; unemployment status of the youth and local unemployment rate; number of siblings; absence of a parent when growing up; and school satisfaction, type and funding level. These variables appear to indicate that financial constraints and school resources are relatively unimportant in determining who goes on to college when other variables are controlled.

IV. Conclusions and Policy Implications

Several conclusions may be drawn from these findings. First, in aggregate, black and Hispanic youth have higher dropout rates and lower probabilities of moving from high school directly to college than do whites. To the extent that these educational decisions affect subsequent labor market success, we can expect continuing racial inequality.

These racial differences in schooling decisions, however, appear due to factors other than race and ethnicity. When other factors are controlled, black youth are less likely than whites to drop out of school, and minority youth are just as likely to move on to college from the 12th grade as are white young people. Apparently, other variables that correlate with race and ethnicity lead minorities to their "negative" educational behavior. Family background variables correlated with minority status which affect schooling decisions include lower education of father, for both blacks and Hispanics; greater incidence of being from poverty homes, absence of mother or father in the home at age 14, and having a child during the year are both correlated and influential for blacks. Also, minorities have poorer schooling situations, i.e., blacks and Hispanics tend to have higher proportions two or more years behind modal grade, much lower knowledge of the labor market scores (our ability proxy), and higher student-teacher ratios.[16] Finally, black youth were more likely to be unemployed.

The implication of these findings is that to improve the schooling situation of minorities, other variables must be changed. Obviously, public policy, particularly as it relates to schools, can do very little to alter some of these variables. For instance, if knowledge of the labor market is actually a measure of basic intelligence, there is little that schools can do to alter it. Similarly, growing up in a single parent household is not easily manipulated by public policy, although government policies other than schooling may impact on this variable. On the other hand, specific background and school-related variables can be influenced by public actions. For instance, the knowledge of the world of work score has been shown to be correlated with race, poverty and age in earlier studies (Parnes and Kohen 1975), indicating that the scale may reflect learned and cultural materials rather than genetically inherited traits. This correlation implies that teaching about the labor market in the schools might reduce dropout rates and increase the proportion of youth going on to college. Obviously, reducing the number of youth who are behind grade level and are dissatisfied with school will also positively affect these decisions. Such changes would in turn lower the overall socioeconomic differences between whites and minorities.

A second finding is that coming from a poverty household and being unemployed while in school tend to increase the probability of dropping out of school, ceteris paribus. The higher dropout probability for poor youth may be the result of their facing substantial economic burdens which do not allow them to continue in school or of the higher marginal utility of income from finding jobs rather than from further schooling. Unemployed youth may similarly have financial burdens which they are trying to shoulder by seeking work, or they may be looking for attractive alternatives to school. Regardless of the reason for the higher dropout rates, it does not appear that programs which increase employment or reduce poverty will have a large direct effect on school enrollment. The effects of these two variables are not large; a reduction of less than 1 percentage point in the national dropout rate would result if there were no poverty and all youth were employed or not in the labor force.

Third, while it should be noted that, on average, youth from poorer families were less likely to attend college, this was probably due to the family background variables of poor youth, such as lower parental education and lower knowledge of the labor market, which were related to college attendance. When these factors were controlled, the percentages of poor youth going on to college were not statistically different from those who were not poor. It would appear that government and other financial aid was sufficient to overcome the strictly monetary problems of students, and financial constraints were not a major impediment to college attendance during 1979-80 among those students who did complete high school. Recent reductions in federal aid to college students may have negated this conclusion, however.

Fourth, school segregation did not affect the dropout rate when other factors were controlled. This implies that integration efforts will not affect this variable directly. On the other hand, minority youth in predominantly white schools were less likely than other minorities to go to college during the following year, a fact which may indicate that integration will raise college attendance rates among minorities.

Fifth, curriculum is a determinant of dropping out of school and going on to college. Students in college preparatory programs have lower dropout rates and higher college attendance rates than students in general studies and vocational curricula. Unfortunately it is not clear to what extent these differences are the result of the programs and how much represent self-selection on the part of the students: students desiring to complete school and go on to college could be expected to seek out college preparatory courses. To some extent the inclusion of the expected level of education controls for self-selection bias, but because expected education probably does not control for all of this bias it is impossible to say if placement of more students in college preparatory tracks would lead to reduced numbers of dropouts.

Plans for the future may reflect a young person's outlook on life but these plans also may be a function of their past experiences. For instance, youth planning to marry are more likely to drop out of school and not to go on directly to college from the 12th grade. It is not clear whether these young people are reducing their education because of their marital expectations or whether failures in high school have turned them away from education and toward other outlets, such as families. Regardless of the flow of causality, however, those youth who plan to marry earlier, join the military, and not to work at age 35, are more likely to leave school than other youth.

Sixth, school characteristics appear to have only limited influence on the three schooling decisions under study here. The dropout rate rises somewhat with student-teacher ratio. Students in schools with student-teacher ratios of less than 18 generally have dropout ratios about 3 percentage points lower than those where the ratio is 19 to 21, and 3 to 4 percentage points below students in schools where the ratio is 22 or more. The relationship is not linear, however, so that the effect of removing one student from each class would not be the same, e.g., going from classes of 23 to classes of 22 would appear to increase the dropout rate by 1 percentage point. Thus, while lowering the student-teacher ratio would lead to some reduction in dropouts, the impact would not likely be very great.

A further finding is that satisfaction with school is a correlate of dropping out; it would appear that if school satisfaction can be increased, dropping out of school can be decreased. Less clear is how this is to be accomplished. In addition to the single question on global satisfaction with school, nine more specific attitude questions were asked. Overall satisfaction was correlated significantly ($.12 \leq r \leq .20$, $P = .001$) with each, however, so that it is not evident that any specific actions such as improving teaching or counseling or school safety will necessarily have a significant impact on dropping out of school.[17]

Finally, teenage pregnancy is one of the major reasons for dropping out of school; having or fathering a child during the year increased the probability by 6 percentage points. Obviously, to the extent that childbearing is delayed until schooling is completed, educational attainment will be increased as will the youth's subsequent labor market success, which has been shown to be correlated with high school graduation. Programs such as sex education and the provision of contraceptive information in the home, school, or another setting, which lead to a reduction in teenage pregnancy, will have substantial impact on the schooling decisions of youth. Further, the provision of services which will permit students with children to continue their education could be helpful.

NOTES

1. By examining the dropout rate for this period, we depart from other studies which compare dropouts with high school graduates or enrollees at a point in time. Our procedure has two advantages. First, it allows us to exploit the longitudinal nature of the data. A major problem with single observation studies is that they measure variables after the dropout has occurred with the result that their measurements may be biased due to inaccurate recall in the case of attitudinal variables, variables for substantially earlier periods, and variables involving details tied closely to specific dates (e.g., employment status in a specific week prior to the dropping out). A second problem is timing of the dropout. If a post-school age group, e.g., 20-21-year-olds, is used, the analysis cannot differentiate persons who dropped out and then returned to school from those who went straight through to graduation. Our method, however, allows us to identify the dropout occurring in a given year and also allows analysis of the returnees.

2. This number compares to 885,000 14-24-year-olds reported by the U.S. Bureau of the Census (1981) to have been enrolled in October 1978 and not enrolled in 1979 without completing the 12th grade. Since the NLS sample was composed of persons who were at least 15, most of the slight difference can be explained by the omission of the 14-year-olds.

3. Approximately one year passed since the vast majority of respondents were reinterviewed 11-13 months after their initial interview.

4. In the following review of variables not all studies are cited which found a significant relationship between dropping out and the variable. Only a few are cited for each variable. The studies which have the most complete lists of variables are Bachman, Green and Wirtanen (1971), McNally (1977), and Rumberger (1981).

5. The NLS finds for youth age 20-21 that 31 percent of Hispanics, 24 percent of blacks and 12 percent of whites did not complete high school. Other studies show minorities have lower rates when socioeconomic background is controlled (Masters 1969). The NLS has aggregate dropout rates of 16 percent for males and 13 percent for females 20-21 years old.

6. The NLS contains a dichotomized global satisfaction with school measure and it would be expected that those students who were dissatisfied with school would more likely be the ones to drop out.

7. The regressions were run without using the sample weights. Due to computer program limitations, not all variables could be included in the probit analysis. Therefore, only those variables significant at P = .10 in the OLS regressions were included. The mean dropout rates are weighted to reflect the national population.

8. Since there were zero-order correlations of many of these variables with the dropout rate, we conclude that they must be correlated with other variables in the analysis which are more important.

9. The percentage point increases or decreases in the probabilities in this chapter are taken from the probit equations evaluated at the means. They represent the average changes for the entire sample holding the other variables constant at their means.

10. If the father was absent at age 14, mother's education was used.

11. It may be argued that the schooling variables are in fact intermediate outcomes of family background and other variables, possibly introducing multicollinearity. Therefore, the OLS equations were run omitting all of the school variables. The major changes were that being male, having moved in 1978, and the index of reading materials and sex were now significant. Also, some of the previously significant variables increased their coefficients and t-values.

12. This section by the authors appeared as "A Note on the Return of Dropouts to High School," *Youth and Society,* Vol. 14, No. 4, June 1983. Reprinted with permission.

13. This was borne out in the study by Larter and Cheng (1979).

14. School satisfaction, which was only measured for those in school, was not included in this equation. A variable for having been married was added to the equation since it was hypothesized that single youth would be more likely to return to school. There were not enough cases of married persons to include this variable in the dropout equation.

Earlier regression runs had also included variables for reason left school and length of time out of school, but these were not statistically significant and are omitted here.

15. To test whether these effects were artifacts of correlations with the school and the expectations for going to college variables, the OLS equation was run without them. The results were even more dramatic; the coefficients for Hispanics, blacks, females, not living in a rural area, the reading materials index, not living in the North Central states, and intending to work at age 35 became positive and significant at P = .05.

16. It should be noted, however, that when the school variables were dropped from the OLS regressions, the same relationships between race and ethnicity and the schooling decisions still occurred.

17. When the nine specific questions were included in earlier regression runs along with the global satisfaction question, none was statistically significant at P = .05.

REFERENCES

Bachman, J., S. Green and I. Wirtanen. 1971. "Dropping Out: Problem or Symptom?" *Youth in Transition, Volume III.* Ann Arbor: Institute for Social Research, University of Michigan.

Christensen, S., J. Melder and B. Weisbrod. 1975. "Factors Affecting College Attendance." *Journal of Human Resources* 10: 174-188.

Conlisk, J. 1969. "Determinants of School Enrollment and School Performance." *Journal of Human Resources* 4: 140-157.

Kolstad, A. 1979. *Influence of High School Type and Curriculum in Higher Education and Postsecondary Training.* Paper available through ERIC system as ED172627.

Larter, S. and M. Cheng. 1979. "Study of Returning Students, Part III." *Characteristics, Opinions and Experiences of Returnees and Non-Returnees.* Paper available through ERIC system as ED188029.

Masters, S.H. 1969. "The Effects of Family Income on Children's Education: Some Findings on Inequality of Opportunity." *Journal of Human Resources* 4: 158-175.

McNally, K.V. 1977. *Estimation of Attrition Behavior: An Analysis of Predictors of High School Dropout Behavior in the United States.* Unpublished doctoral dissertation at Columbia University.

Nam, C., A.L. Rhodes and R. Herriott. 1968. "School Retention by Race, Religion and Socioeconomic Status." *Journal of Human Resources* 3: 171-190.

Parnes, H. and A. Kohen. 1975. "Occupational Information and Labor Market Status: The Case of Young Men." *Journal of Human Resources* 10: 44-55.

Robertshaw, D. and L. Wolfle, 1980. *Discontinuities in Schooling and Educational Attainment.* Paper available through ERIC system as ED186488.

Rumberger, R. 1981. "Experiences in High School and College." In *Pathways to the Future: A Longitudinal Study of Young Americans,* by Borus et al., U.S. Department of Labor.

Shaw, L.B. 1979. *Does Living in a Single-Parent Family Affect High School Completion for Young Women?* Paper available through ERIC system as ED174700.

U.S. Bureau of the Census. 1981. *School Enrollment-Social and Economic Characteristics of Students: October 1979.* Current Population Reports, Series P-20, No. 360. Washington, DC: U.S. Government Printing Office.

Watson, C. 1976. *Focus on Dropouts.* Paper available through ERIC system as ED168123.

Chapter 5
Quantity of Learning and Quality of Life for Public and Private High School Youth

William R. Morgan*

> Even in quantity it is and is likely to remain, altogether insufficient, while in quality, though with some slight tendency to improvement, it is never good except by some rare accident, and generally so bad as to be little more than nominal.
>
> J.S. Mill, *Principles of Political Economy* (1848)

The issue of how much a society should use public or private institutions to educate its citizenry is a fundamental question of democracy. Not surprisingly, its salience increases at times when the educational system as a whole is under attack. John Stuart Mill's dismal assessment of English popular education as it existed in 1848 is strikingly similar to criticisms of American education today. Paradoxically, it was government-subsidized private education which bore the brunt of his criticism then. Mill advocated reducing

*A version of this paper is to appear as "Learning and Student Life Quality of Public and Private School Youth" in *Sociology of Education*. I am grateful to Yu-Hsia Chen for her excellent research assistance.

the role of private schools and giving more support to the better quality, state-run schools.

Mid-nineteenth century England is, of course, quite different from late twentieth century America—at least most of us think so. Instead of a John Stuart Mill attempting to speak out on behalf of the "ignorant poor," the many voices of American public opinion, expressed through polls, school board elections and the popular media, have been clamoring for improved education for their children. In the search for alternatives, many have questioned whether the public schools are performing as efficiently as the private schools. Perhaps public schools should become more "like" private schools, and even more directly, more parents should have the economic opportunity to enroll their children in private schools. Pending Congressional legislation to provide tax credits to parents who send their children to private schools is the most concrete manifestation of this public sentiment.

A basic premise of the current national debate is the belief that the average American child does in fact learn more in private than in public schools. Research by James A. Coleman, the nation's preeminent educational sociologist, at first appeared to substantiate this belief. Coleman, Hoffman, and Kilgore's (CHK) 1981 study of public and private schools has been widely publicized, but also heavily criticized by the social science research community. The specific theoretical and methodological issues under attack are discussed in detail elsewhere (e.g., Olneck 1981; Bryk 1981; Goldberger and Cain 1982; Morgan 1983). In this chapter we shall take a new look at learning in public and private schools, using the fresh data base of the NLS survey and a different theoretical perspective.

Omitted from the CHK study was any reference to existing social science theory on how schooling operates, or to any of the sociological work to which Coleman himself had been an important early contributor (Coleman 1961). What CHK provided was a loose input-output economic metaphor by which to organize their results. Each of the four analytic chapters in their report was addressed to one of the following questions: "Who is in the schools? What resources go into them? What goes on? and What comes out?" (CHK 1981, p. 6). This implicit education production function (Hanushek 1979) needs much greater refinement, however, if it is to move beyond the status of metaphor and provide explicit theoretical guidance in analyzing possible learning differences between public and private school youth.

The first and most important refinement has to do with the assumption that each sector operates in some characteristic total manner on all students to produce learning in varying degrees of efficiency. As Brown and Saks (1981) have recently demonstrated, internal decisions made to allocate resources have a crucial bearing on overall level of learning within classrooms. This argument for resource allocation, although ignored by CHK, also applies at the macro-level of effectiveness in school sector. Overall sector efficiency depends greatly on the decisions each sector makes about resource allocation. Insofar as the private sector devotes a larger share of its instructional time to college preparation, which it certainly does, its average level of cognitive achievement will be higher. Any adequate production function designed to gauge sector effectiveness must incorporate this difference, and the most direct procedure would be to include in the equation a track or curriculum enrollment variable. The important research question thus becomes whether or not private schools are more effective *net* of this resource allocation difference. To omit this variable from the production function, as CHK choose to do, is a serious misspecification.

A second related issue in this production function approach to national educational policy is the question of locus of decisionmaking. Assuming an adequate school sector production function can be estimated, who would use this function to maximize the learning of American youth? Presumably national educational policymakers, yet Coleman has at the same time identified federal regulation of American public education as one of its principal weaknesses. In a popular policy journal, he charged that "public schools have become an overregulated industry, with regulations and mandates ranging from draconian desegregation to mainstreaming of emotionally disturbed children, to athletic activities that are blind to sex differences" (Coleman 1981). When he recommends tuition tax credits for parents who send their children to private schools, he argues it is a deregulation step, giving more parents latitude to choose the type of education they want their children to have. If individual parents are in fact the key policymakers, then it would seem an optimal household education consumption function (Becker 1976) would better inform their sector choice decision than would a national education production function.

Therefore the appropriate education for parents to choose for their child is one which provides the best opportunity to maximize the child's human capital (learning and future earnings), given the constraints on parents of time, income, and production knowledge. The latter would include all factors that enter proper judgments about what type, level, and amount of schooling best maximizes the learning and earnings potential of a particular child. All other things equal, parents uncertain of their child's abilities and interests might prefer a "comprehensive" public high school, providing the maximum flexibility in curricular choice. Parents who estimate their child has below-average ability or taste for schooling would also choose this type of school for its vocational and career training opportunities. Parents who believe their child has high academic ability or interest would prefer schools with a strong college preparatory curriculum. Usually these are either private schools or high quality public schools in more expensive suburban neighborhoods. At least until recently, the extra expenditure for suburban housing and schooling was a more attractive resource allocation choice than private high school tuition payments.

Several social and economic changes may be altering this preference. One is the ever higher cost of suburban housing. Another is the increased number of dual wage-earner households. For working mothers, the preference for minimum commuting time may be a new consideration that offsets the value of larger, more distant housing. More important, the reduced parenting time available in these households may increase the attractiveness of private education where the development of attitudes, motivation, and discipline is a more explicit part of the school curriculum. The private boarding school is the extreme choice wherein affluent parents allocate income to compensate for low parenting time, but most private day schools, especially those offering religious instruction, also emphasize to parents the socialization goals of their curriculum.

The final and most important factor that underlies parents' private school enrollment decisions is the declining confidence in the quality of public school instruction. With the rapid expansion of higher education in the 1960s and 70s, college attendance began to be marketed as the optimal way to maximize human capital for youth of wide levels of ability (Freeman 1976). Higher education policies originally intended to promote minority access became redefined as "universal" access policies. At the high school level, this burgeoned the enrollment in college preparatory courses. Insofar as college preparatory teachers adapted by pitching their group instruction to a broader range of student ability, there was an overall decline in the standard of instruction. Private schools were better able to resist such a decline, screening out weaker students through admissions procedures. Thus the expansion of higher education during the last two decades was a major reason for the disparity today in the academic standards of public and private high schools. This argument proposes that the disparity reflects a difference in resource allocation, however, not in actual instructional resources.

Alternatively, the belief in private school academic superiority may be more mythical than real, reflecting "white flight" racial prejudice and the fallacy among many American consumers of equating market price with product quality. Each generation of ambitious parents seeks new means to give their children a competitive edge, moving from speed reading classes to college entrance examination coaching, from home encyclopedias to home computers. It may be that this is the generation to champion private schooling. CHK's report is the first major study to conclude private education produces superior learning. The findings here, however, do not support so simple a conclusion.

I. Study Design

Table 5.1 presents the unweighted sample frequencies for schools and youth across sectors in both the *High School and Beyond Survey* used by CHK and NLS samples. The HSB sample in CHK included 84 Catholic secondary schools and only 27 non-Catholic private secondary schools. By contrast, the NLS sample, although having only one-fifth as many youth, distributes those youth over more than three times as many secondary schools, including 279 Catholic and 244 other private schools.

After appropriate weighting, the two samples generate comparable population estimates for all but the other private sector. For the public and Catholic sectors, the NLS and HSB estimates are an average of 1 percentage point different from one another. Youth from public high schools are about

14 percent black, 6 percent Hispanic, and 30 percent Catholic, compared to 6 percent black, 6 percent Hispanic, and 90 percent Catholic for those attending Catholic schools. For the other private sector, the discrepancy between surveys averages 4 percentage points. According to NLS estimates, other private sector youth are 9 percent black, 4 percent Hispanic, and 24 percent Catholic.

Table 5.1
Comparison of Unweighted Sample Sizes
of NLS and HSB Surveys, by School Sector

	School Sector			
Unit	Public	Catholic	Other Private	Total
Youth: NLS total youth, aged 14-22 (1979)	11,983	414	299	12,686
HSB total students, sophomores and seniors	51,339	5,528	1,182	58,049
Schools: NLS total schools last attended[a]	2,996	279	244	3,519
HSB total schools currently attended	894	84	27	1,004

HSB SOURCE: Coleman, et al., 1981, table A.1.3, p. A-10.

a. NLS school total equals sum of each distinct "last high school attended" for all youth in sample.

A related sampling problem which has clouded the interpretation of CHK's findings is that the HSB sample is restricted to clusters of 10th and 12th graders who were currently enrolled in the sampled schools. Dropouts were excluded. This means that when CHK average the across-grade achievement differences at each school in order to compare "learning growth" in each sector, they must somehow control for differential selectivity of 12th graders caused by the different dropout rates across sectors.[1] By contrast, the NLS target population is the cohort of all 33 million noninstitutionalized civilian and military youth who were aged 14-21 on December 31, 1978. The availability of the full spectrum of youth, from dropouts to valedictorians, and from high school freshmen to college graduates, permits a more complete assessment of the relative educational impact of the public and private secondary school sectors. This broad sample of youth received cognitive achievement tests administered at one point in time, independent of the youth's age or school status. In the summer of 1980, when the cohort age range was 15-23, 11,878 youth (93.6 percent of the original 1979 sample) took the Armed Services Vocational Aptitude Battery (ASVAB) at over 400 test sites (for a detailed field report and psychometric data quality analysis, see McWilliams 1980; and Bock and Mislevy 1981). Ten subtests constitute the ASVAB. (See table 5.2) All subtests were multiple-choice paper-and-pencil tests, with either four or five alternative choices per item.

Table 5.2
The Armed Services Vocational
Aptitude Battery (ASVAB) Subtests

	Number items	Minutes
1. General Science	20	11
2. Arithmetic Reasoning	30	36
3. Word Knowledge	35	11
4. Paragraph Comprehension	15	13
5. Numerical Operation	50	3
6. Coding Speed	84	7
7. Auto and Shop Information	25	11
8. Mathematics Knowledge	25	24
9. Mechanical Comprehension	25	19
10. Electronics Information	20	9

The ASVAB subtests most similar to the Reading, Vocabulary, and Mathematics tests used in the CHK report are those called Paragraph Comprehension, Word Knowledge, and Arithmetic Reasoning. Table 5.3 reports these test scores for the younger half (15-19) of the NLS cohort together with the comparable scores for the HSB 12th graders. Of particular interest is whether the data sets agree in the assessment of relative achievement across sectors. In both data sets, Catholic and other private school youth score higher than public school youth on all three tests. However, the other private school sample scores consistently lower than the Catholic sector youth in the NLS, and scores higher in HSB. A key difference to be borne in mind in the interpretation of subsequent findings is that the other private schools in the NLS survey are an academically less selective set than the ones included in the HSB study. It is tempting to claim that the 244 schools in the NLS are more representative of the diversity in the other private school sector than the 27 HSB other private schools, but such a claim must be tempered with the realization that the actual respondent sample size is much smaller in the NLS.

Aside from this difference, the consistency across surveys in the public-Catholic achievement comparisons is rather remarkable. As shown in the bottom panel of table 5.3, in both studies Catholic youth score about one-third of a standard deviation higher than public school youth, and in both studies their greatest advantage is in vocabulary. In the NLS survey, however, the other private school sector superiority over public schools averages only one-fourth a standard deviation difference, compared to almost one-half a standard deviation difference in the HSB data.

In summary, the present study has differences from CHK in sampling design, data collection procedures, and measurement instruments. Yet with appropriate weighting and selection of comparable age groups, the two studies yield very

Table 5.3
Comparison of NLS and HSB Achievement Scores for Spring 1980
HSB Twelfth Graders and NLS Youth Aged 15-19 in Summer 1980

Subtest	NLS				HSB			
	Total	Public	Catholic	Other	Total	Public	Catholic	Other
Means:								
Reading	10.33	10.27	11.53	10.94	4.54	4.48	5.00	5.34
Vocabulary	24.18	23.99	27.39	26.68	4.58	4.48	5.35	5.56
Mathematics	16.72	16.58	18.84	18.68	10.80	10.63	12.10	12.74
Standard deviations:								
Reading	3.50	3.52	2.77	3.35	2.10	2.10	1.96	2.04
Vocabulary	7.60	7.62	6.45	7.12	1.97	1.97	1.74	1.94
Mathematics	7.05	7.00	7.14	7.56	4.24	4.24	3.82	4.14
Standard deviate differences:		Catholic-public	Other-public			Catholic-public	Other-public	
Reading		.36	.19			.25	.41	
Vocabulary		.45	.35			.44	.55	
Mathematics		.32	.30			.35	.50	

HSB SOURCE: Coleman, et al., 1982, table 3, p. 69.

similar population estimates of the background composition and achievement scores for youth from two of the three school sectors. Failure to replicate the population estimates for the other private school sector does lend credence to criticisms that the HSB sample of this sector was inadequate.

II. Sector Differences in Quantity Versus Quality of Schooling

The findings in this and the following section are directed toward the basic question of how much, if any, of the observed differences across sectors in cognitive achievement (table 5.3) and other outcomes can be attributed to differences in quality of schooling. This first section reports sector variation in key factors associated with the achievement difference—years of schooling completed, socioeconomic background, curriculum and course enrollment, and school resources. The following section presents a causal analysis of these factors.

For any given youth, the primary determinant of achievement level is quantity of schooling. This seemingly obvious factor is still often ignored by those who ask whether schooling "makes a difference." Table 5.4 groups the 1979 cohort of American youth according to their 1981 level of educational attainment, when they ranged in age from 16-24.[2] At the same time the 33.3 million young persons included an estimated 4.7 million high school dropouts, 8 million currently enrolled high school students, 11.3 million terminal high school graduates, 2.8 million former college students, and 6.5 million currently enrolled college students.[3]

Each of these attainment groups is a sizeable and experientially very different segment of the youth population. Table 5.4 presents the mean cognitive achievement across sectors for each attainment level. The achievement score reported is a composite of four of the ASVAB subtests, representing the

Table 5.4
Mean Achievement and Age of the NLS Youth Cohort
Across Levels of Educational Attainment and School Sector

Educational attainment, 1981	School sector	AFQT	Age 1981	Population (sector %)	Estimate[a] (thousands)
High school dropout	Public	49.9	19.9	97.6	4,592
	Private	51.6	19.4	2.4	111
High school enrollee	Public	65.9	16.9	92.5	7,418
	Private	72.6	16.7	7.5	599
High school graduate, no college[b]	Public	71.1	21.0	95.6	10,784
	Private	78.3	21.2	4.4	497
College, one or more years, no longer enrolled	Public	82.2	21.5	88.0	2,464
	Private	84.5	22.4	12.0	335
College enrollee	Public	85.6	20.3	87.8	5,730
	Private	87.2	20.6	12.2	794
Sector total	Public	70.3	19.8	93.0	30,988
	Private	79.5	19.9	7.0	2,336
Cohort total		71.0	19.8	100.0	33,324

a. 225,000 youth or 0.7 percent of the cohort are unclassified and omitted from total.
b. This category fully defined is high school graduate, not enrolled in college and completed no years of college.

sum of three tests reported separately in table 5.3 (Paragraph Comprehension, Word Knowledge, and Arithmetic Reasoning) and one-half the total score of a fourth subtest, Numerical Operations. This index, known as the AFQT, is the Armed Forces Qualifications Test used to screen military candidates. It has a maximum score of 105 and for this cohort a mean of 71.0 and standard deviation of 20.9.

As expected, for both sectors achievement increased linearly with quantity of schooling. College students scored almost two standard deviations (36 points) higher than high school dropouts. Somewhat surprising was that public and private youth differed substantially only at the two intermediate high school education levels of attainment. High school students and terminal graduates from the public and private sectors both differed 7 points, one-third of a standard deviation. For those who drop out of high school, or go on to college, being from a public or private high school makes a difference in achievement of less than two points, only one-tenth of a standard deviation.

This near-equivalence of sectors within three of five attainment levels must be counterposed with the fact that the cohort as a whole shows a sector difference of 9.2 achievement points. In large part, this difference reflects the tendency for private school youth to be disproportionately represented in the higher levels of educational attainment, where achievement scores are higher. Twelve percent of college students came from private high schools, compared to 7.5 percent of all those currently in high schools, 4.4 percent of terminal high school graduates, and only 2.4 percent of all dropouts. If public and private school youth were distributed the same across attainment levels (using the technique of direct standardization), the overall achievement difference between sectors would drop more than half, to 4.5 points.

But how can the remaining half of this private sector superiority be accounted for? And how can the higher attainment of the private sector youth be explained? The two questions are empirically closely interrelated, and their answers are crucial for understanding the relative strengths of the two sectors. The sector difference may have little to do with the schools themselves, but rather with the differential selection of youth into the sectors. Private sector youth may be socioeconomically advantaged, with greater learning ability and more ambitious educational goals. But if relative school quality is the answer, then either private schools do a more efficient job of instruction, have more resources, or allocate resources more strictly into academic subject areas.

These three possibilities all have varying degrees of support. Private sector youth do have a strong socioeconomic advantage, as indexed by father's education and occupation. Youth in the other private schools are slightly better off than Catholic school youth. Of Catholic and other private youth, 31 percent and 38 percent, respectively, have fathers with 16 or more years of education, compared with only 16 percent of pubic school youth. Similarly, 61 percent and 52 percent, respectively, have fathers with white-collar jobs, compared with 39 percent of public school youth.

Private sector youth are also twice as likely as public school youth to be in a college preparatory curriculum, with Catholic sector youth slightly more so than the other private school youth. The difference is 64 percent and 52 percent, compared with 30 percent. Conversely, youth in the public sector are twice as likely as private sector youth to enroll in a vocational study program, the difference being 14 percent compared with 6 percent of Catholic youth and 7 percent of other private youth. Average differences in educational goals of the youth are equally strong. As measured in 1979 and again in 1981, relative to public school youth, the expected education of Catholic school youth was one and a half years higher, and for other private school youth was one year higher. These constitute differences of about half a standard deviation.

Differences in available resources at the schools of these youth are not ordered as uniformly across sectors as the student characteristics were. If any one sector appears to have an overall resource advantage, it would appear to be the public schools. Public school youth had an average of 1400 students in their schools, compared with 900 and 700 for Catholic and other private school youth. Their teachers' average starting salary in 1980 was 10,900 dollars, 1,900 and 1,400 more than for Catholic and other private school teachers. The sectors are about the same in teachers' degree qualifications. The other private schools, despite having the smallest enrollments, have libraries averaging almost as large as in the public schools. Other private school youth had access to libraries averaging 16,400 volumes, compared with 16,700 volume libraries in public schools and 11,500 volume libraries in Catholic schools. By contrast, the private schools offered extremely limited vocational opportunities. Of seven vocational programs examined (agriculture, business, distributive education, health, home economics, trade, and technical), business was the ony one available to at least half the other private sector youth. Catholic schools were little better, with business and home economics the only programs available to a majority. In the public schools, six of the seven programs were available to at least half the youth. It does appear that the difference between sectors is less a matter of total resources than of resource allocation.

The final comparison pertaining to educational quality examines the academic records of youth who graduated from the college preparatory track of their high schools. Of interest is whether college preparatory programs might be more rigorous in the private schools, in terms of students taking more academic courses and being graded more competitively. This information came from a survey in 1980 of students' final high school transcripts (Campbell, Orth, and Seitz 1981). Credits received during grades 9-12 in the five main academic subject areas—English, mathematics, science, social studies, and foreign language—were coded using the Carnegie credit-unit system, based on one-hour, one-year courses receiving 1.00 credit.

Moderate differences do exist across sectors in the college preparatory curriculum taken by the graduating youth. Overall, Catholic sector youth took one more credit hour of academic coursework than public youth did, and other private school youth took one-half more credit hour. The largest differences were in social studies and foreign languages, with slight differences in English and no significant difference in either mathematics or science. Correspondingly, Catholic and other private sector youth were graded more rigorously, with Catholic sector youth being assigned the lowest grades overall, averaging a quarter-point lower than public school youth, based on a four-point grade scale.

These sector differences in college preparatory coursework lend some slight credence to the educational quality explanation of the higher achievement scores of private sector youth. Translated into a time metric, the average difference of one college preparatory course unit between Catholic and public sectors is a difference of 4 percent of the total high school class time. Compared to coursework differences between curriculum tracks, however, this is at most marginal. For youth from all sectors the average college preparatory course load over grades 9-12 is 16 credits, or four academic courses per year. This means two-thirds of students' total course time is spent in academic courses. By contrast, public sector youth in general and vocational programs average only 11.7 and 10.8 academic course units, respectively, i.e., they spend less than half their class time taking academic courses.[4] This average disparity of more than four course units means general and vocational students spend at least 17 percent less of their total high school hours in academic courses than their college preparatory counterparts.

If quantity of schooling affects cognitive achievement, as we see it did in the case of years of schooling, and cognitive achievement is parents' primary goal for their child, it would seem that the consumer decision to enroll one's child in a college preparatory curriculum is probably going to promote learning more efficiently than would a decision to move the child out of the public sector completely. The next section will estimate the relative gain that can be expected from either of these decisions.

III. Sector and Curriculum Effects

Figure 5.1 presents the causal model used to estimate joint sector and curriculum effects on achievement and college plans, net of background characteristics. The full model is a recursive four equation system. Sector and curriculum enrollment are each determined by a vector of background variables. No causal relationship between the two schooling choice variables is specified other than their joint background determination and correlated residual variation. Achievement is dependent on the background vector, sector, and curriculum enrollment. Expected educational attainment in turn is dependent on these prior variables and achievement. Only the last two equations are estimated in this chapter. Other educational outcomes to be analyzed with these equations include selected vocational achievement scores and ratings of quality of school life.

This relatively simple model is consistent with both the standard status attainment model of sociologists (Blau and Duncan 1967; Sewell, Hauser, and Featherman 1976) and the education consumption approach presented earlier. The attainment model posits schooling as the primary intervening mechanism converting and altering an individual's origin status into destination status. Usually destination status is represented by the adult respondent's educational attainment, occupation, and earnings, origin status by parents' education, occupation, and income, and the individual's preschooling ability level. A social psychological variable, called either significant other's influence or parental encouragement, is also included to capture the impact of differential parental ambition, values, and related factors in mediating the influence of these origin status variables on schooling outcomes. A second social psychological variable, referred to as educational aspirations or expected educational attainments, mediates the outcomes of secondary schooling on final educational attainment.

Figure 5.1
A Causal Model of Sector and Curriculum Effects
on Educational Outcomes

Basic causal model:

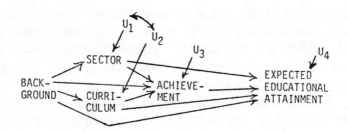

Reduced-form estimation equation:

$$EDEXP = aACH + \sum_{i=1}^{2} b_i SEC + \sum_{i=1}^{3} c_i CUR + dSOI + \sum_{i=1}^{4} e_i INC +$$

$$\sum_{i=1}^{6} f_i MED + \sum_{i=1}^{6} g_i FED + \sum_{i=1}^{2} h_i MOC + \sum_{i=1}^{2} j_i FOC + kSIB$$

$$+ lREL + \sum_{i=1}^{2} m_i ETH + nAGE + oRES + \sum_{i=1}^{8} p_i REG + q$$

From this status attainment perspective, the model in figure 5.1 evaluates the extent to which school sector and curriculum mediate the effects of origin status on the two proximate causes of destination status, academic achievement and expected educational attainment. Their having sizeable effects on the two educational outcomes net of origin status, together with their strong linkage to origin status (as shown in the previous section), would indicate their importance in transmitting social inequality across generations. Alternatively, from the perspective of a household consumption approach, the equations permit an assessment of the production efficiency of parents' expending their resources on either a private high school education or a college preparatory curriculum in order to maximize their children's human capital. The relative value of these two educational policy choices for optimizing various noneconomic attitudinal returns may also be assessed.

Table 5.5 presents the means and standard deviations for all variables used in the achievement and expected attainments equations. The fourteen explanatory variables include the two schooling variables, nine background variables, and three control variables. The background variables are family income, mother's and father's education, mother's and father's occupation, number of siblings, significant other's influence, religion (Catholic or other), and ethnicity (black, Hispanic, or white).[5]

The three control variables included are residence (urban or rural), region (one of the nine Census regions), and age. Although they are not theoretically central to status attainment or to education consumption, the possible effects of these control variables are of substantive interest; and because they correlate with the other background variables, deleting them would bias the estimated effects of these variables.[6]

Table 5.5
Means and Standard Deviations for Variables in Basic Model
of Secondary School Sector Effects
NLS Youth Aged 14-17 in 1979

Variable		X	S.D.
EDEXP		13.96	2.43
AFQT		68.34	20.03
SECTOR (PUB):	CATH	.035	.185
	OTHER	.028	.166
CURR (GEN):	COLL	.315	.464
	VOC	.133	.340
SOI		2.97	.912
INCOME (0-5):	5-10	.116	.320
	10-20	.247	.431
	20+	.400	.490
MOEDUC (0-6):	7-11	.256	.436
	12	.453	.498
	13-15	.106	.308
	16	.075	.263
	17-20	.024	.154
FAEDUC (0-6):	7-11	.234	.423
	12	.333	.471
	13-15	.105	.307
	16	.105	.306
	17-20	.072	.259
MOOCC (NOEMP):	BCOCC	.256	.436
	WCOCC	.275	.447
FAOCC (NOEMP):	BCOCC	.445	.497
	WCOCC	.302	.459
SIBS		3.23	2.23
RELIG (OTHER):	CATH	.321	.467
ETHN (WH):	BLACK	.140	.347
	HISP	.052	.222

Table 5.5 (continued)

Variable		X	S.D.
AGE		15.58	1.08
RESID (RUR):	URB	.772	.419
REGION (PAC):	N ENG	.054	.226
	MATL	.155	.362
	SATL	.177	.382
	ESC	.065	.246
	WSC	.082	.275
	ENC	.238	.426
	WNC	.074	.262
	MTN	.048	.214
NA-CURR		.023	.150
NA-INC		.182	.386
NA-MOED		.047	.212
NA-FAED		.100	.299

N = 4832.

One potentially biasing omission from the vector of background variables is a measure of ability. According to CHK's critics, their failure to control for the probable higher ability of the more selective private school students biased upward their sector effect estimates. This possibility was analyzed on a 20 percent subsample of NLS youth who had at least one intelligence test score available in their high school records. A composite I.Q. index was constructed by taking the first recorded of seven possible intelligence test scores. Scores from the different tests were equilibrated by conversion to national percentiles.[7]

For the achievement equation, addition of the I.Q. index to the background vector uniformly decreased all background and schooling estimates to approximately two-thirds their original size. This reduction reflects the fact the

I.Q. index had a zero-order correlation of .704 with the AF-QT score and moderate correlations with all background variables. Whether these reduced estimates are less biased, however, is by no means certain. The age at which each available intelligence test was administered was variable, but in most cases occurred well into the youths' schooling careers. Two-thirds of the available tests were taken in grades seven through ten, the modal year being grade nine. CHK have argued (1982: 165) that such school-age intelligence tests possess a strong achievement component, and therefore leave unanswered the question of whether such tests measure ability or simply prior achievement. If the latter, the reduced size of the estimated coefficients when the index is in the equation would simply reflect the consistently more modest effects of each variable on achievement *gain* as opposed to achievement *level*. But more important, even if the I.Q. index were a valid ability measure, a nearly uniform one-third adjustment in the size of the coefficients would not alter our overall conclusions on the relative importance of the sector and curriculum effects. Consequently it was decided to leave the estimates unaltered, as presented in table 5.6.

For these schooling equations, the sample has been restricted to the half of the youth cohort who were of school age, 14-17.[8] Eleven of the explanatory variables are expressed in either single or multiple series dummy variable form, and in each case the referent category is denoted in parentheses after the variable name in the table. Eight of these are natural categoric variables. Three interval variables, mother's and father's education and family income, were categorized mainly to permit the inclusion of a no answer category for each, thereby minimizing case loss due to missing data.

This basic model fits the data well.[9] The OLS-estimated equation explains 44 percent of the variation in youth cognitive achievement and 48 percent of the variation in ex-

Table 5.6
Coefficient for Basic Model of Secondary School Sector Effects
on Years of Expected Education and Achievement (AFQT)
of NLS Youth Aged 14-17 in 1979

Explanatory variable		AFQT		ED EXP	
		b	t	b	t
SECTOR (PUB):	CATH	.528	.43	.344	2.61
	OTHER	-1.844	-1.39	.140	.97
CURR (GEN):	COLL	9.14	17.43	1.053	17.95
	VOC	-.271	-.40	-.058	-.79
SOI		1.615	6.42	.544	19.76
INCOME (0-5):	5-10	1.720	1.54	.208	1.71
	10-20	5.667	5.35	.415	3.60
	20+	7.263	6.71	.416	3.52
MOEDUC (0-6):	7-11	3.435	2.59	.126	.88
	12	6.284	4.61	.381	2.57
	13-15	8.281	5.48	.779	4.73
	16	9.572	5.90	.801	4.54
	17-20	14.08	7.02	1.089	4.98
FAEDUC (0-6):	7-11	3.526	3.02	-.083	-.65
	12	5.693	4.81	-.082	-.63
	13-15	7.685	5.77	.168	1.15
	16	10.51	7.54	.534	3.50
	17-20	11.52	7.63	.789	4.77

Table 5.6 (continued)

Explanatory variable		AFQT		ED EXP	
		b	t	b	t
MOOCC (NOEMP):	BCOCC	.497	.91	-.092	-1.55
	WCOCC	1.181	2.14	.088	1.47
FAOCC (NOEMP):	BCOCC	-.991	-1.68	-.095	-1.48
	WCOCC	1.01	1.46	-.017	-.22
SIBS		-.689	-6.51	-.025	-2.16
RELIG (OTHER): CATH		.724	1.36	.100	1.73
ETHN (WH):	BLACK	-15.06	-20.93	.869	10.64
	HISP	-6.485	-5.67	.603	4.83
AGE		2.033	10.04	-.089	-4.00
RESID (RUR):	URB	-1.423	-2.67	.192	3.32
REGION (PAC):	N ENG	2.502	2.14	-.048	-.38
	MATL	-.107	-.12	-.046	-.49
	SATL	-.573	-.66	.060	.64
	ESC	-2.449	-2.22	.215	1.79
	WSC	-.116	-.12	-.023	-.21
	ENC	1.070	1.31	-.076	-.86
	WNC	4.462	4.27	-.043	-.38
	MTN	.726	.61	-.321	-2.49

AFQT	22.46	.035	—	—
NA-CURR	-8.57	-1.398	-9.28	-13.71
NA-INC	3.83	.461	4.29	4.750
NA-MOED	.92	.161	-.22	-.357
NA-FAED	-.64	-.089	1.68	2.127
CONSTANT		10.04		17.43
$\overline{R}^2$		.483		.444
n		4,819		4,832

pected educational attainments. The vector of seven background variables measuring origin status had its expected strong effect on both cognitive achievement and expected years of education. Only father's and mother's occupational position, broadly categorized into the three-fold division of blue-collar, white-collar, or unemployed/out-of-labor force, failed to have an independent effect net of the other variables. The linearity of the parents' education and family income effects is especially striking, as is the strong effect of the social psychological mediator of these origin status effects, significant other's influence.

The five control variables have mixed effects. Being of Catholic origins in itself has no effect on achievement or expectations, and age raises achievement levels and reduces expectations. By contrast, being a member of a disadvantaged minority, either black or Hispanic, strongly lowers achievement and raises expectations. Residing in an urban location also reduces achievement and raises expectations, but only slightly. Finally, the eight dummy variable coefficients measuring regional variation indicate that the regional variation on these two educational outcomes is accounted for reasonably well by the variables already in the equation. Youth from the New England region have the highest observed achievement scores, those from the East South Central the lowest. Net of all other variables in the equation, however, the observed difference between these two extreme regions drops from 13 points to 3 points (see appendix to this chapter).

The two schooling effects were assessed in the context of these background and control variable effects. Table 5.6 indicates that net of the origin status and other control factors, being in a college preparatory instead of general curriculum added an average of 9 points to a youth's total cognitive achievement score. Being in a Catholic or other private school made no difference in achievement scores, the nonsignificant net increment over public schools being .5 for the Catholic and -1.8 for the other private sector. There was a small but significant effect of Catholic sector on expected years of education. Being in the Catholic sector instead of the public added a net average of one-third year more to a youth's expected education. By contrast, being in the other private sector made no significant difference. Being in the college preparatory curriculum added an average of one full year of expected education.[10] The clear conclusion is that being in the college preparatory curriculum of *any* sector is much more critical than sector itself for maximizing these two educational outcomes.

Before accepting this conclusion, several additional analyses were performed. First the analyses were repeated on the older half of the cohort, those who in 1979 were age 18-22. If sector differences appeared in the post-high school years, some type of "sleeper effect" process could be at work, wherein youth in private schools developed study skills or received character training that enabled them to perform better after high school. Table 5.7 shows the two equations reestimated for this older group. The basic model is the same except for the omission of significant other's influence, which is not measured for this age group; for comparison purposes, the 14-17 age group equations were reestimated without significant other's influence. The older youth showed the same basic pattern of effects as the younger, except that the significant effect of Catholic sector on expectations became nonsignificant. The only evidence of a "sleeper effect" is for youth who were in a vocational training program. Having been from such a program gave the older youth a small but significant 3-point achievement advantage over general curriculum youth. Youth in the 14-17 age category, however, showed a nonsignificant achievement disadvantage from vocational training of -.2 points.[11]

The next analysis examined the possibility that estimations made for the total youth population may have concealed

Table 5.7
Secondary School Sector Effects on Achievement (AFQT)
and Expectations Estimated from Basic Model for 14-17 and 18-22 Age Cohorts[a]

Explanatory variable	18-22, no SOI		14-17, no SOI		14-17	
	b	t	b	t	b	t
AFQT						
SECTOR (PUB): CATH	.831	.83	.748	.62	.528	.43
OTHER	1.050	.88	-1.908	-1.45	-1.844	-1.39
CURR (GEN): COLL	11.382	22.82	9.803	19.20	9.143	17.43
VOC	3.121	5.62	-.216	-.33	-.271	-.40
SOI	-				1.615	6.42
AGE	1.506	9.32	1.929	9.72	2.033	10.04
$\overline{R}^2$	.450		.442		.444	
n	6,048		5,094		4,832	
EDEXP						
SECTOR (PUB): CATH	.206	1.82	.366	2.70	.344	2.61
OTHER	.254	1.89	.170	1.15	.140	.97
CURR (GEN): COLL	1.231	21.08	1.211	20.47	1.053	17.95
VOC	.074	.12	-.181	-2.44	-.058	-.79
SOI	-				.544	19.76
AFQT	.045	31.23	.038	24.10	.035	22.46
AGE	-.010	-.54	-.130	-5.79	-.089	-4.00
$\overline{R}^2$	.469		.444		.483	
n	5,990		5,078		4,819	

a. Coefficients for other variables in full equation (see table 5.6) not presented.

significant sector effects for major subgroups of youth. Table 5.8 presents the sector and curriculum effects estimated from the basic model separately for blacks, Hispanics, and whites. The consistency of the college preparatory curriculum effect across subgroups was striking. Taking college preparatory courses helps blacks, Hispanics, and whites about equally, in both achievement and expectations. The net achievement gain over the general curriculum ranges from 7 to 10 points, and the net gain in average expected years of education is one year. The sector effects, on the other hand, are highly unstable across subgroups. The small gain in educational expectations from being in the Catholic sector holds only for white youth. There were no sector effects for black youth, but two suggestive sector effects did appear for Hispanics. Being in Catholic schools raised their achievement scores 7.6 points over public schools, and attending other private schools raised their years of expected education 1.2 years.

In considering the meaning of this Hispanic private sector effect, the first possibility that comes to mind is that the private schools Hispanics attend may do a better job than public schools in dealing with the special verbal needs of Hispanic students. Secondly, the religious instruction in Catholic schools may be an important cultural bridge linking home values with school work. The greater need for this home-school link for Hispanics is suggested by the absence of a significant other's influence effect on achievement for them, compared to strong effects of this variable for both blacks and whites. In order to investigate further the verbal needs explanation, the total achievement score was disaggregated into its four subtest components and the achievement equation was reestimated for each subgroup for each subtest. The sector effect results for each equation are summarized in table 5.9. Note that summing the sector effect for each subtest, using the weighting formula in this table footnote, perfectly reproduces the total AFQT sector effect

Table 5.8
Secondary School Sector Effects on Achievement (AFQT) and Expectations Estimated from Basic Model Separately for Black, Hispanic, and White Youth Aged 14-17[a]

Explanatory variable		Black		Hispanic		White	
		b	t	b	t	b	t
AFQT							
SECTOR (PUB):	CATH	1.025	.30	7.588	2.37	.300	.20
	OTHER	-6.327	-1.93	6.097	1.52	-1.795	-1.08
CURR (GEN):	COLL	10.017	9.70	7.055	4.68	9.159	13.49
	VOC	2.294	1.88	1.811	.95	-.748	-.85
SOI		1.890	4.03	.940	1.31	1.564	4.75
$\overline{R^2}$		.291		.300		.339	
n		1,276		674		2,882	
EDEXP							
SECTOR (PUB):	CATH	-.179	-.43	.289	.82	.382	2.38
	OTHER	.097	.25	1.184	2.61	.068	.39
CURR (GEN):	COLL	1.026	7.93	1.112	6.56	1.050	14.13
	VOC	.098	.67	.057	.27	-.079	-.84
SOI		.419	7.33	.557	6.99	.567	16.11
AFQT		.033	9.60	.043	9.73	.035	17.42
$\overline{R^2}$		.341		.433		.512	
n		1,275		671		2,873	

a. Coefficients for other variables in full equation (see table 5.6) of basic model not presented.

Table 5.9
Secondary School Sector Effects on the Four Subtests of the AFQT Score
for Black, Hispanic, and White Youth Aged 14-17[a]

Subgroup	Sector effect	Subtest					
		Word know.	Parag. comp.	Arith. reas.	Num. oper.	Total AFQT[b]	n
BLACK	CATH	1.441	-.524	.300	-.385	1.025	1276
	OTHER	-2.400	-1.756*	-.191	-3.962	-6.327	
	$\overline{R}^2$	.276	.206	.139	.182	.291	
HISP	CATH	3.409*	1.467*	1.594	2.236	7.588*	674
	OTHER	4.181*	1.426	-.478	1.937	6.097	
	$\overline{R}^2$	.279	.236	.210	.181	.300	
WHITE	CATH	.317	-.076	-.777	1.674	.300	2882
	OTHER	.241	-.448	-.085	-3.005*	-1.795	
	$\overline{R}^2$	.295	.242	.242	.199	.340	
TOTAL	CATH	.530	-.044	-.618	1.319	.528	4832
	OTHER	.201	-.484	-.134	-2.855*	-1.844	
	$\overline{R}^2$	.404	.323	.332	.260	.444	
	$\overline{Y}_{TOT}$	24.41	10.42	16.88	33.25	68.34	
	S.D.TOT	7.46	3.46	7.05	10.55	20.03	

*p .05.
a. Coefficients for other variables in full equation of basic model (see table 5.6) not presented.
b. AFQT = W.K. + P.C. + A.R. + 1/2 N.O.

presented in the right column. These findings confirm the expectation that it is the verbal component of achievement that is most aided by Hispanics' private school enrollment. Sector enrollment has no effect on Hispanic scores in arithmetic reasoning or numerical operations. Being in Catholic schools significantly increases Hispanics' word knowledge and paragraph comprehension scores, and other private sector enrollment also increases their word knowledge scores. No similar pattern holds for the disaggregated scores of black or white youth.

The final analysis of subgroup variation in sector effects substituted vocational achievement for cognitive achievement as the dependent educational outcome. Table 5.10 reports the sector effects for each subgroup on the four vocational subtests from the ASVAB battery—mechanical comprehension, auto and shop information, electronics information, and coding speed. The expectation was that attending a private school would reduce vocational achievement, given the relative absence of vocational training opportunities there. Even after taking into account sector differences in vocational curriculum enrollment, the private school college preparatory and general curriculum youth have fewer opportunities for vocational course electives compared to what is available to their public school counterparts.

The coefficients in table 5.10 indicate a generally consistent pattern of small negative effects of the private sector on vocational achievement. Only 4 of the 24 separate sector effect coefficients are significant, but all 4 show a negative private sector effect. This effect is strongest for white youth, for whom Catholic sector enrollment significantly reduces scores in mechanical comprehension, automobile information, and electronics information. For automobile information only, the coefficients for Catholic and other private sector are negative across all three subgroups. For mechanical comprehension, Catholic sector coefficients are also negative for all three subgroups. Electronics information, which is

Table 5.10

Secondary School Sector Effects on the Four Nonacademic Achievement Tests
for Black, Hispanic, and White Youth Aged 14-17[a]

Subgroup	Sector effect	Subtest				n
		Mech. comp.	Auto. info.	Elec. info.	Coding speed	
BLACK	CATH	-.034	-.731	-.570	1.222	1276
	OTHER	.391	-.932	.356	-6.154*	
	$\overline{R^2}$	.095	.109	.112	.151	
HISP	CATH	-1.003	-1.214	.491	4.456	674
	OTHER	.221	-1.676	.142	2.697	
	$\overline{R^2}$	.142	.180	.163	.138	
WHITE	CATH	-1.123*	-1.300*	-.912*	-.263	2882
	OTHER	-.460	-.467	.315	-1.626	
	$\overline{R^2}$	.135	.098	.149	.140	
TOTAL	CATH	-1.068*	-1.262*	-.842*	.084	4832
	OTHER	-.383	-.572	.332	-1.806	
	$\overline{R^2}$	.250	.231	.250	.205	
	$\overline{Y}$	13.29	12.75	10.35	43.02	
	S.D.	4.99	5.06	4.07	15.16	

*p .05.

a. Coefficients for other variables in full equation of basic model (see table 5.6) not presented.

less "manual" and can be learned in academic as well as vocational settings, has the least consistent pattern of sector coefficients.

IV. Quality of School Life

These findings strongly suggest that increased federal support of private schooling, whether by means of tax credits or some other scheme, will not advance the level of learning among American youth. With the important exception of the Catholic sector effect on verbal achievement of Hispanic youth, enrollment in private schools has no significant net effect on cognitive achievement. What does matter is taking college preparatory courses, and one need not attend private schools to do so. In fact, one could claim that the only justification for federal support of private schooling would be to remedy its deficiencies, particularly in vocational training. From the standpoint of the parent-consumer of education, choice of sector is not a crucial factor in human capital development—choice of curriculum is.

Correspondingly, these findings suggest that in the context of the status attainment model of American society, private schooling is not, and has no special potential for becoming, an important mechanism for fostering social mobility. The degree of social advantage possessed by each youth is not likely to be significantly altered by choice of sector enrollment, however much it may currently determine that choice. By contrast, the uniformly strong effects of curriculum enrollment on schooling outcomes confirms previous studies (e.g., Alexander and McDill 1976; Rosenbaum 1980) which have found this variable to be strongly implicated in the status attainment process.

Why then does the belief in the superiority of private education persist, both among key policymakers and some of the American public? If one assumes, as economists do, that these educational "producers" and "consumers" tend to be rational, and that "bad information" alone is not the answer, there must exist some "nonpecuniary factors" instead of human capital formation that are being optimized by private schooling. Speculation on what the full spectrum of nonpecuniary factors could be is beyond the scope of this report, but one such factor is a general subjective state of well-being, sometimes called "quality of school life" (Epstein 1981). For many parents, the belief that private schools provide an immediate life quality superior to that in public schools might be sufficient justification to expend available income for private school tuition. In order to examine the plausibility of considering the private sector as the best bet for this "nonpecuniary" optimization, six quality of school life indicators were regressed separately on the 14 variables of the basic model. This specification treats general well-being as an attitudinal outcome of schooling parallel to, but very different from, the human capital variable, expected years of education.

The six indicators represent the youths' ratings of the high schools they attended on aspects of school life central to their general well-being—instructional quality, school discipline, learning freedom, personal safety, job counseling, and peer relations.[12] Similar ratings have been used quite differently by CHK, following a long tradition of "school climate" research (e.g., Coleman 1961; McDill and Rigsby 1973). This line of inquiry hypothesizes that these individual attitudes aggregated over the student population of a school constitute the prevailing school climate, which in turn is a key determinant of the academic performance level at the school. The fact that the climate-performance hypothesis has yet to receive any convincing empirical support (Hauser 1970, 1974; Goldberger and Cain 1982) reinforces the theoretical decision to use the ratings only as outcome variables.

Consistent with our previous findings, here we find that being in the college preparatory rather than general curriculum significantly increased all six quality of school life ratings (table 5.11). In addition, being in the vocational curriculum significantly raised ratings on three of the dimensions—instructional quality, learning freedom, and job counseling. But unlike the achievement or expected education findings, all six quality of school life ratings were also significantly affected by sector enrollment. Youth in private schools, net of all background and curriculum enrollment effects, rated more highly than public school youth the quality of their class instruction and strictness of discipline, and slightly more highly their personal safety and friendship opportunities at school. They rated lower than public school youth their degree of learning freedom and opportunities for job counseling.

These sector and curriculum effects on life quality occurred in the nearly complete absence of significant effects from cognitive achievement, the other key schooling variable in the equation. High performing youth tended to rate their personal safety higher, but otherwise youth performance levels were unrelated to their life quality ratings. This contrasts with the strong effect achievement had on the human capital variable, expected years of education.

Some definite nonpecuniary gain is derived from private sector enrollment—the quality of school life is better. Insofar as quality of school life bears the hypothesized relation to youths' subjective state of well-being, this advantage cannot be minimized. Except for Hispanics, however, beliefs about the superiority of private education should be restricted to this domain. Federal policymakers and parents who contemplate investment in private secondary education need to know they will be optimizing student life quality, not learning. Efforts to improve the quality of student life in public schools might be an even sounder investment.

Before proposing any policy interventions, however, further research is needed to determine the range of factors con-

Table 5.11
Secondary School Sector Effects on Six Quality of School Life Ratings Estimated from Basic Model for Youth Aged 14-17 in 1979[a]

Explanatory variable		Instructional quality		School discipline		Learning freedom	
		b	t	b	t	b	t
SECTOR (PUB):	CATH	.162	4.13	.494	7.36	-.434	-6.71
	OTHER	.298	6.97	.442	6.04	-.183	-2.60
CURR (GEN):	COLL	.142	8.20	.070	2.36	.139	4.87
	VOC	.069	3.15	.050	1.34	.141	3.94
SOI		.041	5.01	.032	2.25	.020	1.45
AFQT		-.000	-.26	-.002	-1.93	.000	.16

Explanatory variable		Personal safety		Job counseling		Peer relations	
		b	t	b	t	b	t
SECTOR (PUB):	CATH	.112	1.75	-.148	-2.07	.111	2.11
	OTHER	.195	2.77	-.301	-3.80	.080	1.40
CURR (GEN):	COLL	.085	2.97	.151	4.74	.054	2.33
	VOC	.043	1.19	.232	5.81	-.020	-.67
SOI		-.014	-1.00	.010	.65	-.008	-.70
AFQT		.007	8.70	.001	1.04	.001	1.48

a. Coefficients for other variables in full equation (see table 5.6) not presented.

tributing to the higher quality of life in private schools. Some of these may not be easily transferable to public schools. One of these is the aura of elitism. For example, the label of private school student may in itself convey a sense of privilege and speciality over public school students, causing these youth to attribute a high value to their school life irrespective of its actual quality. Elitism is a psychic resource which, by definition, cannot be widely distributed. Public school systems would only suffer further budgetary problems if parents believed this elitism could be purchased by adding further amenities to their facilities. The democratization of private school enrollment through a tuition tax credit plan might reduce elitism, but would thereby also diminish the value of private schools for many consumers. An alternative to planned democratization of private schools is the natural leveling influences of American popular culture, where symbols of elitism eventually tend to be diffused throughout mainstream society and thereby deflated. A current public high school fad is the "preppy" subculture, wherein students mimic through dress and mannerisms the life style of the private boarding school student.[13]

A related characteristic of many private schools is their greater sense of tradition, and in the case of Catholic and other religious schools, their sacred character. Neither feature can be easily reproduced in public schools, however important they are for quality of student life and general well-being. Constitutional requirements forbid the observance of religion in public schools, and the rapid pace of public school social change and instructional innovation over the past decade has eroded much of the tradition in public school life. As Shils (1981) has argued, the presence of tradition can be crucial in providing a normative ordering that counterbalances the excessive rationalization of modern society. Tradition defines the "natural" way to do things, representing the accumulation of experience tested over time. Informal student folklore, rituals, and formal teacher-student ceremonies operate in place of legalistic student codes of conduct to guide student behavior, providing an interpretive context for the experience of schooling. Waller (1932) has similarly emphasized the importance of tradition in the early-century public high schools.

In addition to normative regulation, school traditions often evoke imagery of past greatness, a heritage of accomplishment worthy of emulation and preservation for future generations of students. Individual striving serves the corporate "student body" extended through time. The existence of an honor roll or portrait gallery of distinguished alumni and former teachers, even the display of athletic trophies dating back to the early history of the school, can add to the quality of life of students. The veneration of past greatness fosters a sense of sharing in this greatness. On the other hand, excessive worship of the past can be a form of escapism that stifles individual freedom and innovation, making youth poorly adapted to the continuing rapid pace of social change in modern society. Learning to cope with the greater social strains, impersonality, and bureaucracy of public school life may be better preparation for the realities of adulthood. These are issues which must be resolved through further research and debate. The present analysis has shown that the substantial sector difference in quality of student life is *not* coupled with any strong sector differences in quantity of learning.

Appendix to Chapter 5
Analysis of Regional Variation

Table 5A.1 shows the regional mean values in achievement and expectations before and after taking into account all the explanatory variables in the basic model. The analysis was restricted to public school youth because of region-specific sample size limitations. Preliminary analyses of the total sample revealed no significant region by sector interaction effect; hence these results should generalize to the private school sector. The expected regional means were calculated by substituting into the regression equations of the basic model region $i = 1$ and $j = 0$ if $i \neq j$ and the means of all other variables in the equation.

Table 5A.1

**Observed and Adjusted Regional Mean Values of Achievement (AFQT)
and Expected Education (Years) for Public Sector Youth
Aged 14-17 in 1979**

Region	Achievement		Expectations	
	Observed	Adjusted	Observed	Adjusted
New Eng.	75.28	69.96	14.55	13.94
Mid. Atl.	68.46	67.07	14.00	13.88
S. Atl.	62.10	66.99	13.64	13.90
E.S. Cen.	60.66	64.78	13.52	14.16
W.S. Cen.	61.91	67.03	13.76	13.93
E.N. Cen.	70.05	68.78	13.84	13.88
W.N. Cen.	73.76	71.66	14.03	13.92
Mtn.	68.28	68.08	13.45	13.61
Pac.	67.72	67.60	14.00	13.95
U.S. total	67.90	67.91	13.93	13.92
S.D.	20.06	-	2.24	-

Looking first at the unadjusted means, public school youth from the three southern regions (South Atlantic, East South Central, and West South Central) average 9 points lower in achievement than youth from the two eastern regions (New England and Middle Atlantic), 10 points lower than youth from the two North Central regions (East and West), and 6 points lower than youth from the two western regions (Mountain and Pacific). If youth were equivalent across regions on all explanatory variables entered in the model (except of course region), these regional differences would become negligible. Looking now at the adjusted regional means, southern youth would differ from eastern youth only 2 points, from north central youth 4 points, and from western youth 2 points.

The basic model also explains most of the regional variation in expected years of education. Clustering the nine census regions into the same four areas, the maximum difference between any two areas of .7 years drops to .2 years after adjustment on the explanatory variables.

NOTES

1. Starting with an estimate that the public school attrition due to dropouts is double that in the private schools, CHK employ an ad hoc adjustment procedure which reduces the across-grade raw differences in achievement scores approximately twice as much for public as for private students. However plausible, there is no way to validate this radical adjustment procedure with the HSB data alone. Because of other serious problems with this "learning growth" approach, particularly its failure to control for test ceiling effects which would bias the growth estimates for initial high-scoring students, no effort has been made here to replicate this particular analysis.

2. The January 1, 1981 age range was 16-23, but as interviews were conducted between the beginning of the year and the spring, some youth were 24 at time of interview.

3. Former students completed one or more years of college and were no longer enrolled. 53.8 percent completed one year only, 27.1 percent completed two or three years, and 19.1 percent completed four or more years of college.

4. Similar track differences appear to hold in the other two sectors, but sample size limitations make the estimates unreliable.

5. Significant other's influence is a four-point scale of perceived degree of approval with a decision not to attend college by the person selected as the most important influence in one's life. High score signifies strong disapproval, i.e., encouragement to attend college. Of the four largest categories of persons chosen, 67 percent were parents, 14 percent friends, 10 percent other relatives, and 3 percent teachers or counselors.

6. One other possible control variable, sex, was uncorrelated with the other explanatory variables, hence its omission had to impact on the other variables estimates. Product terms introduced to test for a possible sex by sector interaction effect were nonsignificant and so were also dropped from the equation.

7. The intelligence tests used, in order of frequency, were the Otis-Lennon, Differential Aptitude, California Test of Mental Maturity, Lorge-Thorndike, Henmon-Nelson, SCAT, Kuhlman-Anderson, Stanford-Binet, and Wechsler.

8. Besides the greater theoretical relevance and comparability with the HSB sample of this age segment, one key variable, significant other's influence, was not measured for the over 17 age group, and the income variable for some members of this older age group signifies the respondent's own destination status income rather than origin status, family income.

9. In addition to this model, results were obtained using two alternative analysis strategies, each of which more closely represented key features of the original design for CHK. For both theoretical and methodological reasons, however, neither was considered preferable to the one reported in the text. One estimated separate production function equations for each sector, and then compared their relative impact by means of component analysis (Althauser and Wigler 1972). The other treated curriculum as a mediator of the sector variable, in a fully recursive structural equations model. Following the conventions of path analysis (Alwin and Hauser 1975), the relative effects of sector and curriculum were then assessed in terms of their total, direct (unmediated), and indirect (mediated) effects. What is important to note here is that results so obtained did not alter any of the substantive conclusions reported in the text.

10. In evaluating the size of these schooling effects, caution must be exercised in taking too literally the absolute values of the coefficients. These values are useful more as a common metric for interpreting the *relative* importance of the different effects.

11. A variety of interpretations for this apparent paradox are possible; for example, it may be that vocational training qualified these youth for cognitively complex post-high school work activity that fostered further cognitive achievement.

12. Instructional quality is a composite of four items: "my schoolwork requires me to think to the best of my ability," "most of my classes are boring," "most of my teachers really know their subjects well," "most of my teachers are willing to help with personal problems." The rest are single item indices—"you can get away with almost anything at this school" (school discipline); "at this school, a person has the freedom to learn what interests him or her" (academic freedom); "I don't feel safe at this school" (personal safety); "this school offers good job counseling" (job counseling); and "it's easy to make friends at this school" (peer relations). All items are coded so a high score corresponds to the variable direction implicit in its label.

13.See Lisa Birnbach, ed., *The Official Preppy Handbook,* New York: Workman, 1980. Ironically, this best-seller among youth advocates the same hedonistic values and disdain of personal achievement which Coleman viewed so critically in his original (1961) study of American high school life.

REFERENCES

Alexander, K.L. and E.L. McDill. 1976. "Selection and Allocation Within Schools: Some Causes and Consequences of Curriculum Placement." *American Sociological Review* 41: 963-80.

Alwin, D.F. and R.M. Hauser. 1975. "The Decomposition of Effects in Path Analysis." *American Sociological Review* 40: 37-47.

Althauser, R.P. and M. Wigler. 1972. "Standardization and Component Analysis." *Sociological Methods and Research* 1: 97-135.

Becker, G. 1976. *The Economic Approach to Human Behavior.* Chicago: University of Chicago Press.

Blau, P.M. and O.D. Duncan. 1967. *The American Occupational Structure.* New York: Wiley.

Bock, R.D. and R.J. Mislevy. 1981. *Data Quality Analysis of the Armed Services Vocational Aptitude Battery.* Chicago: National Opinion Research Center.

Brown, B.W. and D.H. Saks. 1981. "Economic Analysis of Time and School Learning." Paper presented at the National Invitational Conference on Instructional Time and Student Achievement, 18-19 May, 1981, Evanston, Illinois.

Bryk, A.S. 1981. "Disciplined Inquiry or Policy Argument?" *Harvard Educational Review* 51: 497-509.

Campbell, P.B., M.N. Orth and P. Seitz. 1981. *Patterns of Participation in Secondary Vocational Education.* Columbus: National Center for Research in Vocational Education, Ohio State University.

Coleman, J.S. 1961. *The Adolescent Society.* New York: Free Press of Glencoe.

_____. 1981. "Private Schools, Public Schools, and the Public Interest." *The Public Interest* 64: 19-30.

Coleman, J.S., T. Hoffer and S. Kilgore. 1981. *Public and Private Schools.* Report to National Center for Education Statistics. Chicago: National Opinion Research Center.

_____. 1982. "Cognitive Outcomes in Public and Private Schools." *Sociology of Education* 55: 65-76.

Epstein, J.L., ed. 1981. *The Quality of School Life.* Lexington: Heath.

Freeman, R.B. 1976. *The Overeducated American.* New York: Academic Press.

Goldberger, A.S. and G.C. Cain. 1982. "The Causal Analysis of Cognitive Outcomes in the Coleman, Hoffer, and Kilgore Report." *Sociology of Education* 55: 103-122.

Hanushek, E.A. 1979. "Conceptual and Empirical Issues in the Estimation of Educational Production Functions." *The Journal of Human Resources* 14: 351-388.

Hauser, R.M. 1970. "Context and Consex: A Cautionary Tale." *American Journal of Sociology* 75: 645-664.

_____. 1974. "Contextual Analysis Revisited." *Sociological Methods and Research* 2: 365-375.

McDill, E.L. and L.C. Rigsby. 1973. *Structure and Process in Secondary Schools: The Academic Impact of Educational Climates.* Baltimore: Johns Hopkins University Press.

McWilliams, H.A. 1980. *The Profile of American Youth: Field Report.* Chicago: National Opinion Research Center.

Mill, J.S. 1848. *Principles of Political Economy.* New York: Longmans (1923 Ashley edition).

Morgan, W.R. 1983. "Learning and Student Life Quality of Public and Private School Youth." *Sociology of Education* 56: in press.

Olneck, M. 1981. "Are Private Schools Better Than Public Schools?: A Critique of the Coleman Report." *Focus* 5: 1-4, 17-18. Madison: Institute for Research on Poverty, University of Wisconsin.

Rosenbaum, J.E. 1980. "Track Perceptions and Frustrated College Plans: An Analysis of the Effects of Tracks and Track Perceptions in the National Longitudinal Survey." *Sociology of Education* 53: 74-88.

Sewell, W.H., R.M. Hauser and D.L. Featherman, eds. 1976. *Schooling and Achievement in American Society.* New York: Academic Press.

Shils, E. 1981. *Tradition.* Chicago: University of Chicago Press.

Waller, W. 1932. *The Sociology of Teaching.* New York: Wiley.

Chapter 6
The Economic Value of Academic and Vocational Training Acquired in High School*

Russell W. Rumberger
and
Thomas N. Daymont

I. Introduction

The recent report of the President's Commission on Excellence in Education, *A Nation at Risk,* has generated renewed interest in the quality of secondary schooling in the United States. There is particular concern that today's students are not preparing adequately for their future educational and economic lives by taking enough academic courses in such areas as mathematics and science. But what constitutes the best preparation for future work and education? And do curriculum differences in high school lead to differences in the outcomes of schooling?

These two questions have formed the basis for a substantial body of research on the outcomes of schooling. This

*Quoted with permission from *Job Training for Youth* (1982), edited by R. Taylor, H. Rosen and F. Pratzner, The National Center for Research in Vocational Education, The Ohio State University.

research confirms that educational outcomes—the likelihood of attending college, the type of college attended, and even the choice of college major—appear to be influenced by the curriculum followed in high school (Alexander, Cook, and McDill 1978; Polachek 1978; Kolstad 1979). But for those students who do not attend college, differences in high school curriculum appear to have little effect on labor market opportunities (Griffin and Alexander 1978). In particular, students who follow a vocational curriculum in high school enjoy no advantage in labor market opportunities over other students.[1] Recent empirical studies have failed to find systematic advantages to high school vocational training.[2]

The failure to find differences in labor market opportunities from high school curriculum is perhaps most disturbing to promoters of vocational education. They have long held that vocational education provides better preparation than other curricula for direct entry into the labor market immediately after high school. Their faith has spurred increased support for vocational education at both the state and federal levels.

Other observers question whether differences in high school curricula should, in fact, lead to differences in labor market opportunities. On the one hand, if vocational training in high school simply develops specific job skills useful in only a limited number of occupations, then graduates may not receive any relative advantage in earnings or other labor market opportunities, either because the benefits accrue to employers or because initial earnings advantages decline as the number of vocational graduates increase in response to initial advantages (Grubb 1979; Gustman and Steinmeier 1982). On the other hand, if vocational training merely develops more basic skills comparable to skills learned in other curricula, then vocational graduates again may fail to enjoy an economic advantage over other high school graduates (Grubb 1979; Thurow 1979).

Thus, at least in theory it remains unclear whether differences in high school curriculum *should* lead to differences in labor market opportunities. Yet attempts to discern any differences in effect of curriculum remain.

Many past empirical studies of this problem suffer from several shortcomings. First, information on high school curriculum usually comes from students who are asked to identify their program as either college preparatory, vocational, or general. Curriculum differences may be understated because students misperceive their high school program (Rosenbaum 1980; Meyer 1981). More important, using a single measure of curriculum difference may obscure large variations in actual course work. For example, vocational students who follow and complete a full program may be quite different from those who simply take a few unrelated vocational courses (Brown and Gilmartin 1980; Campbell, Orth, and Seitz 1981). Students who identify their program as academic (or college preparatory), vocational, or general frequently take courses in all three program areas (Rumberger 1981; Meyer 1981). Identifying the various curricula with any accuracy thus requires information on specific courses taken by students.

Second, curriculum differences may make little difference in earnings and employment opportunities because high school graduates are frequently employed in low-skilled and low-level occupations (Reubens 1974). Students who prepare for a specific job following high school by completing a legitimate vocational program may, in fact, enjoy an advantage over other graduates if they find a job related to their training. Although several studies have examined the relationship between area of training and the type of job found after high school (Campbell, et al. 1981; Woods and Haney

1981), few have examined the economic advantage of holding a training-related job.

This study addresses both of these limitations, first by looking at differences in high school curricula in greater detail, and second by relating high school training to labor market outcomes more specifically, including an assessment of whether a student's vocational training was used on the job.[3]

We also examine race and sex differences in both high school vocational training and labor market opportunities. If vocational training shows little effect on labor market outcomes, then race and sex differences in curriculum may explain little of the observed differences in labor market opportunities among these groups. Yet, if certain areas of vocational training do provide access to better paying jobs, then differences in high school curricula may be telling. Vocational training opportunities in high school are clearly divided along sexual lines, with women more likely to enroll in office occupations training and young men more likely to pursue training in technical and industrial areas (Rumberger 1981). To a lesser degree there are also racial differences in vocational training opportunities. Thus, in some instances, race and sex differences in high school curricula may explain some of the differences in post-school labor market opportunities.

During the 1979 NLS interview, respondents were asked to identify the high school they were currently attending, or last attended. For those respondents who were 17 to 21 years old in 1979 and who had last attended an American high school (8,420 out of 11,406 respondents), efforts were made to collect high school transcripts and school information. Complete transcript data were collected for 6,591 respondents (78 percent of those eligible). We further restricted the sample to those respondents who were not enrolled full-time during the second interview, who had completed 9 to 12 years of schooling, and for whom complete transcript data were available for all years of school completed.[4] These further restrictions resulted in a sample of 1,857 respondents. Throughout the analysis, observations were weighted by their sample weights to adjust for the oversampling of blacks, Hispanics, and disadvantaged whites.

II. Academic and Vocational Training in High School

We grouped courses into three areas: academic, vocational, and other. Academic courses include language arts, foreign languages, mathematics, natural sciences, and social sciences; vocational courses include agriculture, distributive education, health occupations, home economics, office occupations, and technical, trades and industry.[5] All remaining courses, including business, industrial arts, art, music, and physical education, fall into the "other" category.[6] These major divisions differentiate between the general skills acquired from academic courses and the specific skills acquired from vocational training.

Graduates completed a total of 15.4 credits during their last three years of high school, whereas dropouts completed an average of only 5.4 credits (table 6.1). Graduates completed an average of eight credits in academic subjects (52 percent of their total credits), 3.5 credits in vocational subjects (23 percent), and 3.9 credits in other subject areas (25 percent). As we might expect, students in college preparatory programs took more academic subjects than other students, while vocational students took more of their course work in vocational areas. College preparatory students had the most credits in language arts and social sciences; vocational students had the majority of their credits in home economics, office occupations, and trades and industry.

Table 6.1
Mean Number of High School Credits by Graduation Status,
Self-Reported Program, and Curriculum Area[a]

Curriculum area	Graduates				Dropouts	Total
	College prep	Vocational	General	Total		
Academic	9.87	7.01	7.75	7.95	2.59	7.06
Language arts (05)	3.13	2.70	2.84	2.86	.99	2.54
Foreign languages (06)	.77	.24	.29	.37	.05	.32
Mathematics (11)	1.67	.96	1.09	1.16	.43	1.04
Natural sciences (11)	1.81	.94	1.10	1.19	.44	1.07
Social sciences (15)	2.49	2.16	2.43	2.37	.67	2.09
Vocational	2.16	5.08	3.14	3.49	.98	3.05
Agriculture (01)	.06	.16	.25	.19	.14	.18
Distributive ed. (04)	.11	.24	.16	.17	.06	.16
Health occupations (07)	.05	.08	.05	.06	.02	.05
Home economics (09)	.63	.80	.80	.77	.24	.65
Office occupations (14)	1.01	2.11	1.17	1.40	.20	1.20
Tech., trades & industry (16, 17)	.30	1.70	.70	.90	.32	.80

Other	3.56	3.51	4.29	3.93	3.61
Business (03)	.18	.23	.22	.22	.19
Industrial arts (10)	.46	.78	.89	.78	.71
Art, music (02, 12)	.90	.66	1.02	.90	.81
Miscellaneous (08, 18-22)	2.03	1.82	2.16	2.05	1.91
Total	15.60	15.59	15.18	15.38	13.72

a. Tabulations based on a weighted sample of 17 to 21 year olds who were not enrolled in school full-time in the winter of 1980, who completed 9 to 12 years of school, and for whom complete transcript data were available (N=1857). One credit corresponds to a standard, full-year course. Only credits for courses taken in grades 10-12 are included. Numbers in parentheses refer to major curriculum areas designated by the Office of Education (Putnam and Chismore 1970).

Students also took a number of courses in miscellaneous areas such as health, driver education, and physical education.

Because students in all three program areas often take both academic and vocational courses, program designation may reveal little about the actual academic and vocational preparation a student receives in high school. This causes a problem for research, one which may be especially acute when we are looking at vocational areas that involve specific training. In order to assess the effectiveness of vocational training accurately, we must identify vocational students: one way to do this is to find what proportion of those who identify themselves as vocational students actually complete a given number of credits in the vocational area in which they are training.[7]

Such an examination reveals that a significant proportion of vocational students have taken less than three credits in the specific area in which they were training (table 6.2). In fact, the transcripts of some students show that they have not received credit for a single course in their specific area. The proportions of students receiving given numbers of credits also vary widely by area—three-quarters of vocational students in office occupations had completed three or more credits in that area, whereas about one-third of vocational students in distributive education and health occupations had done so. Some students in other vocational areas and in college preparatory and general programs have also completed three or more credits in more specific vocational areas.

Instead of the program designation offered by students themselves, the benchmark of three credits will be used in the next part of this study to identify vocational students.[8] Of course not everyone who has completed three credits of vocational courses in a specific area has completed a pro-

Table 6.2
High School Vocational Credits by Graduation Status, Program, and Curriculum Area

| Vocational curriculum area | Graduates | | | | Dropouts | Total |
| | Academic | Vocational | | General | | |
		Specific[a]	Total			
Percent with some credits						
Agriculture	4	75	9	13	11	10
Distributive education	7	71	11	11	7	10
Health occupations	3	43	3	2	1	2
Home economics	44	81	50	60	19	46
Office occupations	56	96	59	61	21	53
Tech., trades & indus.	11	67	38	24	14	24
Percent with 3 or more credits						
Agriculture	1	56	2	4	1	3
Distributive education	1	40	4	2	1	2
Health occupations	1	32	1	1	1	1
Home economics	5	56	8	8	0	6
Office occupations	13	78	4	15	0	17
Tech., trades & indus.	5	54	7	12	6	13
Percent with 6 or more credits						
Agriculture	0	10	0	0	0	1
Distributive education	0	8	1	0	0	0
Health occupations	0	20	1	0	0	0
Home economics	1	27	12	1	0	3
Office occupations	1	31	14	2	0	4
Tech., trades & indus.	1	32	15	4	1	6

a. Students whose specific vocational program corresponded to the vocational curriculum areas that are listed.

gram in that area. Each vocational program consists of a particular sequence and number of courses. Although the benchmark of three credits only provides an approximate indication of students who have completed a vocational program, it offers a marked improvement over the program identification used in most previous studies.

The mean numbers of credits in various curriculum areas for specific race-sex groups of high school graduates are shown in table 6.3. Other than the observation that white young women seem to be more likely than minorities to take vocational training in office occupations, little systematic racial difference appears among high school curricula. Not surprisingly, we find large sex differences in types of vocational courses taken: young women tend to concentrate in office occupations and home economics and young men in trades and industries.

III. Effects on Labor Market Outcomes

The effects of high school curriculum were estimated through a series of equations that expressed several measures of labor market success as a linear function of high school course work and an array of control variables. Estimates were derived using ordinary least squares regression. Course work represents the number of credits completed in various subject areas and was expressed in varying degrees of detail. Unlike previous studies that use dummy variables to distinguish between vocational, academic, and general curriculum areas, we were able to measure the actual *amount* of course work taken by each person in specific subject areas. Because our sample consists of persons who have completed from 9 to 12 years of schooling, the number of credits completed in grades 10-12 varies from zero to over 20. Thus we can estimate the incremental effects of taking additional course work in various curricula as well as the relative effects

Table 6.3
Mean Number of High School Credits by Sex, Race, and Curriculum Area[a]

	Females			Males			Total
	Black	Hispanic	White	Black	Hispanic	White	
Academic	8.25	8.27	7.89	7.93	8.07	7.97	7.95
Language arts	2.94	2.81	2.89	2.98	2.80	2.81	2.86
Foreign languages	.43	.96	.45	.20	.58	.27	.37
Mathematics	1.31	1.10	1.04	1.30	1.25	1.26	1.16
Natural sciences	1.23	1.07	1.17	1.06	1.09	1.24	1.19
Social sciences	2.33	2.32	2.35	2.39	2.35	2.40	2.37
Vocational	3.58	3.38	4.23	2.88	2.48	2.84	3.49
Agriculture	.03	.05	.11	.21	.34	.29	.19
Distributive education	.28	.17	.13	.24	.05	.22	.17
Health occupations	.11	.03	.11	.01	.00	.00	.06
Home economics	1.39	1.13	1.14	.57	.36	.39	.77
Office occupations	1.46	1.83	2.45	.41	.34	.44	1.40
Tech., trades & indus.	.31	.17	.29	1.45	1.39	1.51	.90
Other	3.27	4.02	3.51	4.36	5.22	4.32	3.93
Business	.16	.17	.25	.14	.09	.20	.22
Industrial arts	.08	.11	.12	.85	1.39	1.52	.78
Art, music	.73	.94	1.17	.85	.81	.71	.90
Miscellaneous	2.30	2.80	1.97	2.53	2.93	1.90	2.05
Total	15.10	15.67	15.64	15.18	15.78	15.13	15.38

a. High school graduates only (N = 1429).

of taking more courses in one or another area (e.g., vocational versus academic).

In each equation the same set of control variables were included to minimize any bias due to students of different backgrounds and abilities selecting different high school subjects.[9] Background variables included a measure of parental education and a cultural index indicating the presence of newspapers, magazines, and a library card in the respondent's original home. The respondent's grade point average in the ninth grade was used as a measure of early ability.[10] Additional control variables included race, marital status, presence of children, sex-children interaction, and post-school experience.[11]

In order to examine different dimensions of labor market behavior and success, we analyzed three labor market outcome variables: hourly earnings in the 1980 survey week, the number of weeks unemployed in the previous year, and the number of hours worked in the previous year.[12]

Estimates were derived for respondents in our basic sample (1,857 cases) who had complete information on the dependent variables and information on most of the independent variables.[13] Males and females were analyzed separately, since they tend to have different labor market experiences and generally acquire different vocational training in high school. Estimates for each of the three dependent variables are shown in separate panels in table 6.4 for males and in table 6.5 for females.

As a reference point, the first equation in each table shows the effects of the standard measure of educational attainment—years of school completed. The effect of years of school completed on hourly earnings (.047 for males and .055 for females) is slightly lower but fairly consistent with previous studies using a similar measure of educational attainment (e.g., Griliches 1976). However, precise comparisons with the results of previous studies are difficult because we observe earnings very early in the work career and restrict our analysis to those who do not go on to college. Although not shown in the tables, the years completed equation was also estimated with an additional "diploma" variable to test for a credentialism effect: surprisingly, there was no evidence of such an effect.[14] In the second equation in each panel, we substituted total credits for years completed and found fairly consistent results for both men and women. As expected, both variables have positive effects on hourly earnings and hours worked and negative effects on weeks unemployed. Given that a normal school year usually consists of five or six credits, the size of the coefficients for years completed and total credits correspond very closely for women and moderately well for men. The main exception is that the effect of total credits on hourly earnings is quite small for men.

In the third equation, we partition credits into our categories: academic, vocational, and other. In most cases, academic and vocational course work have similar effects. For hourly earnings, the effects of both types of course work are insignificant for men and significant for women. The coefficients for women imply that a half-day's course work for a school year (i.e., about three credit hours) of either academic or vocational courses would increase hourly earnings by about 3 percent. For weeks unemployed, the results imply that a half day's course work would reduce unemployment by about one to one and one-half weeks per year, with the effects of academic training being stronger for men and the effects of vocational training being slightly stronger for women. Both academic and vocational training have strong effects on annual hours worked for women: a half-day's course work of either is associated with working about 150 more hours per year, the equivalent of almost four weeks of full-time work. The biggest difference in effects is for hours

Table 6.4
The Effects of Curriculum on Labor Market Success
for Young Men Who Do Not Go On to College[a]

	Equation				
	(1)	(2)	(3)	(4)	(5)
	(Log) hourly earnings				
Years completed	.047*				
Total credits		.004			
Academic			.007	.008	.008
Vocational			.005		
Vocational (nonprogram)				-.009	-.010
Vocational (program)				.004	
Vocational (program, not used)					-.001
Vocational (program, used)					.007
Other			-.001	-.0005	-.0005
R² (adj.)	.12	.11	.11	.11	.11
N	713	713	713	713	713

Weeks unemployed

	(1)	(2)	(3)	(4)	(5)
Years completed	-2.620**				
Total credits		-.404**			
Academic			-.575**	-.583**	-.584**
Vocational			-.305*		
Vocational (nonprogram)				.148	.151
Vocational (program)				-.304*	
Vocational (program, not used)					-.264
Vocational (program, used)					-.325*
Other			-.196	-.221	-.220
R^2 (adj.)	.08	.07	.08	.08	.08
N	515	515	515	515	515

Hours worked

	(1)	(2)	(3)	(4)	(5)
Years completed	239.90**				
Total credits		32.797**			
Academic			14.149	13.940	14.222
Vocational			52.331**		
Vocational (nonprogram)				67.859*	66.554*
Vocational (program)				52.281**	
Vocational (program, not used)					35.263*
Vocational (program, used)					61.758**
Other			47.156**	45.238**	46.127**
R^2 (adj.)	.14	.12	.13	.13	.13
N	515	515	515	515	515

a. One asterisk indicates statistical significance at the .05 level, and two asterisks indicate significance at the .01 level.

Table 6.5
**The Effects of Curriculum on Labor Market Success
for Young Women Who Do Not Go On to College[a]**

	Equation				
	(1)	(2)	(3)	(4)	(5)
			(Log) hourly earnings		
Years completed	.055*				
Total credits		.010*			
Academic			.011*	.011*	.012*
Vocational			.010*		
Vocational (nonprogram)				.003	.002
Vocational (program)				.009	
Vocational (program, not used)					-.002
Vocational (program, used)					.015**
Other			.008	.008	.009
R² (adj.)	.06	.06	.06	.05	.06
N	648	648	648	648	648

Weeks unemployed

	(1)	(2)	(3)	(4)	(5)
Years completed	-2.190**				
Total credits		-.356**			
Academic			-.435**	-.433**	-.457**
Vocational			-.503**		
Vocational (nonprogram)				-.546*	-.523*
Vocational (program)				-.509**	
Vocational (program, not used)					-.362**
Vocational (program, used)					-.658**
Other			-.056	-.054	-.079
R^2 (adj.)	.05	.05	.06	.06	.06
N	565	565	565	565	565

Hours worked

	(1)	(2)	(3)	(4)	(5)
Years completed	257.86**				
Total credits		38.710**			
Academic			47.321**	44.929**	51.138**
Vocational			55.942**		
Vocational (nonprogram)				95.967**	88.388**
Vocational (program)				60.519**	
Vocational (program, not used)					17.073
Vocational (program, used)					104.24**
Other			4.734	2.139	10.645
R^2 (adj.)	.35	.34	.35	.35	.39
N	576	576	576	576	576

a. One asterisk indicates statistical significance at the .05 level, and two asterisks indicate significance at the .01 level.

worked for men: while the effect of vocational training is as strong as it is for women, the effect of academic training is insignificant.

Although not directly comparable, our results are fairly consistent with several previous studies of the relative effects of vocational and academic courses. Using a set of dummy variables to measure curriculum, Grasso and Shea (1979) found that, net of the control variables, the labor market experiences of "the average male graduate of a vocational program who did not go on to college was not substantially different from that of the average general program graduate" (p. 156). Results such as these have often been interpreted as negative evidence of the effectiveness of vocational education. But this interpretation requires one also to conclude that a general curriculum is ineffective. Our specification and results suggest that a more appropriate interpretation is that, in general, *both* academic and vocational curriculum have a significant positive impact on labor market success.

Other course work appears to have relatively small effects on labor market success. The main exception is for hours worked where other course work had a substantial positive effect for men. In addition, the effect of other courses on hourly earnings is nontrivial for women, although it is not statistically significant at traditional levels.

We also performed parts of the analysis with the sample restricted to those who graduated from high school and in which academic, vocational, and other credits were coded as proportions of total credits. Since academic, vocational, other, and total credits are linearly dependent, the academic credits variable was omitted from the analysis and thus serves as a reference for evaluating the effects of vocational and other credits. This specification corresponds more closely to the traditional specification used by Grasso and Shea (1979) and others. The results from this alternative specification are similar to those discussed above in that the only instance in which the effects of vocational training are significantly different from academic training is the stronger and more positive effects of vocational training on hours worked for men (table 6.6).

Because vocational training develops specific job skills, the labor market benefits of vocational courses that are part of a complete program may be higher than the benefits from unrelated courses. In order to examine this issue, we counted all of a student's vocational credits either in a program variable (if the student completed at least three credits in one specific vocational area), or in a nonprogram variable. The results for the equations in which these were substituted for the general vocational variable are shown as equation (4) in tables 6.4 and 6.5. The effects of the program variable for men were in the anticipated direction for all three labor market outcome variables, although its effect was not significant for hourly earnings. On the other hand, the nonprogram variable had a detrimental effect on hourly earnings and unemployment, although its effect on hours worked was positive and significant. These results generally support the hypothesis that participating in a specific vocational program does pay off in the labor market while an occasional vocational course does not. The evidence for women is less conclusive: the effects of nonprogram training on weeks unemployed and hours worked is as strong or stronger than that of training related to a specific vocational program. Only for unemployment is the effect of the vocational program variable somewhat stronger.

Again because vocational training develops specific job skills, its economic benefits may also depend on whether or not the individual is employed in an occupation where it can be used. To test this notion, program credits were further partitioned into two categories: one for program credits related to the respondent's occupation, the other for the re-

Table 6.6
Effects of High School Curriculum on Labor Market Success Among High School Graduates: Proportional Specification[a]

	Males			Females		
	(1)	(2)	(3)	(1)	(2)	(3)
			(Log) hourly earnings			
Vocational	-.081			-.009		
Vocational (nonprogram)		-.248	-.258		-.098	-.118
Vocational (program)		-.052			-.044	
Vocational (program, not used)			-.185			-.239*
Vocational (program, used)			.010			.066
Other	-.121	-.090	-.087	-.049	-.052	-.030
Total credits	-.006	-.008	-.008	.006	.006	.006
R^2 (adj.)	.12	.12	.12	.04	.04	.05
N	579	579	579	582	582	582

Weeks unemployed

	(1)	(2)	(3)	(4)	(5)	(6)
Vocational	4.311			-2.571		
Vocational (nonprogram)		12.409**	12.681**		-1.538	-1.135
Vocational (program)		3.568			-1.265	
Vocational (program, not used)			5.990*			.487
Vocational (program, used)			2.356			-2.821
Other	4.418	3.200	3.291	7.177**	8.326**	7.996**
Total credits	-.086	-.036	-.029	-.288*	-.312*	-.308*
R² (adj.)	.06	.06	.06	.04	.04	.04
N	407	407	407	464	464	464

Hours worked

	(1)	(2)	(3)	(4)	(5)	(6)
Vocational	603.78*			297.43		
Vocational (nonprogram)		435.74	397.33		516.20	352.31
Vocational (program)		597.00*			250.41	
Vocational (program, not used)			251.29			-411.25
Vocational (program, used)			774.93**			827.88**
Other	355.63	346.26	334.06	-648.00**	-779.90**	-635.62**
Total credits	-20.229	-21.259	-22.098	10.720	14.378	13.015
R² (adj.)	.12	.12	.12	.33	.33	.37
N	407	407	407	467	467	467

a. All curriculum area credits are the proportion of total credits in this area. One asterisk indicates statistical significance at the .05 level, and two asterisks indicate significance at the .01 level.

maining credits. The occupational and educational code crosswalk prepared by the National Occupational Information Coordinating Committee (1979) was used to partition program credits. For each specific vocational area, the crosswalk provides a list of occupations that were judged to use the skills taught in that area.[15] These two variables were substituted for the vocational program variable in equation (5) of tables 6.4 and 6.5. These results show that for both men and women and for each labor market outcome, the effect of vocational training used on the job is significant and substantially greater than the effect of vocational training not used on the job. Thus, vocational training seems to yield a higher payoff for those individuals who are employed in jobs where their training can be utilized.

How many men and women hold jobs related to their area of high school vocational training? Table 6.7 shows the proportion of students taking (or not taking) vocational programs in specific areas whose occupation corresponded to that area. For example, the top row of the table indicates that among men who took a vocational program in agriculture, 42 percent held an occupation in 1980 that corresponded to that area, while only 17 percent of other men held that type of job. In most areas, vocational training substantially increases the likelihood of an individual's obtaining related employment. Apparently, either these programs are teaching important job-related skills or at least many employers think they do. Two exceptions to this general finding are trades and industry and home economics: for both men and women, the likelihood of students finding employment in these areas is about the same for students with and without vocational training.[16]

The variation across programs in the degree that training was used on the job raises the question of whether the labor market returns to vocational training varied by specific area of study. To examine this issue, we further partitioned our vocational training variables into detailed areas while retaining the distinctions among program, nonprogram, and job-related training.

Table 6.7
Percentages of Students Taking (or Not Taking) Vocational Programs in Specific Areas Who Obtained a Job in an Occupation That Corresponded to That Area by Specific Area and Sex[a]

Vocational and occupational area (No. of students in program)[b]	Specific vocational program participation	
	Yes	No
Males		
Agriculture (40)	42	17
Distributive education (16)	38	27
Health occupation (0)	-	5
Home economics (13)	4	6
Office occupation (16)	54	19
Trade and industry (191)	65	59
Females		
Agriculture (9)	3	7
Distributive education (16)	66	28
Health occupation (16)	40	6
Home economics (97)	15	13
Office occupation (248)	60	35
Trade and industry (34)	26	32

a. For example, the entry in the top row in the left hand column indicates that 42 percent of students who participated in an agricultural vocational program obtained an occupation that utilizes skills developed in an agricultural vocational training program. The entry in the top row in the right hand column indicates that 17 percent of students who did not participate in an agricultural vocational program (i.e., either participated in another vocational program area or did not participate in any vocational program) obtained an occupation that utilizes skills developed in an agricultural vocational training program.

b. The entries for the number of students in a program are unweighted while the main entries are weighted percentages.

For men, it appears that the types of vocational training have no significant effect on hourly earnings or unemployment, but do have a substantial favorable impact on hours worked. For women, training in office occupations stands out as having the strongest favorable effect on each dimension of labor market success. Although training in home economics appears to increase hours worked and decrease unemployment for women, its effect on hourly earnings is not significant.

Another question we explored is whether different types of course work are more or less helpful to different types of students. For example, it is widely believed that the students who are at a disadvantage either because of race, ethnicity, social background, or cognitive abilities will be the primary beneficiaries of vocational training. Our sample is already restricted to those who do not go on to college and thus already contains an overrepresentation of disadvantaged students. However, to further explore this issue, we reestimated the effects of academic, vocational, and other credits (i.e., equation (3) in tables 6.4 and 6.5) on labor market outcomes for several subsamples which distinguish between individuals who might be considered to be either disadvantaged or not, based on their race, ethnicity, social background, or cognitive ability. This analysis was not disaggregated by sex because the size of some of these subsamples is already quite small and because the results presented so far have suggested only small sex differences in the relative effects of academic and vocational course work. In terms of race and ethnic differences, little systematic pattern appears. However, there is some evidence that the effects of both academic and vocational training on hourly earnings are lower for blacks than for whites and Hispanics. It also appears that the effects of both these types of course work are weaker for Hispanics on unemployment and stronger for hours worked than they are for other individuals (table 6.8). The bottom four rows of table 6.8 show the

Table 6.8
Effects of High School Curriculum on Labor Market Success
for Different Samples Defined According to Race,
Ethnicity, Socioeconomic Background, and Mental Ability[a]

Sample	Academic	Vocational	Other
	(Log) hourly earnings		
Total (1361)	.010**	.007*	.002
Whites (926)	.010*	.009*	.002
Blacks (242)	.006	-.007	.015
Hispanics (193)	.018*	.014	-.001
GPA ninth grade≤2.2 (674)	.012*	.004	-.0004
Parents' education<12 (455)	.018**	-.010	.008
GPA ninth grade>2.2 (687)	.010*	.011*	.004
Parent's education≥12 (906)	.008	.012*	-.0002
	Weeks unemployed		
Total (1080)	-5.14**	-.412**	-.133
Whites (727)	-.577**	-.446**	-.155
Blacks (207)	-.441	-.442	-.323
Hispanics (146)	-.031	-.337	-.461*
GPA ninth grade≤2.2 (564)	-.511**	-.413**	-.314*
Parents' education<12 (386)	-.450**	-.551**	.121
GPA ninth grade>2.2 (516)	-.628**	-.520**	-.085
Parents' education≥12 (694)	-.615**	-.420**	-.288**
	Hours worked		
Total (1091)	29.871**	55.997**	25.365**
Whites (725)	26.117**	57.510**	23.129*
Blacks (215)	38.544*	51.133*	46.736
Hispanics (151)	53.516*	75.538**	21.464
GPA ninth grade≤2.2 (573)	34.036**	44.217**	53.322**
Parents' education<12 (391)	38.616**	81.314**	31.947*
GPA ninth grade>2.2 (518)	30.697**	71.685**	4.302
Parents' education≥12 (700)	27.350**	47.244**	23.309*

a. One asterisk indicates statistical significance at the .05 level, and two asterisks indicate significance at the .01 level. The control variables included in the regressions are described in the text.

results for those who are above and below average for our sample in terms of social background or cognitive ability.[17] On unemployment and hours worked, no systematic differences appear between the disadvantaged and the not-disadvantaged groups in the relative effects of academic and vocational training. On hourly earnings, vocational training has stronger effects than academic training in the not-disadvantaged groups relative to the disadvantaged groups, which if anything contradicts the hypothesis that the disadvantaged are the primary beneficiaries of vocational training and suggests that perhaps the most important need for disadvantaged students is training in basic skills.

IV. Conclusion

Our study of the economic value of academic and vocational education acquired in high school uses detailed information on course work available from high school transcripts. We attempted to discern whether differences in high school curricula lead to differences in labor market opportunities for persons who completed 10 to 12 years of schooling and acquired no post-secondary training. The economic variables were hourly wage rates, annual weeks unemployed, and annual hours worked. Consistent with other studies, the results varied between men and women.

For women, academic and vocational training showed equally strong effects on the different dimensions of labor market behavior that we examined. Although they should be interpreted with caution, our results suggest that an additional half-day's course work for a school year (i.e., about three credit hours) of either academic of vocational course work would lead to about 3 percent higher hourly earnings, one to one and one-half fewer weeks of unemployment per year, and 150 more hours worked per year.

For men, the results vary depending on which outcome variable is being examined. The effects of both types of training on unemployment are as strong for men as for women, but their effects on men's hourly earnings are smaller and statistically insignificant. Although the effect of vocational training on hours worked was as strong for men as it was for women, the effect of academic training on hours worked was insignificant.

The payoff to vocational training appears to vary in several other aspects. Vocational training that constitutes a specific program has a greater impact on labor market outcomes than vocational training in unrelated areas. In addition, the payoff to a program of vocational training is higher for persons employed in jobs where their training can be used. Moreover, vocational students were substantially more likely than other students to obtain employment in occupations that utilized their vocational skills except in the area of trades and industry, and home economics. These results suggest that in order to measure the payoff to vocational training, it is necessary to have more detailed information on the type of vocational training taken and the area of employment. Of course, very large sample sizes are needed to estimate the relative effects of curriculum on labor market success with any precision.

The strongest vocational training effects were associated with training in office occupations. We suspect that these high returns result from the recent growth in the service and clerical sectors of the economy where this type of training is particularly demanded. In any event, this finding suggests that the demand side of the youth labor market should be considered more carefully.

We observed substantial sex differences in the types of vocational training taken, with men concentrating in trades and industries and women concentrating in office occupations and home economics. This sex segregation in vocational training surely contributes to sex segregation in occupations. Although the relative payoff to the types of training taken by women appears to be at least as high as the payoff to the types of training taken by men, this segregation may help perpetuate inequality indirectly by contributing to the idea that it is natural for men and women to do different work. Greater access to all program areas should be afforded both men and women. Important parts of this effort would be to better inform boys and girls of career opportunities in both traditional and nontraditional areas, and to provide additional support for students in nontraditional areas once they have entered them.

Racial differences in economic outcomes appear minimal. The effects of vocational training on hourly earnings were lower for blacks than for whites, but the effects of vocational training on unemployment and hours worked are similar for blacks, Hispanics, and whites. Since members of each of these groups take similar types of high school courses, vocational training appears to have little impact on racial and ethnic inequality.

Our results compare quite closely with those of other recent studies. Like these studies, ours did not find systematic advantages to any single type of high school curriculum, particularly vocational. This lack of evidence does not mean that vocational training has no economic value, only that it has no more than any other training acquired in high school. In other words, both vocational and academic curricula have positive results.

Of course the present analysis focused only on the immediate economic payoff to high school curricula for students who acquire no additional post-secondary training. A more complete assessment of the economic value of different high school curricula should include its long term benefits as well as its effects on subsequent training opportunities and the economic benefits that accrue from them

(Meyer 1981). Additional educational benefits may include the impact of various curricula on keeping students in school who otherwise might drop out (Reubens 1974). In all cases, the benefits should be assessed relative to their costs. Since vocational education is generally more costly than other forms of education (Hu and Stromsdorfer 1979), its benefits should exceed those from other types of secondary schooling. That did not prove to be the case in the present analysis.

The results of this research suggest that policies designed to improve the secondary school curriculum may improve the educational outcomes of high school, but do little to improve the economic outcomes. Only in some cases did we find that vocational training provides economic outcomes superior to other kinds of high school course work. In other cases vocational and academic course work may simply be substitutes for each other, with each developing general as opposed to specific skills (Grubb 1979; Thurow 1979).

It appears that the specific courses taken in high school, whether academic or vocational, may be less important in determining success in the labor market than other types of learning, such as appropriate work habits and attitudes. Recent surveys of employers suggest such qualities are indeed more desirable than specific job skills (Maguire and Ashton 1981; Wilms 1983). In that case, schools should offer a variety of academic and vocational courses to meet the various interests of students in order to help them to complete school.

NOTES

1. Reviews of earlier empirical studies are found in Reubens (1974), Hu and Stromsdorfer (1979), and Mertens, et al. (1981).

2. There has been a rash of recent empirical studies, generated in part by the availability of more detailed data and by recent federal interest in reviewing the value of vocational education. Studies include Grasso and Shea (1979), Wiley and Harnischfeger (1980), Campbell, et al. (1981), Meyer (1981), Gustman and Steinmeier (1982), Woods and Haney (1981).

3. This study focuses on individual differences in high school experiences and their effects on opportunities after leaving school. Another body of literature examines the effects of school characteristics and resources on students' performance and outcomes (e.g., Spady 1976; Griffin and Alexander 1978).

4. The last requirement dictated that a student's transcript showed three or more credits of course work for each year of school completed. For example, high school graduates were required to have transcript information for grades 10-12 in order to be included in the sample.

5. Because so few students had completed credits in technical areas, this category was combined with trades and industry.

6. Course categories correspond to standard curriculum areas (Putnam and Chismore 1970).

7. Students who identified their program as vocational were also asked to identify the specific vocational area of their program: agricultural, business or office, distributive education, health, home economics, trade or industrial, or other.

8. Three credits represent a half day of vocational training taken for a full year. This is the minimum amount of vocational training required to complete a program in certain subject areas. Other areas require more preparation.

9. Of course this approach only controls for selection bias associated with measured control variables. Systematic selection on unmeasured variables such as motivation or parental encouragement that is independent of the measured controls may also produce bias in the effects of high school curriculum on labor market success.

10. Indicators of mental ability, primarily IQ test scores, were collected along with the transcripts. Although these test scores were preferred on a conceptual basis, we decided not to use them because of the low response rates (about 50 percent), differences in the kinds of tests taken, and the wide range in the age when the test was taken.

11. More specifically, the control variables were measured as follows: Parental education was the number of years of school completed by either the respondent's mother or father, whichever was greater. The cultural index was the sum of three dichotomous variables each indicating the presence ($=1$) or absence ($=0$) of newspapers, magazines, or a library card in the household when the respondent was 14 years old. Grade point average was computed from all courses taken in the ninth grade in which the student received a passing grade. Passing grades were converted to numerical equivalents, with $A=4$, $B=3$, $C=2$, $D=1$, and $F=0$. The two race variables included an indicator for being black ($=1$; 0, otherwise) and an indicator for being Hispanic ($=1$; 0, otherwise). Marital status equals 1 if married, spouse present; 0, otherwise. Children is the number of children living with the respondent. The sex-children interaction is the product of sex and children. Post-school experience is the number of months between the date the respondent last left school and the date of interview.

12. Since our sample ranges in age from 18 to 22 years of age, these variables measure labor market standing in most cases from 1 to 7 years after leaving school. Our results may be influenced by differences in the number of years since leaving school (although we control for this) as well as the particular year in which we measure labor market outcomes (1980). See the discussion by Gustman and Steinmeier (1982).

13. Observations were excluded from an equation if they had missing data on any variable included in the equation except parental education, the cultural index, and grade point average for the ninth grade. Race-sex specific means were substituted for missing data on parental education and the cultural index. Values were imputed for missing data on grade point average for the ninth grade based on a regression equation including the following explanatory variables: black, Hispanic, sex, parental education, cultural index, knowledge of the world of work, age, early mental ability test score, and a dichotomous variable indicating missing data on any early ability test score. In addition, observations were eliminated from the weeks unemployed last year and hours worked last year regressions if they had not been out of school for at least 12 months as of the date of interview.

14. The coefficient for the diploma variable (equal to one if the respondent received a high school diploma and equal to zero if not) was insignificant in five of the six equations and had the unexpected sign in half of them. More specifically, for men, the coefficients (and t values) were -.053 (-.7), -.38 (-.2), and -317 (-1.9) for hourly earnings, weeks unemployed, and hours worked respectively. For women, they were .065 (.8), 2.72 (1.6), and -213 (-1.3).

15. Although the crosswalk matches occupations to detailed vocational course categories, we only attempted to match respondents' occupations (1970 Census codes) to broad vocational categories (e.g., agriculture). For some of the more heterogeneous occupational categories (i.e., managerial, not elsewhere classified), we also required a match between the industry listed in the crosswalk and the respondent's industry.

16. This may be partly due to the broad and heterogeneous nature of the trades and industry category of occupations. About 60 percent of all the occupations held by the men in our sample required skills related to trades and industry vocational training. Perhaps a matching of more detailed breakdown of these program areas and occupations would yield different results.

17. Social background is measured using parental education; cognitive ability is measured using ninth grade GPA. See footnote 11 for a description of these variables.

REFERENCES

Alexander, Karl L., Martha Cook and Edward L. McDill. 1978. "Curriculum Tracking and Educational Stratification: Some Further Evidence." *American Sociological Review* 43 (February): 47-66.

Brown, Lawrence L. and Kevin J. Gilmartin. 1980. *Measures of Participation in Vocational Education: Course Enrollments, Students and Contact Hours.* Washington, DC: Office of Planning and Budget, U.S. Department of Education.

Campbell, Paul B., Mollie N. Orth and Patricia Seitz. 1981. *Patterns of Participation in Secondary Vocational Education.* Columbus: The National Center for Research in Vocational Education.

Campbell, Paul B. et al. 1981. *Employment Experiences of Students With Varying Participation in Secondary Vocational Education.* Columbus: National Center for Research in Vocational Education.

Chismore, W. Dale and Quentin M. Hill. *A Classification of Educational Subject Matter.* Washington, DC: U.S. Government Printing Office, 1978.

Grasso, John T. and John R. Shea. 1979. *Vocational Education and Training: Impact on Youth.* Berkeley: Carnegie Council on Policy Studies in Higher Education.

Griffin, Larry J. and Karl L. Alexander. 1978. "Schooling and Socioeconomic Attainments: High School and College Influences." *American Journal of Sociology* 84 (May): 319-47.

Griliches, Zvi. 1976. "Wages of Very Young Men." *Journal of Political Economy* 84 (August): S69-S85.

Grubb, W. Norton. 1979. "The Phoenix of Vocational Education: Implications for Evaluation." In *The Planning Papers for the Vocational Education Study.* Washington, DC: National Institute of Education.

Gustman, Alan L. and Thomas L. Steinmeier. 1982. "The Relation Between Vocational Training in High School and Economic Outcomes." *Industrial and Labor Relations Review* 36, 1 (October): 73-87.

Heyns, B. 1974. "Social Selection and Stratification in Schools." *American Journal of Sociology* 79 (May): 1434-51.

Hu, Teh-Wei and Ernst W. Stromsdorfer. 1979. "Cost-Benefit Analysis of Vocational Education." In Theodore Abramson, Carol Kerr Tittle and Lee Cohen, eds., *Handbook of Vocational Education Evaluation.* Beverly Hills: Sage.

Jencks, Christopher S. and Marsha D. Brown. 1975. "Effects of High Schools on Their Students." *Harvard Educational Review* 45 (August): 273-324.

Kolstad, A.J. 1979. "The Influence of High School Type and Curriculum on Enrollment in Higher Education and Postsecondary Training." Paper read at annual meetings of American Educational Research Association, 8-12 April 1979, San Francisco, California.

Maguire, M.J. and D.N. Ashton. 1981. "Employers' Perceptions and Use of Educational Qualifications." *Educational Analysis* 3 (Spring): 25-36.

Mertens, Donna M. et al. 1980. *The Effects of Participation in Vocational Education: Summary of Studies Reported Since 1968.* Columbus: National Center for Research in Vocational Education.

Meyer, Robert H. 1981. *An Economic Analysis of Vocational Education.* A report prepared for the National Commission for Employment Policy. Washington, DC: The Urban Institute.

Meyer, Robert H. and David A. Wise. 1981. "High School Preparation and Early Labor Market Experience." In Richard B. Freeman and James L. Medoff, eds., *Youth Joblessness and Unemployment.* Chicago: University of Chicago Press.

National Occupational Information Coordinating Committee. 1979. *Vocational Preparation and Occupations, Vol. 1: Occupational and Educational Code Crosswalk.* Interim Edition. Washington, DC: National Occupational Information Coordinating Committee.

National Opinion Research Center. 1980. "The School and Transcript Survey: Technical Report." Chicago: National Opinion Research Center (mimeo).

Polachek, Solomon William. 1978. "Sex Differences in College Major." *Industrial and Labor Relations Review* 31 (July): 498-508.

Putnam, John F. and W. Dale Chismore. 1970. *Standard Terminology for Curriculum and Instruction in Local and State School Systems.* Washington, DC: U.S. Government Printing Office.

Reubens, Beatrice G. 1974. "Vocational Education for All in High School?" In James O'Toole, ed., *Work and the Quality of Life*. Cambridge: MIT Press.

Rosenbaum. J.E. 1980. "Track Misperceptions and Frustrated College Plans: An Analysis of the Effects of Tracks and Track Perceptions in the National Longitudinal Survey." *Sociology of Education* 53: 74-88.

Rumberger, Russell W. 1980. "Experiences in High School and College." In *Pathways to the Future,* edited by Michael E. Borus, pp. 301-68. Columbus: Center for Human Resource Research, Ohio State University.

_____. 1981. "Why Kids Drop Out of High School." Paper presented at the annual meeting of the American Educational Research Association, Los Angeles, April 13-17.

Smith, Gene M. 1967. "Usefulness of Peer Rating of Personality in Educational Research." *Educational and Psychological Measurement* 27 (Winter): 967-84.

Spady, William G. 1976. "The Impact of School Resources on Students." In William H. Sewell, Robert M. Hauser and David L. Featherman, eds., *Schooling and Achievement in American Society.* New York: Academic Press.

Thurow, Lester C. 1979. "Vocational Education as a Strategy for Eliminating Poverty." In *The Planning Papers for the Vocational Education Study.* Washington, DC: National Institute of Education.

U.S. National Commission on Excellence in Education. 1983. *A Nation at Risk: The Imperative for National Reform.* Washington, DC: U.S. Government Printing Office.

Wiley, David E. and Annegret Harnischfeger. 1980. *High School Learning Vocational Tracking, and When Then?* Final Report prepared for NCES Contract No. 300-78-0541. Evanston, IL: CERMEL.

Wilms, Wellford W. 1983. "Technology, Job Skills, and Education." A study prepared for the Los Angeles Area Chamber of Commerce. Los Angeles: Higher Education Research Institute, University of California.

Woods, Elinor M. and Walt Haney. 1981. *Does Vocational Education Make a Difference?* Final report prepared for NIE Contract No. 400-79-0026. Cambridge, MA: Huron Institute.

Chapter 7
The Time-Use Behavior
of Young Adults

Ronald D'Amico*

I. Introduction

The modern industrial age has become increasingly time-conscious, with the beginnings and endings of daily activities regulated by the clock to an extraordinary degree. In recent years, social scientists have come to appreciate that such synchronization of our daily lives affords unique research opportunities across a range of research areas. At the macro level, for example, time expenditures bear important implications for the quality of life. Thus, how much time is spent on household chores, or in transportation, or in leisure activities, and how time is apportioned while at work might all well serve as useful social indicators. Similarly, time-use patterns constitute useful measures of the preferences and constraints of societies or individuals, especially given time scarcity as an endemic social problem (Linder 1970).

At the micro level, time allocations are also of considerable interest. Economists investigate how time "inputs" are converted to "outputs" of various sorts. For example, family members are hypothesized to apportion their time

*Special thanks to Paula Baker for very capable research assistance, to Joel Rath for programming expertise and to Sherry Stoneman for excellent clerical help.

between market and nonmarket activities in order to maximize the family's consumption of market and home goods (see, for example, Becker 1965; and Gronau 1973). Elsewhere, parent-child interactions are viewed as investments in the child's human capital development (see, for example, Fleisher 1977). For both analyses, quantifying time expenditures becomes necessary for estimating rates of return. Indeed, the possible applications of time-use data are as unbounded as the imagination of creative researchers, as recent work in family sociology (Berk 1979), education (Biddle, et al. 1981), and social ecology (Melbin 1978) attests.

Unfortunately, the time-use research now available is quite fragmentary, largely reflecting the inadequate data on the time expenditures of individuals. Increasingly, however, this inadequacy is being overcome by systematic data collection efforts, where careful measurement strategies are used to record time allocations for large, representative samples of individuals. The research described here represents the fruits of one such endeavor, the time-use data collected in the third wave of the National Longitudinal Survey (NLS). The goals of this chapter are two-fold: (1) to describe briefly the time allocations of young American adults across a set of activities, and (2) to investigate some of the determinants and/or covariates of time-use expenditures.

II. Measuring Time-Use in the NLS

The third wave of the National Longitudinal Survey was administered primarily in the winter and early spring of 1981 to a nationally representative sample of over 12,000 respondents. The sample members were 16-24 years of age at the time. Data on time-use behavior in these critical years of transition to adult roles has heretofore not been available for large samples of respondents. Because the paucity of time-use research derives partly from inherent measurement difficulties, a brief discussion of how some of these difficulties were dealt with in the NLS is appropriate here.

The earliest efforts at eliciting time-use information in social research consisted of questions asking respondents to estimate their "usual time" expenditures across a range of activities. While some interesting findings emerged from this research, subsequent investigations have shown this measurement approach to be notoriously unreliable in that respondents consistently overestimate their actual time expenditures. An alternative methodology, found to minimize such reporting errors, is the so-called "time-diary" approach, which asks respondents to report what they were doing minute by minute for a single twenty-four hour period.

A series of methodological studies (Robinson 1977; Juster and Stafford 1983) has shown that the time diary does in fact provide a very reliable indicator of what the respondent was doing and for what length of time for the day in question. Moreover, the time diary is unparalleled in producing time estimates across a very detailed set of activity categories. Nevertheless, the diary has certain limitations which makes its use somewhat problematic. To begin with, the open-ended format of the time diary allows respondents considerable discretion in the way they describe their activities. Many respondents, for example, report "time at work" and "time at school" as homogeneous categories, and make no differentiation according to type of job activity (e.g., type of job task, coffee breaks, training time) or school activity (e.g., class time, study time, extracurricular activities). In-depth analyses of work time or school time then become rather uncertain. Second and more important, the time-use information elicited for a single day might be atypical of the way each respondent *usually* allocates time, making each respondent's time expenditure data highly dependent on the day for which the diary was administered. Indeed, Robinson

(1977) reports that a substantial proportion of respondents report their diary day is atypical in important respects. This imprecision in measurement is of minimal consequence if one is interested in describing time-use behavior in the aggregate, since the deviations presumably cancel out when averaged across respondents. However, since the NLS is primarily used for micro-level analyses, this instability can result in seriously downwardly biased effect coefficients.

For these reasons, the time diary was deemed inappropriate for the NLS and an alternative was devised. The approach used asks respondents to report their time expenditures on select activities "during the last seven days." Its advantage derives from the ability to tailor questions to focus in-depth attention on a few activities of greatest general interest. Additionally, as a measurement device it was believed to incorporate some of the desirable characteristics of both the time diary and "usual time" approach. By asking about a specific and recent time period, the recall problems plaguing the "usual time" approach should be minimized; at the same time, by broadening the focus beyond interest in just a single day, the instability of time-use estimates should be attenuated relative to a time diary approach. Finally, asking about a week's activities seems to correspond more closely to the way people actually schedule and organize their time. (For a fuller discussion of the tradeoffs involved in choosing a time-use methodology, see Baker, et al. 1983). A methodological study conducted on pretest data, which explicitly compared time diary and seven-day time estimates, lent further credence to the utility and reliability of adopting a seven-day approach for select activities (Baker, et al. 1983).

Accordingly, the NLS asked respondents in-depth questions about their time expenditures during the last seven days in a number of activity areas. These areas include:

(1) Time at work—Questions asked respondents about total
     time spent working for pay in each of the last seven days
     for each of several jobs. Additional items probed what
     percent of their work time for their major employer was
     spent reading or writing, working with tools, and deal-
     ing with people, and whether they were participating in
     a formal apprenticeship or job training program while
     at work. Finally, respondents were asked to estimate the
     length of time and miles of their usual trip to work.

(2) Time at school—Respondents reported their time spent
     at school for each of the last seven days. Of the total
     time spent at school, estimates were then given for the
     time spent actually attending classes or labs and time
     spent studying at school. Other time spent studying in
     the last seven days, as well as distance and usual time
     spent traveling to school are also available.

(3) Time in government or private training programs—
     Respondents enrolled in such programs were asked
     about the time spent attending training sessions, study-
     ing for the program and in transportation in the last
     seven days, in a series of questions parallel to those ask-
     ed of students in regular schooling.

(4) Job search—An extensive series of questions on job
     search behavior was asked of those looking for work.
     This sequence asks which of 10 specific methods the
     respondent actually used (e.g., placed or answered
     newspaper ad, checked with friends, used a state
     employment agency, etc.) and which led to contacts
     with employers. Time spent on each method in the last
     seven days was also elicited.

(5) Time spent sleeping in the last seven days.

(6) Time spent watching TV in the last seven days.

(7) Additional information was elicited on the respondent's
     responsibility for household chores and child care. This

included a scale inquiring whether the respondent was usually the one in the household who did each of a number of chores, including child care. Answers were in response categories ranging from "do it almost never" to "do it almost all of the time." Because pretest results showed that the reliability of time estimates for household chores and child care dropped off sharply when respondents were asked to recall beyond a single day, time-use estimates for these activities were elicited for the day preceding the interview day only.

(8) Finally, time spent reading "yesterday" was also estimated by all respondents.

III. The Concomitants of Time-Use

Following Robinson (1977), time allocations can be conceptualized as being determined by four sets of factors: (1) personal characteristics, including race and social background; (2) role obligations, including whether the respondent is employed, a student, a parent, a spouse, and so on; (3) ecological characteristics, including the respondent's living arrangements; and (4) resources, such as income and the utilization of labor-saving technology. The way each of these relate to time-use expenditures on the activities described above will be considered in the following sections. Since the relationship between sex and time use is certain and strong, all cross tabulations will be presented separately for males and females.

Personal Characteristics

The first set of comparisons regarding the relationship of personal characteristics to time-use behaviors is presented in table 7.1, which reports time-use breakdowns by ethnic origin. Turning first to sex differences in employment characteristics, substantial differences in the proportion of

Table 7.1
Time-Use for Selected Activities: Results by Ethnic Origin and Sex

Activity	Black		Hispanic		White	
	M	F	M	F	M	F
Working for pay						
% with a job	56.1*	41.6 †	63.8	49.6†	68.1	61.7
Hours spent working for pay	32.48	30.31†	35.09	30.84†	32.95	28.44
% time writing/reading[a]	21.5	36.7	17.9	42.4	18.5	38.9
% time working w/hands[a]	75.1	71.4	80.0	72.0	78.1	72.3
% time with people[a]	53.0	60.0†	47.6	65.0	50.7	67.8
Hours spent for trip to work (one-way)	.29	.33†	.27	.28†	.27	.23
Time at school						
% enrolled in school	40.0*	44.6	40.6*	37.2	45.7	42.1
Hours spent at school	29.68*	25.29	24.50*	24.55	27.92	26.16
Hours spent in class	21.77*	19.37	18.35	18.57	19.01	18.92
Hours spent studying at school	4.64	3.81	3.55*	3.10†	5.05	4.37
Other time at school	3.27	2.11	2.60	2.88	3.86	2.87
Hours spent studying not at school	7.88	8.07†	6.70	7.66†	7.49	9.04
Total hours spent studying[b]	12.52	11.88†	10.25*	10.76†	12.54	13.41
Hours spent for trip to school (one-way)	.39*	.37†	.31	.36	.29	.30

Table 7.1 (continued)

Activity	Black		Hispanic		White	
	M	F	M	F	M	F
Training programs[d]						
% participating in programs	3.3	4.5	4.2	3.0	4.1	3.3
Hours spent at training programs	16.12	18.64	15.61	21.94	16.37	15.19
Hours spent in class	12.59	15.00	12.56	18.70	13.34	13.23
Hours spent studying at program	1.05	1.83	1.12	.66	1.64	1.38
Other time at program	2.48	1.81	1.93	2.58	1.39	.58
Hours spent studying away[b]	4.45	5.86	4.82	6.72	3.06	5.86
Total hours spent studying[b]	5.50	7.69	5.95	7.38	4.70	7.24
Hours spent for trip to program (one-way)	.29	.39	.36	.42	.36	.33
Leisure						
Hours spent reading (not for school)[c]	6.52*	5.30	5.78	5.29	4.93	5.23
Hours spent watching TV	13.35*	18.60†	12.53	16.04†	11.92	14.28
Hours spent sleeping	51.19*	53.34	53.90*	55.34†	52.22	52.90

Hours spent on household chores[c]	9.06*	17.98†	8.55	18.67†	8.17	15.03
N	1555	1525	950	959	3620	3586
Total by race	3080		1909		7206	

UNIVERSE: Youth age 16-24 on interview date. (N=33,517,000)

NOTE: All time estimates are hours per last seven days; digits to the right of the decimal point are fractional hours.

a. These items represent percent of time at work spent doing each of these three tasks and were adapted from Kohn (1969). To allow for a respondent to be doing multiple job tasks simultaneously, the question wording for these items specifically permitted double counting. Accordingly, percents sum to greater than 100.

b. These figures are the sum of time studying at school (program) and time studying at home.

c. Since time estimates for these activities were asked of "yesterday" only, time estimates were first weighted to produce a uniform frequency distribution across days of the week, and then multiplied by seven to arrive at an hours per last seven days estimate.

d. Includes government training programs (e.g., CETA) and "special" schools (e.g., technical schools, barber schools).

*T-tests for significant differences between males of different ethnic origin treat white males as the reference group. An asterisk indicates that the starred value is different from the corresponding value for white males at the .05 level.

†T-tests for significant differences between females of different ethnic origin treat white females as the reference group. A cross indicates that the marked value is different from the corresponding value for white females at the .05 level.

respondents who are employed appear. Regardless of ethnic group, males are anywhere from 6 to 14 percentage points more likely to work than are females. Notable racial differences in employment status also emerge, with blacks least likely and whites most likely to be employed. Hispanics occupy an intermediate position between these two groups.

Among those who work, however, the length of the average workweek shows only modest variance across race and sex groups. Hispanic males have the longest workweek, at 35 hours, while white females have the shortest week, at 28 hours. Across all racial groups, women not only have lower labor force participation rates but also work from 2 to 4 fewer hours per week than do males. Presumably these sexual differences in work intensity reflect in part the proclivity of married women, even at this age range, to work only part time while keeping house. Among men, the fact that the average workweek is as low as it is doubtless reflects the inclusion in the sample of students, who also tend to work only part time.

Looking at the kinds of tasks youth perform on their jobs, we see marked sex differences but fairly modest race differences. Females of all race groups spend about twice as much time as males reading and writing; indeed, no more than about one-fifth of the average male workweek involves such tasks. Women similarly spend considerably more time than males dealing with people while on their jobs. Interestingly, males and females spend about equal amounts of time working with their hands, with such tasks comprising the largest part of the workweek for all race and sex groups.

These figures correspond well to what might be expected, given the well-known sex differences in distributions across occupational categories. The clerical and sales positions, at which women typically labor, are reflected in the high time expenditures in reading and writing and working with hands, in the former case, and dealing with people, in the latter.

Similarly, the disproportionate representation of young males in manufacturing and craft positions explains their intensive involvement with manual tasks. In any case, these data provide an informative and useful way of quantifying the sexual division of labor in the American workforce. Along these lines, the surprisingly close correspondence of job task time expenditures across racial groups is noteworthy. Perhaps, as others have found with respect to wages (e.g., Rosenfeld 1980), the races begin to diverge markedly in their job tasks only further along in their careers.

Turning to the results for time at school, Hispanic and white males are more likely to be enrolled than female Hispanics and whites, but the opposite pattern holds true among blacks. Indeed, 45 percent of all black females are enrolled, second only to the 46 percent figure for white males. With the exception of black males, all groups spend roughly the same amount of time per week attending classes, just short of four hours per school day. However, there are notable discrepancies in total amount of time various groups spend actually at school per week, suggesting that some groups spend more time in extracurricular or other leisure activities at school. In particular, black and white males spend more time at school than do females, and Hispanics of both sexes spend the least amount of time there. Some of these differentials represent the greater amounts of study time which black and white males spend at school, but equally as notable is their proclivity to spend unstructured "other time" at school, that is, time at school spent neither studying nor attending classes. Apparently, black and white males strongly gravitate towards their neighborhood schools as foci for recreation and leisure time activities. Interestingly, this pattern does not hold for Hispanic males, who spend among the least time of all groups in "other time" at school. Indeed, with their low time expenditures in classes, studying at school, and, at least for males, spending other time at school, Hispanics in general seem least involved in schools as institutions.

Finally, with respect to the school section, some modest differences in total study time emerge across race and sex groups. Whites, and especially white females, study somewhat more on average than do others. Not surprisingly, given their low time investments in educational institutions, Hispanics spend the least total time studying of all groups.

Turning to the results for participation in government sponsored or other vocational training programs (excluding those sponsored by employers or unions), note that Hispanic and white males are about 1 percentage point more likely to participate in such programs than their female counterparts. Surprisingly, this sex differential in participation rates is reversed for blacks. In any case, no more than about 4 percent of any race-sex group participated in such programs in spring 1981. While these data show no notable overall race differences in levels of participation, previous work with NLS data has shown marked race differences in participation rates by *type* of program.

Because of the low participation rates, cell sizes are so small that estimates of participation are somewhat unreliable. Nonetheless, the patterns that do emerge suggest that trainees invest substantial time in these programs, both attending classes and studying, with total time involvements exceeding 20 hours per week.

Elsewhere in table 7.1, American youth are shown to spend substantial parts of their week watching TV, with females watching about 2.3 hours a day and males about 1.8 hours. Blacks, and especially black females, seem to watch a bit more TV per week than either whites or Hispanics.

In contrast to this rather substantial leisure time expenditure, youth spend strikingly little time reading during their week. Including the reading of newspapers, magazines, and all other materials not directly related to school, respondents report spending less than three-quarters of an hour per day on these activities.

Finally, in table 7.1, youth are shown to sleep about 7.5 hours per night, and apparently have some modest responsibility for household chores. On this latter score, unsurprisingly, women of all races spend about twice as much time as males in domestic activities. Time expenditures on household chores will be investigated in more detail in a subsequent section.

Table 7.2 extends the investigation of the relationship between personal characteristics and time-use expenditures by reporting results by family socioeconomic status (SES). While any number of measures of background status could have been used, we chose the Duncan status score of the head-of-household's occupation when the respondent was age 14. The Duncan status measure was chosen because of its long history as a measure of socioeconomic status in social science research (e.g., Blau and Duncan 1967) and because it is a variable for which few sample cases have missing data. Head-of-household's Duncan score was divided into three categories for purposes of this analysis: low (scores from 0 to 30), medium (scores from 31 to 60), and high (scores from 61 to 100).

Note first the concave shape to the relationship between labor force participation and family background status. The heightened participation rate of those from middle-ranking socioeconomic background may well derive from the difficulty those from the least advantaged families have finding a job, on the one hand, and high college enrollment rates of those from the most privileged backgrounds, on the other. Indeed, that many of the employed from high-status families are actually students working part time is suggested by the relatively short average workweek of this group.

The work experiences of youth from various background statuses differ in other important ways. In particular, differences in the way these youth apportion their time while at work are striking. Those from high socioeconomic status

Table 7.2
Time-Use in Hours for Selected Activities: Results by Sex and Duncan Score of Occupation Held by Head of Household When R was 14

| | Duncan of head | | | | | |
| | Low | | Medium | | High | |
Activity	M	F	M	F	M	F
Working for pay						
% with a job	67.4	56.2†	69.3*	64.5†	65.6	60.8
Hours spent working for pay	34.32*	29.82†	34.16*	29.29†	30.20	27.48
% time writing/reading[a]	16.8*	37.2	19.9	40.0	20.8	40.0
% time working w/hands[a]	81.2†	76.1†	78.1*	72.8†	71.9	65.2
% time with people[a]	50.5	65.6	49.9	69.1	53.1	67.6
Hours spent for trip to work (one-way)	.27*	.24	.26	.23	.25	.23
Time at school						
% enrolled in school	34.7*	33.9†	44.5*	40.8†	60.6	57.5
Hours spent at school	27.90	25.82	27.74	25.54	28.05	26.23
Hours spent in class	20.95*	19.85†	19.54*	19.60†	17.36	17.96
Hours spent studying at school	4.22*	3.60†	4.61*	3.84†	5.96	4.56
Other time at school	2.73*	2.37†	3.59*	2.10†	4.73	3.71
Hours spent studying not at school	6.43*	7.84†	6.57*	8.96†	9.54	10.19

Total hours spent studying[b]	10.65*	11.44†	11.18*	12.80†	15.50	14.75
Hours spent for trip to school (one-way)	.33	.33	.29	.30	.30	.31
Training programs[d]						
% participating in programs	4.4*	3.4	4.4*	3.1	2.7	3.3
Hours spent at training programs	17.20	15.96	17.69	13.72	13.33	18.17
Hours spent in class	13.11	14.09	13.36	10.15†	12.10	16.12
Hours spent studying at program	1.61	.86	1.48	2.41	1.39	1.44
Other time at program	2.48*	1.01	2.85*	1.16	0	.61
Hours spent studying away	2.73	5.73	2.73	4.07†	4.99	8.60
Total hours spent studying[b]	4.34	6.59†	4.21	6.48	7.38	10.04
Hours spent for trip to program (one-way)	.35	.35	.39	.28	.36	.25
Leisure						
Hours spent reading (not for school)[c]	4.45*	4.87†	5.37	5.42†	5.94	6.93
Hours spent watching TV	13.60*	16.86†	11.65*	14.97†	9.81	10.83
Hours spent sleeping	52.66*	54.00†	52.07*	52.55	51.19	52.19

(continued)

Table 7.2 (continued)

Activity	Low		Duncan of head Medium		High	
	M	F	M	F	M	F
Hours spent on household chores[c]	8.67	17.41†	7.61	14.44†	8.08	13.34
N	2489	2459	1199	1165	1109	1088
Total N by Duncan category	4948		2364		2197	

UNIVERSE: Youth age 16-24 for which occupation of head of household when respondent was 14 was reported; excludes respondents with head of household in military. (N = 27,785,000)

NOTE: All time estimates are hours per last seven days; digits to the right of the decimal point are fractional hours.

a. These items represent percent of time at work spent doing each of these three tasks and were adapted from Kohn (1969). To allow for a respondent to be doing multiple job tasks simultaneously, the question wording for these items specifically permitted double counting. Accordingly, percents sum to greater than 100.

b. These figures are the sum of time studying at school (program) and time studying at home.

c. Since time estimates for these activities were asked of "yesterday" only, time estimates were first weighted to produce a uniform frequency distribution across days of the week, and then multiplied by seven to arrive at an hours per last seven days estimate.

d. Includes government training programs (e.g., CETA) and "special" schools (e.g., technical schools, barber schools).

*T-tests for significant differences between males of different background status treat high status males as the reference group. An asterisk indicates that the starred value is different from the corresponding value for high status males at the .05 level.

†T-tests for significant differences between females of different background status treat high status females as the reference group. A cross indicates that the marked value is different from the corresponding value for high status females at the .05 level.

families spend substantially less time than youth from less privileged backgrounds working with their hands. Indeed, the workweek of those of high status, of both sexes, involves about 10 percentage points less time investment in such activities than those in the lowest SES category. By contrast, males from low SES backgrounds are less likely to be writing or reading in their jobs. These results suggest that labor market stratification by socioeconomic group (if not by race) begins at quite an early age.

A high proportion of those from high SES backgrounds are enrolled as full-time students as of the survey date, suggesting that such youth have assimilated the achievement orientation of their parents or at least are confronted with more propitious opportunity structures. Interestingly, total time spent at school shows little variation across socioeconomic groups, but this uniformity masks important differences in the way youth actually spend time while at school. High status youth spend significantly less time attending classes, presumably representing the fact that a higher proportion of them are college rather than high school enrollees. Additionally, the curriculum offered by the high schools attended by those of higher SES may be less structured and offer more opportunity for independent study. In any event, while these youth spend less time attending classes than others, they spend more time studying and spending free time at school. Apparently, because these youth are presumably less alienated from societal institutions, they carry on more extensive social interactions within the school environment.

This section of table 7.2 shows that high SES youth spend about 2 to 5 more hours studying per week than those of low SES families. Conceivably the higher expectations of the parents and teachers of the former group, and their fewer household and employment obligations, account for their greater diligence.

Finally, table 7.2 shows that time expenditures for TV watching significantly decrease and reading time increases as family background status increases. Nevertheless, even in the highest SES category, youth spend nearly twice as much time watching TV as reading. Sleeping time and time on household chores show ony modest variation across SES category, though it is worth noting that the sex differential on time expenditures for household chores is narrowest for those from the highest SES backgrounds.

Enrollment Status

Table 7.3 presents the first set of comparisons showing the relationship between respondents' role obligations and time-use expenditures. This table presents the relation between the youth's enrollment status and time allocations, once again shown separately by sex.

Not surprisingly, the first rows of this table show that a larger percentage of nonstudents are employed and that employed nonstudents work twice as long in their workweek as employed students. What is surprising, however, is the extent of the work involvement of both high school and college full-time enrollees. About one-half of high school and college students of both sexes held a job during the survey week, and for each of these groups the length of the workweek is on average about sixteen hours for females and about eighteen hours for males.

While each of the three groups shown in this table demonstrates substantial work commitment, the nature of the job tasks of each noticeably varies. Moreover, important sex-by-enrollment status interactions emerge. Among males, high school students perform the most manual tasks of the three groups and are least likely to be writing or reading or dealing with people on the job. Just the opposite is true for male college students; they are least likely to be working with their hands and are most likely to be dealing with paper work and with people. Nonstudents occupy an intermediate position between these two extremes.

For women, the situation is somewhat more complicated. As with males, high school women are most likely and college women least likely to be engaged in manual tasks. In a departure from the pattern observed for males, however, nonstudents are most likely to be reading or writing on the job and least likely to be dealing with people. These sex differentials undoubtedly reflect the fact that female nonstudents of college age are frequently employed in clerical positions, while male nonstudents of like age are more likely to be employed in blue-collar occupations. Also of interest in these rows of table 7.3 is the observation that the sex differences in job tasks remain fairly constant across enrollment status. Among nonstudents, females are nearly as likely as males to work with their hands but are substantially more likely to be dealing with paper work and with people. As if in anticipation of their post-student roles, the sex differences in job tasks remain much the same for both high school and college enrollees. Apparently, the sex typing of job tasks extends even to the very youngest employees with only casual labor force attachments.

In the sections dealing with time at school in table 7.3, note that about 5 percent of nonfull-time students are enrolled part time. However, the total time investment of this subset in school-related activities, including time at school and time studying, is not inconsequential, amounting to over two and one-half hours per week day. Elsewhere, across all enrollment categories, males spend more time at school than females. As observed in a previous table, however, this finding primarily reflects the greater amounts of "other" time males spend at school, rather than any actual sex differences in time attending classes. High school students of both sexes spend more time at school and more time actually attending classes than college goers, but the latter group spends about twice as much time as the former in total time studying.

Table 7.3
Time-Use in Hours for Selected Activities: Results by Sex and Enrollment Status

Activity	High school		College		Nonstudents	
	M	F	M	F	M	F
Working for pay						
% with a job	47.3	44.7	50.4	49.4†	78.8*	65.4†
Hours spent working for pay	17.31	15.40	19.22*	16.64	39.54*	34.56†
% time writing/reading[a]	11.4	25.3	22.6*	34.4†	20.0*	42.9†
% time working w/hands[a]	84.7	77.2	69.7*	63.4†	77.7*	72.7†
% time with people[a]	49.2	78.1	60.0*	71.0†	49.5	63.5†
Hours spent for trip to work (one-way)	.19	.17	.20	.20†	.31*	.27†
Time at school						
% enrolled in school	100	100	100	100		
Hours spent at school	30.80	29.33	27.23*	24.56†	9.40*	8.77†
Hours spent in class	23.52	23.26	15.46*	15.34†	6.85*	6.44†
Hours spent studying at school	3.51	3.18	7.49*	6.19†	2.07*	1.81†
Other time at school	3.77	2.89	4.28	3.03	.48*	.52†
Hours spent studying not at school	5.14	6.85	11.19*	12.15†	5.99	6.40
Total hours spent studying[b]	8.65	10.03	18.68*	18.34†	8.06	8.21†
Hours spent for trip to school (one-way)	.33	.35	.25*	.27†	.41	.31

Training programs[d]

% participating in programs	5.8	2.7	1.5*	1.8	3.9*	4.1†
Hours spent at training programs	11.41	10.47	e	e	18.72*	17.16†
Hours spent in class	10.72	9.27	e	e	14.60*	14.41†
Hours spent studying at program	.86	.68	e	e	1.72	1.59
Other time at program	0.00	.52	e	e	2.40*	1.16
Hours spent studying away	1.08	1.73	e	e	4.49*	6.66†
Total hours spent studying[b]	1.94	2.41	e	e	6.21*	8.25†
Hours spent for trip to program (one-way)	.33	.22	e	e	.36	.38†
Leisure						
Hours spent reading (not for school)[c]	4.68	5.54	6.83*	5.44	5.04*	5.24
Hours spent watching TV	12.85	13.54	8.80*	8.07†	12.86	17.42†
Hours spent sleeping	54.38	54.28	50.59*	50.52†	51.71*	53.38†
Hours spent on household chores[c]	6.66	10.68	7.64*	11.64†	9.14*	16.16†
N	1423	1262	814	838	3888	3970
Total N by enrollment status	2685		1652		7858	

(continued)

Table 7.3 (continued)

UNIVERSE: Youth age 16-24 on interview date. (N = 33,517,000)

NOTE: All time estimates are hours per last seven days; digits to the right of the decimal point are fractional hours. Those classified as "High school" and "College" are full-time students only. Part-time students, as well as the nonenrolled, are classified as "nonstudents."

a. These items represent percent of time at work spent doing each of these three tasks and were adapted from Kohn (1969). To allow for a respondent to be doing multiple job tasks simultaneously, the question wording for these items specifically permitted double counting. Accordingly, percents sum to greater than 100.

b. These figures are the sum of time studying at school (program) and time studying at home.

c. Since time estimates for these activities were asked of "yesterday" only, time estimates were first weighted to produce a uniform frequency distribution across days of the week, and then multiplied by seven to arrive at an hours per last seven days estimate.

d. Includes government training programs (e.g., CETA) and "special" schools (e.g., technical schools, barber schools).

e. Fewer than 25 respondents fall in this category. Time estimates are not reported due to unacceptable instability.

*T-tests for significant differences between males of different enrollment status treat high school males as the reference group. An asterisk indicates that the starred value is different from the corresponding value for high school males at the .05 level.

†T-tests for significant differences between females of different enrollment status treat high school females as the reference group. A cross indicates that the marked value is different from the corresponding value for high school females at the .05 level.

Turning to the training section, male high school students and nonstudents of both sexes are the prime beneficiaries of training programs. While participation rates are quite small for all groups, time investments among those who do participate are substantial, especially for nonstudents. Moreover, total time spent studying is also quite marked for this group. Differences in study time across enrollment status doubtless reflect the fact that high schoolers are most likely to be enrolled in CETA or other government sponsored programs, while nonstudents are mostly attendees of business or technical schools.

Finally in table 7.3, note that high schoolers spend the most time sleeping of all groups, while college students spend the least time watching TV and, for males, the most time doing nonschool-related reading. Time expenditures on household chores vary significantly but not markedly between high school and college goers, but nonstudents, and especially nonstudent females, spend substantially longer than any other group on such tasks. Doubtless this reflects the fact that a substantial number of this group are housewives.

Employment Status

In order to consider in somewhat greater detail the time expenditures of nonstudents, table 7.4 reports time-use estimates for this group separately for the employed, the unemployed, and those out of the labor force. The working for pay figures for the employed, shown in this table, are the same as those already shown as column three of table 7.3; accordingly, these data will not be described anew.

Of interest elsewhere in table 7.4 is the finding that such a small proportion of the unemployed and out of the labor force are part-time enrollees or are involved in a training program of any sort. Indeed, the employed are actually more likely to be participating in such programs than the

Table 7.4
Time-Use in Hours for Selected Activities: Results by Sex and Employment Status, Universe of Nonstudents and Part-time Enrollees

Activity	Employed		Unemployed		Out of labor force	
	M	F	M	F	M	F
Working for pay						
% with a job	100	100	0*	0†	0*	0†
Hours spent working for pay[a]	39.54	34.56	-	-	-	-
% time working/reading[a]	20.00	42.92	-	-	-	-
% time working w/hands[a]	77.66	72.69	-	-	-	-
% time with people[a]	49.51	63.51	-	-	-	-
Hours spent for trip to work (one way)	.31	.27	-	-	-	-
Time at school						
% enrolled in school	5.5	6.4	3.1*	3.3†	8.7	3.6†
Hours spent at school	8.46	7.00	e	e	e	e
Hours spent in class	6.33	5.34	e	e	e	e
Hours spent studying at school	1.75	1.22	e	e	e	e
Other time at school	.41	.44	e	e	e	e
Hours spent studying not at school	6.00	5.42	e	e	e	e

Total hours spent studying[b]	e	e	e	e	6.64	7.75
Hours spent for trip to school (one way)	e	e	e	e	.33	.46
Training programs[d]						
% participating in programs	4.3	14.5*	3.9	3.0	4.1	3.0
Hours spent at training programs	22.34†	28.09*	e	e	14.97	13.90
Hours spent in class	19.21†	21.36*	e	e	12.67	10.75
Hours spent studying at program	1.62	2.85	e	e	1.50	1.31
Other time at program	1.51	3.88	e	e	.80	1.84
Hours spent studying away	8.58†	6.81*	e	e	5.12	3.41
Total hours spent studying[b]	10.20	9.66*	e	e	6.62	4.72
Hours spent for trip to program (one way)	.41	.36	e	e	.37	.39
Leisure						
Hours spent reading (not for school)[c]	4.42†	5.56	5.96†	6.88*	5.38	4.91
Hours spent watching TV	26.98†	16.54*	23.96†	19.80*	12.78	11.28

(continued)

Table 7.4 (continued)

Activity	Employed		Unemployed		Out of labor force	
	M	F	M	F	M	F
Hours spent sleeping	50.91	52.28	54.46*	55.16†	55.36*	55.49†
Hours spent on household chores[c]	8.11	14.34	15.82*	22.10†	12.10*	28.10†
N	2946	2414	617	517	325	1039
Total N by employment status	5360		1134		1364	

UNIVERSE: Youth age 16-24 who were part-time students or not enrolled in school at interview date. (N=20,046,000)

NOTE: All time estimates are hours per last seven days; digits to the right of the decimal point are fractional hours.

a. These items represent percent of time at work spent doing each of these three tasks and were adapted from Kohn (1969). To allow for a respondent to be doing multiple job tasks simultaneously, the question wording for these items specifically permitted double counting. Accordingly, percents sum to greater than 100.

b. These figures are the sum of time studying at school (program) and time studying at home.

c. Since time estimates for these activities were asked of "yesterday" only, time estimates were first weighted to produce a uniform frequency distribution across days of the week, and then multiplied by seven to arrive at an hours per last seven days estimate.

d. Includes government training programs (e.g., CETA) and "special" schools (e.g., technical schools, barber schools).

e. Fewer than 25 respondents fall in this category. Time estimates are considered unreliable and are not reported.

*T-tests for significant differences between males of different employment status treat employed males as the reference group. An asterisk indicates that the starred value is different from the corresponding value for employed males at the .05 level.

†T-tests for significant differences between females of different employment status treat employed females as the reference group. A cross indicates that the marked value is different from the corresponding value for employed females at the .05 level.

unemployed. And while those out of the labor force show the highest involvements in such programs, at least among males, still at least 75 percent of them are neither enrolled in school part time nor participating in training programs. The females among them are likely to be full-time housewives; the males among them may well be mostly discouraged job seekers.

With their daily time-use largely unaccounted for by any structured activities (at least those measured in this survey), the unemployed and those out of the labor force spend more time than the employed sleeping, watching TV, and performing household chores.

Job Search

Also of interest, especially for the unemployed, is the nature of and time investment in job search activities. Table 7.5 shows time expenditures in various job search methods for unemployed nonstudents and for those full-time students and employed nonstudents who were looking for work. These results show, as one might have expected, that the unemployed spend more time on job search than either of the other two groups. At the same time, however, unemployed males report spending only about 5.7 hours and females about 3.4 hours on all job search activities per week.

These results also give some sense of the wide range of job search methods which are utilized, especially by the unemployed. The most commonly used method by all categories of job seekers is checking with friends or relatives. Substantial numbers also contact state employment agencies, check newspaper ads, and apply directly to employers. Once again, with scant exception, unemployed nonstudents are more likely to use each method (except checking with teachers or school counselors) than are students or employed job seekers; by implication, the unemployed are more likely to utilize multiple job search methods.

Table 7.5
Time-Use in Hours and Percent Using Various Job Search Methods
Results by Sex and Enrollment and Employment Status

Activity	Full-time students		Nonstudents & part-time enrollees			
			Employed		Unemployed	
	M	F	M	F	M	F
% looking for work	26.4*	23.5†	19.3*	18.6†	100.0	100.0
Hours spent looking for work last week (all methods)	2.27*	1.87†	3.30*	2.69	5.67	3.41
N	632	502	542	399	585	471
% checked with state employment agency	12.1*	12.5†	31.3*	20.8†	52.9	41.7
Job contact (%)	19.5*	33.6	31.9	44.2	35.3	38.3
Job offer (%)	6.5	11.6	8.2	9.6	8.7	8.0
% checked with private employment agency	8.5*	7.6†	14.6*	21.2	26.0	20.2
Job contact (%)	57.0	46.8	55.3	52.5	44.6	45.0
Job offer (%)	20.2*	14.2	16.6	29.2†	8.6	12.4
% checked with friends or relatives	75.6*	77.1	86.1	78.4	84.3	79.9
Job contact (%)	51.0*	47.2	53.9*	48.8	44.2	48.4
Job offer (%)	15.0	10.1	20.3*	16.0	12.6	12.4

% checked with newspaper ads	31.7*	39.9†	44.7*	52.9†	57.1	61.9
Job contact (%)	56.3	54.9	64.8*	57.9	55.7	62.5
Job offer (%)	10.9*	12.4	20.8*	18.1	5.7	12.7
% took Civil Service test or filed for government job	4.8*	6.2	11.4	11.5	11.9	8.9
Job contact (%)	40.3	52.8†	35.6	29.8	41.1	28.0
Job offer (%)	2.1	22.6†	1.3	6.7	1.8	3.6
% checked with CETA or community action group	5.2*	8.8†	8.9*	5.3†	15.2	14.3
Job contact (%)	36.7	25.3	28.9	a	19.7	34.7
Job offer (%)	13.5	13.0	9.2	a	9.4	5.4
% checked with school placement office	21.6†	24.8†	6.0	9.4†	7.8	4.5
Job contact (%)	51.5*	39.1	38.4	37.9	26.6	a
Job offer (%)	10.7*	10.7	5.7	17.9	2.9	a
% checked with teachers or professors for job leads	22.7*	24.4†	9.4	7.3	11.8	6.8
Job contact (%)	26.8	22.8†	38.5	19.1†	38.2	45.2
Job offer (%)	5.1	7.7	6.8	6.0	12.0	20.2

(continued)

Table 7.5 (continued)

| Activity | Full-time students | | Nonstudents & part-time enrollees | | | |
| | | | Employed | | Unemployed | |
	M	F	M	F	M	F
% checked with labor union	1.6*	.9	7.1	.6	10.1	1.3
Job contact (%)	a	a	33.5	a	38.2	a
Job offer (%)	a	a	17.2*	a	3.8	a
% applied directly to employers	68.9*	70.0	68.5*	67.7	77.9	71.6
Job contact(%)	21.5*	16.7†	22.5*	22.8†	11.5	10.7
Job offer (%)	-	-	-	-	-	-

UNIVERSE: Youth age 16-24 who reported they were looking for work at time of interview or within last 4 weeks. (N = 8,530,000)

NOTE: Time estimates are hours per last seven days; digits to the right of the decimal point are fractional hours. For each method the percentage figures are: % of job seekers who used that method in the last 4 weeks, % of those using the method who had a job contact result, and % using the method who had a job offer result.

a. Fewer than 25 respondents used this method. Estimates are considered unreliable and are not reported.

*T-tests for significant differences between males treat nonstudent unemployed males as the reference group. An asterisk indicates that the starred value is different from the corresponding value for unemployed nonstudent males at the .05 level.

†T-tests for significant differences between females treat unemployed nonstudent females as the reference group. A cross indicates that the marked value is different from the corresponding value for unemployed nonstudent females at the .05 level.

Using these data to draw inferences regarding the success of job search methods is rather hazardous. This sequence of job search questions was asked only of those looking for work; currently employed nonjob-seekers were not asked how they found their jobs. Accordingly, we have here a sample of recent or longer term unsuccessful job seekers (more recent NLS data can be used to address the issue of method of job finding, however; see Wielgosz 1983). This explains why the unemployed appear by these data to be the least successful in eliciting job offers. Employed or student job seekers are in all probability in less need of a (new) job and therefore have the luxury of turning down job offers once made. By contrast, unemployed nonstudents are more likely to accept whatever job offers they receive, and thus those who have been made an offer are less likely to appear in our sample.

At the same time, these data are suggestive of the effectiveness of alternate job search methods. If one takes the goal of any search to be putting one in contact with employers, differences in effectiveness across methods are striking. By this standard, information from friends or relatives, newspaper ads, and private employment agencies are all reasonably effective. For students, school placement services are also rather successful in putting students in contact with employers. As others have shown, state employment services are relatively ineffective in leading to job contacts or job offers, though this may reflect the employability of those who use the state services (Wielgosz 1983).

Working Versus Nonworking Students

We have thus far looked at time expenditures of those with various role obligations. Given that time-use is a zero-sum proposition, it is interesting to observe which time-use tradeoffs are implemented for youth as multiple role obligations accumulate. Must students who work, for example, sacrifice valuable study time to carry out their employment obligations? Or do they forsake leisure time activities? Table 7.6 addresses these and related issues by comparing the time expenditures of nonworking high school students, nonworking full-time college students, working high school students and working full-time college students.

As shown previously, employed high school and college youth work on average from about 16 to 20 hours per week. The time for this employment seems to be taken away from a range of activities rather than from any one or two. Employed students spend less time at school, less time actually attending classes (perhaps some are work-study students), less time studying and less "other" time at school (males only), less time sleeping, less time watching TV, less time doing leisure reading (except for college females) and less time doing chores, and most of these differences are significant. Indeed, with the scant exception noted, employed students spend less time on every other category of activity for which time estimates are collected in the NLS. Interestingly, the time-use tradeoffs made by employed male and female high school and college students appear quite similar, though males may sacrifice more study time than females, and high schoolers seem to sacrifice a greater proportion of their TV watching.

Ecological Factors

This section of the paper focuses on the role of ecological factors, and, especially, living arrangements on the household and child care responsibilities of youth. Table 7.7 reports the mean time expenditures and also the degree of responsibility for various household and child care tasks. These results show the greater time expenditure committed by women to household chores across all categories of living arrangements. This sex differential is 2-5 hours for those living alone, with peers or with parents, but is fully 13.5 hours for those who are married. These data dramatically illustrate the extent of the sexual division in the burdens of household obligations.

Table 7.6

Time-Use in Hours for Selected Activities: Results by Sex, Employment Status and Enrollment Status, Universe of Full-Time Students Only

| | Employed full-time students | | | | Nonworking full-time students | | | |
| | High school | | College | | High school | | College | |
	M	F	M	F	M	F	M	F
Working for pay								
% with a job	100*	100†	100*	100†	0	0	0	0
Hours spent working for pay[a]	17.31	15.40	19.22	16.64	-	-	-	-
% time writing/reading[a]	11.36	25.32	22.56	34.36	-	-	-	-
% time working w/hands[a]	84.73	77.16	69.75	63.39	-	-	-	-
% time with people[a]	49.25	78.12	59.99	71.05	-	-	-	-
Hours spent for trip to work (one-way)	.19	.17	.20	.20	-	-	-	-
Time at school								
% enrolled in school	100	100	100	100	100	100	100	100
Hours spent at school	28.65*	27.63†	23.93*	23.51†	32.73	30.71	30.60	25.57
Hours spent in class	22.89*	21.63†	14.60*	14.62†	24.08	24.58	16.34	16.03
Hours spent studying at school	2.83*	3.07	5.90*	5.77	4.12	3.28	9.09	6.59
Other time at school	2.93*	2.93	3.43*	3.12	4.53	2.85	5.17	2.95
Hours spent studying not at school	4.81*	6.73	10.07*	11.70	5.44	6.95	12.33	12.58
Total hours spent studying[b]	7.64*	9.80	15.97*	17.47	9.56	10.23	21.42	19.17
Hours spent for trip to school (one-way)	.33	.33	.29*	.29	.34	.35	.21	.25

Table 7.6 (continued)

	Employed full-time students				Nonworking full-time students			
	High school		College		High school		College	
	M	F	M	F	M	F	M	F
Training programs[d]								
% participating in programs	5.5	3.1	.5*	1.0	5.9	2.8	2.1	2.2
Hours spent at training programs	10.36	7.73	16.53	16.42	12.26	12.17	23.54	20.17
Hours spent in class	9.24	5.54†	11.41	15.53	11.53	11.57	15.94	21.11
Hours spent studying at program	1.19	1.29	1.50	.67	.59	.31	4.32	1.84
Other time at program	0	.90	3.62	.22	.14	.29	3.28	0
Hours spent studying away[b]	1.66*	1.18	6.41	5.63	.61	2.06	5.26	8.91
Total hours spent studying[b]	2.85	2.47	7.91	6.30	1.20	2.37	9.58	10.75
Hours spent for trip to program (one-way)	.25*	.12†	.31	.42†	.38	.28	.35	.21
Leisure								
Hours spent reading (not for school)[c]	4.38	4.78†	6.07*	5.75	4.94	6.23	7.91	5.07
Hours spent watching TV	10.98*	11.06†	8.38	7.39†	144.51	15.56	9.23	8.73
Hours spent sleeping	53.28*	53.37†	50.19	49.59†	55.36	55.02	51.00	51.43
Hours spent on household chores[c]	5.75*	8.92†	7.07*	10.12†	7.56	10.44	8.43	13.36
N	623	486	412	422	800	776	402	416
Total N by employment status	1109		834		1576		818	

UNIVERSE: Youth age 16-24 who were full-time students at interview date. (N = 13,471,000)

NOTE: All time estimates are hours per last seven days; digits to the right of the decimal point are fractional hours.

a. These items represent percent of time at work spent doing each of these three tasks and were adapted from Kohn (1969). To allow for a respondent to be doing multiple job tasks simultaneously, the question wording for these items specifically permitted double counting. Accordingly, percents sum to greater than 100.

b. These figures are the sum of time studying at school (program) and time studying at home.

c. Since time estimates for these activities were asked of "yesterday" only, time estimates were first weighted to produce a uniform frequency distribution across days of the week, and then multiplied by seven to arrive at an hours per last seven days estimate.

d. Includes government training programs (e.g., CETA) and "special" schools (e.g., technical schools, barber schools).

*There are two reference groups for males in this table; employed high school males are compared with nonworking high school males and employed college males are compared with nonworking college males. An asterisk indicates that the starred value is different from the corresponding value for nonworking high school/college males at the .05 level.

†There are two reference groups for females in this table; employed high school females are compared with nonworking high school females and employed college females are compared with nonworking college females. A cross indicates that the marked value is different from the corresponding value for nonworking high school/college females at the .05 level.

Table 7.7

Time-Use Behaviors for Household Chores and Child Care: Results by Sex and Living Arrangement

Chores and child care	R's living on own away from parents						R's living with parents or guardian	
	Alone or with kids		With spouse		With adult (nonspouse)			
	M	F	M	F	M	F	M	F
Household chores								
Hours spent on all chores	9.42*	11.48b	12.55*	25.96b	8.64*	13.92†	7.29	11.85
Degree of responsibility for:c								
meals	3.68*	4.40†	1.71*	4.51†	2.53*	3.35†	1.45	2.04
dishes	3.77*	4.62†	1.69*	4.53†	2.61*	3.49†	1.60	2.79
laundry	3.75*	4.68†	1.55	4.59†	3.02*	3.89†	1.53	2.48
cleaning	4.05*	4.69†	1.84*	4.53†	2.69*	3.45†	1.76	2.80
shopping	4.10*	4.56†	2.54*	4.23†	2.74*	3.42†	1.43	1.84
errands	4.28*	4.47†	3.18*	3.50†	3.02*	3.09†	2.40	2.53
outdoor chores	3.35*	2.97†	3.74*	2.20†	2.70*	1.85	2.84	1.84
house repairs	3.80*	3.42†	4.16*	1.96†	2.92*	1.95†	2.57	1.56
paperwork	4.14*	4.25†	2.82*	3.52†	2.35*	2.69†	1.23	1.38
Child care								
% with own children in home	0*	38.5†	45.0*	54.5†	2.9*	13.9†	1.2	9.5
Degree of responsibility for care of own childrenc	a	4.86†	2.40	4.43	a	4.61	2.62	4.49
Hours spent dressing and feeding	a	20.13	7.01*	22.27†	a	19.59	3.32	19.03
Hours spent reading and playing	a	21.25	15.21	22.04	a	22.59	15.56	21.42
Other time in supervision	a	45.49	13.11*	46.02†	a	45.38	8.72	39.61

% with siblings or other children in home	1.4*	.1†	2.0*	.9†	12.9*	8.3†	41.7	40.1
Degree of responsibility for care of other children^c	a	a	a	a	1.84	2.54†	1.72	2.16
Total hours spent taking care of children in home	a	a	a	a	11.54*	14.78†	2.98	5.83
Hours spent dressing/feeding	a	a	a	a	1.89*	2.43†	.22	.90
Hours spent reading/playing	a	a	a	a	4.13*	7.14†	1.37	2.51
N	315	478	754	1387	697	726	3632	3099
Total N by living arrangement	793		2141		1423		6731	

UNIVERSE: Youth age 16-24 not living in dorms, barracks, or other group quarters. (N = 30,456,000)

NOTE: All time estimates are hours per last seven days; digits to the right of the decimal point are fractional hours. Since time estimates for household chores and child care were asked of "yesterday" only, time estimates were first weighted to produce a uniform frequency distribution across days of the week, and then multiplied by seven to arrive at an hours estimate for the last seven days.

a. Fewer than 25 respondents in the cell. Estimates are considered unreliable and are not reported.

b. To make the inter-sex comparison for those "living alone" more meaningful, this time estimate refers to those "living alone" with no children in the home. This was done because only a very small number of males "living alone" have children living with them, and the time-use of women "living alone" with and without children differs drastically.

c. The degree of responsibility for each chore was assessed by asking respondents to place themselves on a five-point scale, with 1 = R almost never does the chore to 5 = R has almost sole responsibility for doing this chore.

*T-tests for significant differences between males with different living arrangements treat males living with their parents as the reference group. An asterisk indicates that the starred value differs from the corresponding value for males living with their parents at the .05 level.

†T-tests for significant differences between females with different living arrangements treat females living with their parents as the reference group. A cross indicates that the marked value differs from the corresponding value for females living with their parents at the .05 level.

The within sex comparisons across ecological arrangements are also revealing. In general, youth allocate the least time to household responsibilities when they are living with their parents, but surprisingly this burden increases only modestly for youth living alone or with friends. Presumably youth living alone occupy modest accommodations and are able to keep necessary household chores to a minimum. By contrast, living with one's spouse leads to a proliferation of house management responsibilities. Indeed, wives spend over 100 percent and husbands nearly 35 percent more time on household chores than their peers who live alone. Looked at another way, a male and female married and living together spend between them over 38 hours per week on chores, but only about 20.5 hours per week on average if unmarried and living apart.

Questionnaire items also ask respondents to assess their degree of responsibility for individual chores on a five-point scale from 1, —almost never does the chore, to 5, —has almost sole responsibility for it. For preparing meals, doing dishes, doing the laundry, cleaning house and shopping, women report a greater level of responsibility than males in every type of living arrangement. Similarly, regardless of living arrangement, men claim a greater level of responsibility for outdoor chores and house repairs. For the remaining chores listed, doing paperwork and running errands, relative responsibility level varies depending upon the ecological arrangement. Differentials in responsibility levels are most extreme in the case of married couples, where the division of labor is clearcut for most chores, and narrowest for those living alone, where both males and females report high responsibility levels for all chores.

Looking at within sex differences, youth of both sexes report the lowest absolute levels of responsibility when living with parents. For females, those levels show a marked jump for those living with others and a still further increment, to the highest levels reported for females, for those living alone or with a spouse. This pattern differs noticeably for males. Starting from the lowest responsibility levels for males living with parents, the level of obligation increases modestly for most household chores for those who are married and for those living with others. A still further jump is detected for those living along, bringing male responsibility levels nearly up to or greater than those reported by females.

Turning to the time-use estimates for child care in table 7.7, once again a marked, if not unexpected, sexual difference in time expenditures emerges, especially for those with their own child. Among parents, women claim notably higher levels of responsibility for child care and report spending over three times as long as males in dressing/feeding the child and in supervision time. The sexual inequalities are reduced somewhat when playing with the child is considered, but they remain pronounced.

Youth report remarkably little time taking care of their siblings (under age 14) and here the sexual disparities are far more modest. Females living in their parents' dwelling unit with younger siblings in the household report spending only about 5.8 hours per week on child care and supervisory activities of all sorts. For males, this figure is about three hours per week.

Table 7.8 extends this investigation by considering whether husbands assume more responsibility for household chores as wives accumulate additional role obligations. The universe in this table is restricted to those nonenrollees who have their own children. Time expenditures are reported for working and nonworking women and for males whose spouses are working and nonworking.

As table 7.8 shows, males whose wives work spend a nonsignificant two additional hours per week on household chores than males whose wives are not employed. Moreover, the variables measuring degree of responsibility for various chores show an only occasionally significant shifting of

Table 7.8

Time-Use Behaviors for Household Chores and Child Care: Results by Sex and Wife's Employment Status Universe of Nonstudents and Part-Time Enrollees with Children

Chores and child care	Nonstudents and part-time enrollees with own children				
	Males with children		Females with children		
			Spouse present		No spouse present
	Wife not working	Wife working	R not working	R working	
Household chores					
Hours spent on all chores	11.7	13.12	34.54	25.36†	24.72†
Degree of responsibility for:[a]					
meals	1.44	1.60*	4.64	4.41†	3.69†
dishes	1.38	1.49	4.74	4.31†	3.98†
laundry	1.41	1.41	4.76	4.57†	4.00†
cleaning	1.63	1.81*	4.72	4.37†	4.14†
shopping	2.43	2.37	4.27	4.29	3.64†
errands	3.06	3.11	3.48	3.58	3.58
outdoor chores	3.71	3.66	2.28	2.20	2.44
house repairs	4.03	4.15	2.03	1.86	2.48†
paperwork	2.82	2.46	3.50	3.68	2.97†
Child care					

Degree of responsibility				
for child care	2.34	2.47	4.67	4.10†	4.62
Hours spent dressing and feeding children	6.17	5.57	24.67	19.30†	19.58†
Hours spent reading and playing with children	16.03	14.28	21.86	22.46	14.76
Other time in supervision	14.55	11.12	52.35	37.16†	41.60†
% with a job	83.8	87.1	0	100†	34.1†
Hours spent working for pay	40.2	43.6	-	29.9	34.3
Hours spent reading (not for school)	3.9	3.5	4.2	2.7†	3.7
Hours spent watching TV	17.1	14.9	29.7	17.5†	23.3†
Hours spent sleeping	51.9	52.0	54.7	52.7†	53.0†
N	200	220	439	323	718

UNIVERSE: Youth age 16-24 with children who were part-time students or not enrolled in school at interview date. (N = 4,235,000)

NOTE: All time estimates are hours per last seven days; digits to the right of the decimal point are fractional hours. Since time estimates for household chores, child care, and reading were asked of "yesterday" only, time estimates were first weighted to produce a uniform frequency distribution across days of the week, and then multiplied by seven to arrive at an hours estimate for the last seven days.

a. The degree of responsibility for each chore was assessed by asking respondents to place themselves on a five-point scale, with 1 = R almost never does the chore to 5 = R has almost sole responsibility for doing this chore.

*T-tests for significant differences between males treat males whose wives are not working as the reference group. An asterisk indicates that the starred value is different from the corresponding value for males whose wives are not working at the .05 level.

†T-tests for significant differences between females treat women who are not working for pay as the reference group. A cross indicates that the marked value is significantly different at the .05 level from the corresponding value for women not working for pay.

responsibility such that wives who work claim somewhat less responsibility for several chores than wives who do not work and males whose wives work claim somewhat more responsibility on meal preparation and cleaning than males whose wives are not employed. In all these cases, however, the shifting in responsibility is slight. Perhaps most dramatic in this table, however, is the substantial drop in the amount of time working women spend doing chores relative to nonworking wives. Since we have just shown no such dramatic increase in males' contribution to household maintenance where both spouses work, we can conclude that third parties, including the service economy, assume some of these housekeeping burdens (e.g., an increased number of meals are eaten out) or that a downward redefinition of what are considered essential household chores occurs. In any event, working wives are still shown to spend nearly twice as long as their spouses discharging household obligations.

Something very much like this scenario applies where child care is concerned. Males report slightly more, females slightly less responsibility for child care where the wife is employed. The woman's time expenditure for dressing and feeding and supervising her child drops markedly when she is employed, though her time spent playing with the child remains essentially unchanged. Interestingly, the husband's time expenditure on all facets of child care also tends to decline somewhat when his spouse is employed. Thus, these findings suggest that when a wife is employed, a greater burden of child care does not devolve to the husband. Instead one can assume that third parties (e.g., relatives or day care facilities) take up the slack.

Looking at the various other relevant components of time-use which the NLS provides, we note that mothers who work apparently must sacrifice substantial parts of their leisure activities. Such women sleep somewhat less on average, watch considerably fewer hours of TV, and read a bit less per week than mothers who are not employed. Nonetheless, in the context of husbands' time expenditures for these activities, the reductions seem less dramatic; indeed, working mothers sleep as much as their husbands do and still watch about three more hours of TV per week. In any event, even granted that working wives work only about two-thirds of the workweek of their husbands, the combined burden of employment and household and child care responsibilities seems very onerous.

Resources

Finally we investigate the relationship between resources and time-use expenditures. One of the most straightforward of these relationships is the effect of ownership of the means of transportation on time expenditures for transportation. Table 7.9 shows mean times for trips to work and school (one-way), distances (also one-way) and distances per unit of time by mode of transportation used. The results are striking. Those who use an automobile or motorcycle to get either to work or school make the trip in substantially less time than those who use any other mode except walking. Moreover, the efficiency of private transportation by auto or motorcycle as judged by the average miles per hour criterion seems clear; this mode is substantially and significantly more efficient than practically any other mode.

Riding a school bus is also a relatively time efficient mode of transportation for high schoolers. A trip to school by bus takes somewhat more time than a trip by private auto, but the average one-way distance is over a mile longer. Walking or riding a bicycle may be relatively quick for some people, but this advantage seems to be entirely due to the fact that the destination for the users of this mode is on average quite short. Aside from walking, the mode of transportation shown to be consistently least efficient is public transportation. Users of this mode can expect to average no more than 13 (for trips to school) or 18.4 (for trips to work) miles per hour. Policy efforts aimed at encouraging use of mass

Table 7.9
Time-Use in Hours for Transportation: Results by Mode of Transportation

	Mode of transportation				
	Auto/ motorcycle	Public transpt./taxi	School bus	Walk/ bicycle	Mixed mode
Trip to high school					
Mean time one-way	2.9	.45*	.42*	.40*	.57
Mean distance in miles	4.34	4.82	6.42*	1.65*	7.08
Miles/time	24.12	12.59*	17.07*	8.21*	22.44
N	981	295	813	420	41
Trip to college					
Mean time one-way	.38	.66*	a	.30*	a
Mean distance in miles	9.70	8.19*	a	1.62*	a
Miles/time	28.68	12.93*	a	10.78*	a
N	645	166	13	322	24
Trip to work					
Mean time one-way	.27	.59*	-	.24*	.43*
Mean distance in miles	8.80	9.68	-	2.80*	18.58*
Miles/time	30.31	18.39*	-	19.62*	65.79
N	4642	511	-	1014	344

UNIVERSE: Youth age 16-24 (excluding respondents living on campus or school grounds) who spent any time at work or at school within last 7 days of interview date. Estimates for trip to high school and college are based on reports from full-time students only. A number of respondents, most of whom used the "walk/bicycle" mode, reported that their trip to school (work) took no time and that their distance from school (work) was zero miles. These respondents were deleted from all calculations. (N = 23,989,056)

a. Indicates fewer than 25 respondents used this method. Figures are considered unreliable and are not reported.

*T-tests for significant difference by mode treat "auto/motorcycle" as the reference group. An asterisk indicates that the starred value is different at the .05 level from the corresponding value for those using the "auto/motorcycle" mode.

transportation might do well to consider ways of improving the efficiency of this mode.

IV. Conclusion

The tables described in this paper have provided an interesting sketch of the time-use behavior of young adults. Additionally, we have shown a number of interesting concomitants of time expenditures. Time allocations have been shown to bear systematic relationship to race, family background status, role obligations and ecological arrangements, in addition to some of the more predictable time-use variants by sex. A descriptive and tabular presentation of this sort cannot, of course, claim to pinpoint causal relationships. As with any exploratory and descriptive undertaking, the effort is nonetheless deemed well-served if it succeeds in drawing attention to provocative relationships that merit more careful analytic scrutiny.

REFERENCES

Baker, Paula, Ronald D'Amico, and Gilbert Nestel. 1983. "Measuring Time-Use: A Comparison of Alternate Measurement Strategies." Columbus: Center for Human Resource Research, Ohio State University.

Becker, Gary. 1965. "A Theory of the Allocation of Time." *The Economic Journal* 75 (September): 493-517.

Berk, Sara Fenstermaker. 1979. "Husbands at Home: Organization of the Husband's Household Day." In Feinstein, ed., *Working Women and Families.* Beverly Hills: Sage.

Biddle, Bruce, Barbara Bank, D. Anderson, John Keats and Daphne Keats. 1981. "The Structure of Idleness: In-School and Dropout Adolescent Activities in the United States and Australia." *Sociology of Education* 54 (April): 106-119.

Blau, Peter and Otis Dudley Duncan. 1967. *The American Occupational Structure.* New York: Wiley.

Fleisher, Belton. 1977. "Mother's Home Time and the Production of Child Quality." *Demography* 14 (May): 197-212.

Gronau, Reuben. 1973. "The Intrafamily Allocation of Time: The Value of the Housewives' Time." *American Economic Review* 63 (September): 634-651.

Juster, F. Thomas and Frank Stafford. 1983. *Time, Goods, and Well Being.* Ann Arbor: Institute for Social Research.

Kohn, Melvin. 1969. *Class and Conformity.* Homewood, IL: Dorsey Press.

Linder, Staffan. 1970. *The Harried Leisure Class.* New York: Columbia University Press.

Melbin, Murray. 1978. "Night as Frontier." *American Sociological Review* 43 (February): 3-22.

Robinson, John. 1977. *How Americans Use Time.* New York: Praeger.

Rosenfeld, Rachel. 1980. "Race and Sex Differences in Career Dynamics." *American Sociological Review* 45 (August): 583-609.

Wielgosz, John. 1983. "The Effectiveness of Job Search and Job Finding Methods of Young Americans." In Borus, ed., *Pathways to the Future,* Vol. IV. Columbus: Center for Human Resource Research, Ohio State University.

Chapter 8
Delinquency and Employment
Substitutions or Spurious Associations
Joan E. Crowley

Few would quarrel with the proposition that delinquency and employment are related. After all, if youths can obtain money on the streets, why should they put up with the hassles of the types of entry level jobs available to them? Conversely, why should an employer put up with a difficult adolescent when there are so many law-abiding ones to choose from? Actually measuring the relationship between delinquency and employment, however, is a challenging task. The 1980 National Longitudinal Survey of Youth Labor Market Experience (NLS) included newly developed instruments to gauge both criminal behavior and the extent of involvement of youth with the criminal justice system. The NLS now includes the largest nationally representative sample survey of delinquent behavior available in the published literature.

The first goal of this chapter is to present the picture of crime and delinquency in the youth population which emerges from the distributions of the NLS data. The second goal is to find out whether and to what extent delinquent activity directly reduces labor force participation by providing substitute income and other rewards (e.g., social status)

239

when factors known to be causally associated with both types of behavior are taken into account.

I. Measuring Delinquency

Traditional criminology has separated crime from delinquency according to the age of the offender: offenses committed by legal minors are delinquency; offenses committed by legal adults are crime. The NLS second wave youth cohort, ranging in age from 15 to 23, crosses these age boundaries. Because 15 appears to be the peak age for delinquent activity (Berger, et al. 1975; Ageton and Elliott 1978), the NLS sample is quite old relative to the subjects of most delinquency studies. This paper will continue to refer to delinquent behavior, but readers must keep in mind that a large proportion of the respondents are legally adults.

It is important to distinguish between participation in delinquent or criminal behavior and the consequence of being caught and officially processed as a delinquent or a criminal. Some criminologists argue that official processing as delinquent or criminal tends to lock people into criminal behavior (Farrington 1977). The criminal justice system itself has been labeled a training ground for criminal behavior, as apprentice thieves learn from more experienced "colleagues." Similarly, being "bad" enough to get oneself thrown out of school could have longer range consequences than would less public versions of misbehavior. Potential employers may ask whether an applicant has a police record and use this information to deny employment to ex-convicts, but criminal behavior which has not led to a conviction would not have such public consequences.

Delinquent Behavior[1]

The measurement of delinquent behavior in a nationally representative sample such as that used by the NLS is a relatively rare phenomenon. Most studies of delinquency have been done on small and specially selected groups, with measures tailored to the specific research focus. A new index had to be developed that would suit the NLS interview setting and that would avoid some of the problems identified in the use of earlier delinquency measures.[2] The items used in the delinquency scale are shown in table 8.1. The first three items, running away from home, truancy, and drinking alcohol describe status offenses, i.e., behaviors forbidden only to minors, and were asked only for youths under the age of 18.

Because simply asking the precise number of times the respondent had participated in a prohibited activity was not feasible, respondents selected categories to indicate the range of their frequency of participation in various activities. The responses cannot be interpreted as absolute frequencies of activity; they should instead be interpreted as scale scores, with a higher score indicating a higher level of participation in delinquent activity.

The items in the NLS self-reported delinquency instrument were analyzed for empirical typologies, using factor and cluster techniques.[3] Excluding the status items, three groups of offenses emerged: property crime, drug use and sale, and assault. Probably because many youths reporting sale of marijuana are selling small quantities to their friends, this item fits in best with drug use. Sales of drugs other than marijuana, however, seem much more profit-oriented and associated with serious property crimes. Robbery fits both into property and assaultive clusters. Table 8.1 shows the items included in each offense classification.

The proportion of youths participating in a particular offense declines as offenses become more serious: use of "soft" drugs, fighting, and petty theft are relatively common, but grand theft, selling hard drugs, and aggravated assault are relatively rare, both in terms of proportion of the

Table 8.1
Self-Reported Delinquency Items and Summary Subscales by Sex

Abbreviated title	Item[a]	Female Mean	Female % zero	Male Mean	Male % zero	Ratio of means Male/Female
1. Runaway[s]	Run away from home?[b]	.20	90	.22	91	1.1
2. Truant[s]	Skipped a full day of school without a real excuse?	3.11	56	4.49	51	1.4
3. Drinking[s]	Drank beer, wine or liquor without your parents' permission?	8.56	37	12.00	31	1.4
4. Fighting[v]	Gotten into a physical fight at school or work?[c]	.30	88	1.67	61	5.6
5. Robbery[v]	Used force or strong arm methods to get money or things from a person?	.08	98	.36	92	4.5
6. Assault[v]	Hit or seriously threatened to hit someone?	1.21	74	2.49	52	2.1
7. Aggravated assault[v]	Attacked someone with the idea of seriously hurting or killing them?	.18	94	.76	86	4.2
8. Using marijuana[d]	Smoked marijuana or hashish (pot, grass, hash)?	9.38	54	13.09	49	1.4
9. Using hard drugs[d]	Used any drugs or chemicals to get high or for kicks, except marijuana?	2.05	80	2.92	77	1.4
10. Selling marijuana[d]	Sold marijuana or hashish?	.62	93	2.05	84	3.3
11. Selling hard drugs[d]	Sold hard drugs such as heroin, LSD, cocaine (total number of all hard drug sales)?	.12	99	.45	97	3.8
12. Vandalism[p]	Purposely damaged or destroyed property that did not belong to you?	.22	90	1.28	71	5.8
13. Shoplifting[p]	Taken something from a store without paying for it?	.85	76	1.46	70	1.7

14. Petty theft[p]	Other than from a store, taken something not belonging to you worth under $50.00?	.40	86	1.11	73	2.8
15. Grand theft[p]	Other than from a store, taken something not belonging to you worth $50.00 or more?	.03	99	.43	92	14.3
16. Fraud[p]	Tried to get something by lying to a person about what you would do for him, that is, tried to con someone?	.78	82	1.44	75	1.8
17. Breaking & entering[p]	Broken into a building or vehicle to steal something or just to look around?	.03	98	.50	89	16.7
18. Fencing[p]	Knowingly sold or held stolen goods?	.17	95	.82	82	4.8
19. Auto theft	Taken a vehicle for a ride or drive without the owner's permission?	.16	95	.44	89	2.8
20. Gambling	Helped in a gambling operation, like running numbers or policy or books?	.05	99	.38	96	7.6
SUBSCALES						
Status[e]		11.86	27	16.75	23	1.4
Violence[f]		1.76	68	5.29	40	3.01
Drugs[f]		12.15	53	18.51	47	1.52
Property[f]		2.47	57	7.01	41	2.84

a. Response categories were never, once, twice, 3-5 times, 6-10 times, more than 50.
b. Items 1-3 are status offenses, only illegal for minors. UNIVERSE: Civilians age 15-17 on interview date (N = 11,200,000).
c. Items 4-20 were asked of the total sample. UNIVERSE: Civilians age 15-23 on interview date (N = 31,600,000).
e. UNIVERSE: Civilians age 15-17 as of the interview date who responded to all items on the questionnaire (N = 11,200,000).
f. UNIVERSE: Civilians age 15-23 as of the interview date who responded to all items on the questionnaire (N = 30,800,000).
d. Item included in drugs subscale.
p. Item included in property subscale.
s. Item included in status subscale.
v. Item included in violence subscale.

population ever participating in the activity and in the mean levels of involvement. Creating summary scales using simple sums could result in a youth who has committed five armed robberies being counted as less delinquent than a youth who admits to ten petty thefts, clearly a distortion of the desired result. A scaling procedure was used which resulted in all items contributing approximately equally to their appropriate scales, regardless of overall frequency, effectively weighting each item by its seriousness (Crowley 1982).

Table 8.1 shows the distributions of the self-reported delinquency items by sex,[4] showing both the percent of respondents who denied participation in the activity within the previous year and the mean level of involvement with the activity. The distributions of the involvement scores (not presented here) show that most youths have either never participated in the activity or have participated only a few times. The only exceptions to this pattern are use of marijuana or alcohol: the frequency distributions for use of these drugs show that youths tend to report either very low levels of use, once or twice, suggesting experimentation, or very high levels, suggesting habitual use.

Among minors, truancy and drinking are fairly common occurrences, and almost half of the total sample reported using marijuana or its derivatives. For both males and females, assault was the second most common nonstatus (illegal regardless of perpetrator's age) offense; half the young men and a quarter of the young women reported at least one incident.

Most young people report participation in some sort of delinquent activity; about half of the population under eighteen is estimated to have committed at least one status offense, and a full three-quarters of youth have committed at least one adult offense. Consistent with the mean scores for the individual items, the summary scale means show that drug use tends to have the highest levels of involvement.

Large differences appear between young men and young women in the levels of delinquency (table 8.1, last column). For the status offenses and for less serious offenses, the ratios of involvement between males and females are fairly low, but they are much higher for offenses involving substantial violence or relatively large sums of money. For most offenses, not only are young men more likely to participate in delinquent activities, but they are also more likely to participate more often than do young women.

Because the difference in crime rates between the sexes is a universal pattern in criminology, all the remaining data are presented separately by sex. Other key demographic patterns to be explored include distributions by age (where adults are defined as being 18 and older and minors are younger than 18), ethnicity, poverty status, and enrollment status.

Demographics of Self-Reported Illegal Behavior

Previous studies have indicated that delinquent activity declines after age 15. The NLS data support this pattern, with the exception of items on drug use. Adults (respondents over the age of eighteen) are about a third less involved in nondrug illegal activities than are minors. For drug use, on the other hand, adults actually report higher use levels than their younger counterparts.

There is a popular image of delinquents as youth from homes impoverished both financially and emotionally. The NLS joins a growing body of work seriously questioning this image.[5] Table 8.2, which breaks down the delinquency items by race, poverty, school enrollment, and sex, shows a higher involvement of whites in delinquent activity than blacks. Certainly the whites, both male and female, report higher levels of involvement with status offenses than do either blacks or Hispanics. This pattern is largely due to the much higher reports of alcohol use by whites. Indeed, whites

Table 8.2
Mean Response for Delinquency Scales
by Sex, Race, Poverty, and School Enrollment Status

	Female				Male			
	Status[a]	Violence[b]	Drugs[b]	Property[b]	Status[a]	Violence[b]	Drugs[b]	Property[b]
Race								
Black	4.47	2.48	7.87	2.64	8.02	5.10	12.02	6.18
Hispanic	9.72	1.33	6.60	1.91	13.29	4.46	11.60	6.63
White	13.30	1.67	13.45	2.49	18.57	5.38	20.09	7.18
Poverty Status								
Nonpoverty	12.38	1.62	12.34	2.44	17.42	5.29	18.67	7.30
Poverty	8.84	2.56	10.87	2.74	13.60	5.03	15.05	6.15
School Enrollment Status								
High school dropout	18.53	2.37	16.67	2.72	31.50	8.54	30.28	11.65
High school student	11.19	2.35	9.10	2.93	15.26	6.20	11.88	7.73
College student	13.42	.88	12.29	2.02	33.44	2.61	16.65	3.69
Nonenrolled high school graduate	23.80	1.41	13.78	2.17	48.54	4.27	23.47	6.10

a. UNIVERSE: Civilians are 15-17 as of the interview date who responded to all items on the questionnaire.
b. UNIVERSE: Civilians are 15-23 as of the interview date who responded to all items on the questionnaire.

report much higher levels of drug use in general, including hard drugs, than do blacks or Hispanics.

Few major differences appear along ethnic lines when we look at the remaining offenses. Black females tend to be more likely than white or Hispanic females to report personal violence (fighting, assault). Among males, however, whites are more likely to report involvement in fights and assaults. Generally, for both sexes, Hispanics are either intermediate between blacks and whites, or the lowest of all groups in reported level of involvement in offenses.

It is clear, however, notwithstanding some potential for underrepresentation of the ratios of offenses between blacks and whites, that criminal offenses are not limited to any one race group.[6] The few items on which black males report higher levels of involvement than do white males include three of the most serious offenses: grand theft, robbery, and aggravated assault. However, the data show a fairly high degree of involvement of all race-sex groups in various types of activities that would be punished if they became known.

Despite the popular assumptions about the link between poverty and delinquency, Table 8.2 shows that, generally, when there is a difference among males between the poor and the nonpoor (using the Current Population Survey definition of poverty), it is the nonpoor who are most delinquent. This pattern holds particularly true for the drinking and drug use items, no doubt reflecting the use of discretionary income for recreational chemicals. Males from nonpoor families are also more likely to report vandalism, shoplifting, assault, and fraud.

As usual, the pattern is much different for females. More affluent women, like their male counterparts, are more likely to report alcohol and drug use than are poor women. However, the only other offense reported substantially more frequently by nonpoor women is petty theft. Poor women report more involvement with offenses involving personal violence—fighting, assault, and aggravated assault.

Poor youths, both male and female, report higher levels of running away and truancy. While any finding based on such simple analysis must be interpreted cautiously, the implication of greater disturbance in family relationships among poor youth may have significance for the perpetuation of poverty. Perhaps the most important observation to be made from this table is the lack of evidence for the assumption that poverty per se breeds crime.[7]

In contrast to the results for poverty, delinquent activity is clearly associated with enrollment status. Among males, dropouts report high levels of delinquent activity relative to students and high school graduates in each offense category. Like minors, they report high levels of violence against people and property. Like adults, they report high levels of drug use and of drug sales. Conversely, college students, youth grouped as the most successful academically, have the lowest levels of delinquent involvement.

Among females, differentiation by enrollment status is much less pronounced. Dropouts report higher levels of delinquent involvement than do students and graduates for 13 of the 20 offenses, which is still a majority but far from the consistent pattern for males. Although the NLS contradicts the popular view that race and poverty are strongly associated with delinquency, the results do support the popular view that those who do less well in school have higher levels of criminal involvement.

The sex difference in the relationship between illegal activities and enrollment status may be due to sex differences in the reasons for dropping out of school. For young women, dropping out is often due to family considerations, such as marriage or pregnancy. For young men, on the other hand, dropping out is more likely to reflect difficulties with school or with the adult authorities who control schools.

Illegal Income

The key link between crime and employment logically lies in the degree to which crime serves as an alternative source of income. Youth who can make a good living "on the street" should spend less time in the labor force and should have a higher reservation wage, ceteris paribus, than youth who are less adept at hustling.

It is clearly not reasonable to expect that thieves who have no accountability to the tax collector or anyone else will know with any accuracy how much they earn from their activities over any extensive period of time. However, we attempted to gauge subjectively the degree to which the youth looked to crime as a source of income by asking what fraction of their total support was derived from such activities as those described on the delinquency form. It should be noted in interpreting the results that the same amount of income represents a smaller proportion of support for affluent youth than for poor youth.

Most youth do not report a profit from their activities, but a substantial minority, slightly over 20 percent of the young men and 10 percent of the young women, get at least some of their support from "crime." About 1 male in 20 reports getting one-fourth or more of his support from such sources. The expected race and income difference exist but are fairly small, especially when the base levels of income are taken into account. As with the reports of delinquent behavior, the variables most consistently related to illegal income are sex and enrollment status. One-third of the male high school dropouts and one-fifth of the female dropouts get at least some income from crime. The group with the lowest frequency of illegal income of all categories investigated is, as expected, college students.

Reported Police Contacts

Delinquent activity may or may not lead to involvement with the police and with the courts. Table 8.3 shows the distributions of police and criminal justice involvement broken down by sex, poverty status, and race.[8] The first row of the table shows the proportions of each group who report any contact with police. The remainder of the table refers to the proportions of those who report any contact and who further report various levels of involvement with the criminal justice system. This method allows comparisons of levels of involvement across groups independent of the proportion of each group who manage to stay completely out of the system.

Over a third of the young men report some police contact; the proportion for young women is closer to one-tenth. Of those who do come in contact with the police, the sex difference is much less pronounced; but even given an initial contact with police, young women are less likely than young men to be charged, convicted, placed on probation, or incarcerated. Females do report referral to counseling programs more often than males.

Some significant patterns emerge when the levels of involvement by poor and nonpoor youths are considered. There is no difference by income in frequency for males in being stopped by police without further processing, and poor females are actually somewhat less likely than more affluent females simply to be stopped by police. However, poor youth are consistently more likely to be formally charged, convicted, and put on probation or incarcerated than are nonpoor youth. In fact, the more serious the level of involvement with the criminal justice system, the more discrepant the rates by income status. Of those who come into contact with the police, about one-fifth of both poor and nonpoor males report being convicted of an offense, but poor males are almost three times as likely as nonpoor youth to report

Table 8.3
Incidence of Being Stopped, Charged or Convicted
by Sex, Poverty Status and Race

Seriousness	Female					Male				
	Non-poverty	Poverty	Black	Hispanic	White	Non-poverty	Poverty	Black	Hispanic	White
Percent of population	42	8	7	3	40	43	7	7	3	40
Stopped, charged or convicted[a]	10	14	8	13	11	33	37	36	36	34
Among those ever stopped, charged or convicted[b]										
Stopped	79	70	79	78	76	82	82	81	83	82
Charged	31	47	31	35	36	41	53	41	49	45
Charged as adult	12	16	14	12	13	19	21	19	20	22
Convicted	15	23	10	19	18	23	32	22	25	26
Convicted as adult	6	8	*	9	7	12	15	12	11	13
Counseling	27	31	23	24	29	20	25	16	19	22
Probation	13	17	15	11	14	23	36	28	26	26
Incarcerated	5	7	*	*	6	7	19	12	13	9
Incarcerated as youth	4	7	*	*	5	4	12	7	7	5
Incarcerated as adult	*	0	*	0	*	4	9	8	7	5

*Percentage is 0.1-0.5.
a. UNIVERSE: Civilians age 15-23 on interview date.
b. UNIVERSE: Civilians age 15-23 on interview date who reported ever being stopped, charged, or convicted.

incarceration. The pattern for females is similar, although less dramatic. These results contrast sharply with the greater involvement with delinquent behavior reported by nonpoor youth.

Table 8.3 also presents criminal justice involvement broken down by race and shows a pattern subtly similar to the one shown for income: while black youth are actually less likely than whites to be charged with offenses or convicted, blacks are more likely to be put on probation or incarcerated. Interpretation of these results must be extremely cautious at this time, since there is no control for the type of offense with which individuals are charged, and type of offense is the single major determinant of sentence severity. Among the young men in the sample, major traffic offenses, vandalism, and possession of marijuana were mentioned more frequently by whites than by blacks, but blacks were more likely to report a conviction for assault or robbery. The direction if not the magnitude of these differences in conviction rates by race are echoed in the frequency of report of the individual offenses on the delinquent behavior measure.

Out-of-school youths, particularly dropouts, have the highest levels of involvement: over half of the male dropouts have come in contact with the police. Of these, two-fifths report a conviction for an offense, and one-quarter report a conviction as an adult. Probation and incarceration are also fairly common among dropouts. Perhaps the most useful group for comparison with the dropouts is nonenrolled high school graduates.[9] The same sort of increasing differentiation of level of involvement with the criminal justice system appears as was noted for poverty. Among males with police contact, there is a moderate difference between high school dropouts and high school graduates in the percent charged with an offense—two-thirds of the dropouts compared with half of the high school graduates. Dropouts are, however, almost four times as likely to be incarcerated as are high school graduates, and are over seven times more likely to report being incarcerated in juvenile institutions. The patterns are quite similar for females, allowing for their generally lower level both of initial contact and of serious involvement following contact.

The results for poverty and enrollment status, which are quite consistent with the general image of youths in the criminal justice system, encourage confidence in the validity of the responses to the interview. This very consistency, however, raises questions of inequity in view of the lack of relationship between poverty and delinquent behavior as reported by the youth.

The results for poverty and race support the observation that poor and minority youth face an accumulation of disadvantage when they enter the criminal justice system (McNeeley and Pope 1981). At each stage where discretionary decisions are to be made, there is a tendency for youths from poorer backgrounds to be treated more harshly than youths from white or middle class homes. The differences at each stage are slight, but the cumulative effect is that at the most severe level of punishment—incarceration—blacks, Hispanics, and the poor are concentrated beyond their proportions in reported criminal behavior. To the extent that the general population uses the publicized descriptions of the incarcerated population to form their concepts of the attributes of the minority and poor members of society, this distorted image will affect the perpetuation of disadvantage in society at large.

II. Crime and Work

Traditionally, delinquency has been primarily the province of sociologists. Recently, however, economists have expanded their area of concern to include time allocation to illegal as well as legal sources of income. The next section will attempt to synthesize and distinguish the insights of these two fields in conceptualizing the link between delinquency and employment.

The analysis is presented in the three following sections, based on the design of the NLS research. First, a cross-sectional analysis is offered describing the patterns of delinquent activity reported by NLS respondents and presenting first-order correlations between measures of delinquency and measures of employment. A 2-wave analysis follows, presenting a fairly standard multiple regression approach to estimating the relationship between employment and crime, net of other factors known to be associated with each. Finally, a path analysis is presented using three waves of the NLS. The third analysis attempts both to build on the results of the cross-sectional and 2-wave analyses and to take advantage of the structure of the panel study to untangle the reciprocal effects of employment and crime.

Theories of Delinquency

Economic approaches to crime regard each individual as trying to maximize utilities from legal and illegal activities. The emphasis is on the choice of activities based on rational calculations. The greater the rate of return to illegal activities as compared to the returns from legal activities, the greater the time allocated to crime. Of course, crime involves expected costs, in the form of possible arrests, fines, and convictions, which are not attached to legitimate employment. Some of these costs have been entered into models of criminal behavior, in the form of arrest and conviction rates.[10] The analogous costs of legitimate employment in reduction of leisure time and autonomy are not considered explicitly. The usual human capital indicators, education and work history, are predicted to be related to crime because they determine the returns to employment. Conditions that are expected to lead to higher levels of criminal activity include low expected wages, high rates of unemployment, low probability of arrests and other legal sanctions, and "tastes" for the nonpecuniary rewards of crime—risk taking, for example.

It is assumed in the economic analysis of crime that the more time is allocated to crime, the less is allocated to employment, and vice versa. What is not considered explicitly is the fact that most delinquent or criminal activity involves a very brief time commitment (Hirschi 1969). Time spent in criminal activity may substitute for other leisure activities, rather than for time in the labor force.

The sociological approach presented in the literature on social control also assumes that people are essentially hedonistic and rational. However, the factors considered in evaluating the costs and benefits of a particular course of action are defined in terms of the emotional bonds of individuals to important people in their lives—parents, peers, spouses, children—and to conventionally valued goals—occupational advancement, marriage, respectability. Illegal activities threaten attachment bonds and chances of obtaining conventional goals, and so these bonds and goals help to control hedonistic behavior (c.f., Hirschi 1969; Hindelang 1973; Minor 1977).

Although economic approaches describe rational calculations of utilities and the control approach focuses on the emotional bonds of youths to other people, aspirations, and institutions, closer inspection shows that they make virtually identical predictions about the way that various experiences of youths may affect delinquency. Both, for example, stress the role of education. For economists, education is a major part of human capital accumulation. For sociologists, commitment to educational goals and attachment to the individuals and institutions associated with school are threatened by delinquent behavior. In fact, the relationship between school performance and delinquency is solidly established (Noblit 1976; Gold and Mann 1972).

Employment itself fits into control theory as a source of attachments to co-workers and commitment to job advancement, both of which should reduce the level of criminal activity. This factor is independent of the substitution of time allocation that is central to economic formulations. Conversely, control theory can be used as a framework for specifying the predicted costs of criminal activity. Neither economic theory nor control theory, however, is particularly useful for specifying nonpecuniary benefits associated with various types of crime.

Use of three measures of illegal activities allows refining of the hypotheses about the links between employment and crime. The economic model, where returns to illegal activities are balanced against returns to employment, applies conceptually to crimes against property—chiefly the various forms of theft. Therefore, we expect that, for adults at least, property crime will be related to lower levels of weeks worked and longer periods of unemployment and nonparticipation in the labor force.

Violence has been related to labor force participation in two ways. Unemployment has been associated in particular with violence within the family, e.g., wife abuse and child abuse (Monahan and Klassen 1982). Bachman (1978) found that men who were high in violent behavior tended to have poorer work histories in terms of sporadic and low status jobs. These two findings imply different causal directions—unemployment may lead to violence and violent behavior may lead to employment instability.

On the other hand, we expect drugs to be more commonly used by those with reliable sources of income, and thus positively associated with employment. The high frequency of drug use reported in the sample indicates that most of the users are not the junkies of skid row, but rather are people who use drugs as a part of rather ordinary life. The effect of income in facilitating drug purchase should lead to a net positive association between drug use and weeks worked, and a corresponding negative association with unemployment.

Reservation wage, a subjective judgment rather than a behavioral measure subject to constraints outside the control of the individual, may provide some differentiation in the effects of criminal activity on employment. If crime provides income, the marginal value of wages should be reduced, so that a higher wage would be required before the individual will accept a job. There is no clear reason that nonincome producing types of crime would have the same effect, although it could be argued that the expense of maintaining a drug habit would also increase the reservation wage.

Measures of Employment and First Order Relationships

Several employment-related measures are explored, the primary focus resting on the supply of labor. The NLS data base includes measures of the proportion of weeks worked, weeks unemployed, and weeks out of the labor force (OLF), between January 1978 and the 1981 interview. These allow continuous measures of the amount of labor provided by the respondent in the periods before, during, and after the period for which delinquent activity is measured.

The analysis includes reservation wage—the wage at which an unemployed person would accept a job—in part because it is not restricted by external constraints. The logic of the connection between crime and work is similar for reservation wage and weeks unemployed. The higher the income and other returns derived from criminal behavior, the higher the reservation wages.

Table 8.4 shows the first-order correlations between employment and crime for each of two designated universes. The first is restricted to high school youth over the age of 16. The age restriction reflects legal age restrictions on employment. The second universe is nonenrolled youth over the age of 18.[11] College students are omitted from the adult group because they are not expected to be primarily oriented towards employment. Dropouts under the age of 18, while

Table 8.4
Correlations Between Delinquency Scales and Employment Indicators[a]

Employment variable	Females				Males			
	Violence	Drugs	Property	Illegal income	Violence	Drugs	Property	Illegal income
High school students[b]								
Weeks worked	-.02*	.13**	.04**	.02	.01	.05**	.04*	.01
Weeks unemployed	.02†	.09**	.05*	.09**	.05	.05	.04	.04
Weeks OLF	.02*	-.16**	-.06**	-.04*	-.01	-.07**	-.04†	-.02
Reservation wage	.10*	.09	-.04	.03	.05	-.02	-.00	.02
Nonenrolled adults[c]								
Weeks worked	-.07**	.05	.02	-.07*	-.08*	-.02	-.07*	-.17**
Weeks unemployed	.07*	.04	.04*	.08**	.10**	.03	.05†	.10**
Weeks OLF	.04**	-.04**	-.02*	.06**	.02	.03	.05	.05**
Reservation wage	.01	.03	.04	.01	-.01	.01	.05	.05

a. Coefficients for weighted data. Significance estimated without weights.
b. UNIVERSE: High school students 16 years and older.
c. UNIVERSE: Nonenrolled civilians, 18-22 years old.
†p .10.
*p .05.
**p .01.

presenting major problems for law enforcement, are excluded from the analysis to avoid confounding age with school completion. Within each of these major universes, all analyses are run separately by sex.

Predictions are weakly supported, if at all. What is not expected is the greater consistency and magnitude of the correlations for young women than for young men. For three of the four sex-status groups, drugs tend to be positively associated with weeks employed and negatively related to being OLF, which tends to confirm the association between drug use and disposable income. Also as predicted, violent behavior tends to be negatively associated with weeks employed, although the relationship is very weak for young men. As with drugs, youths reporting higher levels of property crime tend to report more weeks employed or unemployed, and correspondingly fewer weeks out of the labor force. Only among adult males are higher levels of property crime associated with fewer weeks worked. Illegal income has the predicted negative association with weeks worked only for adults.

These seemingly contradictory findings make some sense for high school youths in a context of role expectations. Students, particularly girls, who spend more time out of the labor force report less of all types of delinquent activity. The greater time delinquent youth spend in the labor market is consistent with the observations that delinquent youth tend to adopt adult behavior patterns earlier than their more law abiding contemporaries (Hirschi 1969). Among high school students, then, work and delinquent activity may both be ways of moving out of the dependent roles of child and student into more autonomous lives. For those who are past their school years, on the other hand, illegal income acts as would be predicted if crime competes with employment as a source of revenue. The expected negative relationship between violence and weeks worked is also clearer among adults.

Reservation wage, although intuitively appealing as a means of measuring willingness to work given illicit income, seems almost totally unrelated to criminal activity. The signs are inconsistent, and, with the exception of the correlation with violence for high school females, the coefficients are miniscule.[12]

Crime and Work: Regression Analysis

Predictions based on both sociological and economic considerations were used to develop a model of the relationship between employment and delinquency, predicting labor market outcomes as functions of human capital considerations, family background, current family roles and relationships, school experience and performance, and urban residence. Indicators of criminal behavior and of official crime records were then used to see if they contribute any explanatory power to the model once these background functions have been entered. Conversely, the model and the employment indicators were used to predict delinquent behavior. This is an admittedly crude style of analysis, but serves as a first approximation of the relationship between crime and employment net of their known correlates.

Separate models have developed for each of the two universes, students and adults. The estimators of human capital for high school students were age and weeks worked between January 1, 1978 and the initial interview date. Among students, age and educational level are highly collinear, so only one of these variables could be used. For the out of school sample, age and education are not as closely correlated, so both age and dummy variables for less than 12 years of education and more than 12 years were used, with high school graduates the comparison group.

The work history available on the NLS was divided into two sections: weeks worked in the period between January 1978 and the 1979 interview, and weeks worked in the period between the 1979 and 1980 interviews. Since the delinquency

scales covered the calendar year preceding the 1980 interview, the between-interview period provides a good estimate
of the supply of labor that was concurrent with the delinquent activity. The first period is used as a measure of work
history, and provides an indicator of work attachment that
does not have the ambiguous causal relationship which
potentially biases the estimated relationship between crime
and work when they are measured over the same time span.

The NLS has a number of measures of the family environment in which the youth lived at age 14. Intactness of the
family is based on whether the youth lived with both a father
and a mother figure or in some other living situation.[13] For
youth under 18, that is, for the high school sample, the attachment to the family of origin was assessed by looking at
whether the youth had run away from home in the past
year.[14]

For the adults, dummy variables for marital status and
whether the youth were living with their own children tapped
the acquisition of adult family roles. The available evidence
on the effect of marital status on crime is inconsistent. In
studies of released offenders, those with continuing family
ties, including marriages, are somewhat less likely to
recidivate than are others (Monahan and Klassen 1982). On
the other hand, Farrington (1982) reports little association
between getting married and official arrest records or self-
reported criminal behavior, although marriage did tend to
reduce activities associated with crime, such as drinking and
sexual promiscuity.

The human capital effects of schooling are usually
measured as years of school completed. The quality of the
school experience, on the other hand, has long been identified as a key factor in delinquent behavior.[15] The NLS includes an assessment of satisfaction with various aspects of
the school experience that was included in the analysis of the
high school sample. The school discipline scale was coded
zero if the respondent had never been suspended or expelled,

1 if the respondent had been suspended only, and 2 if the respondent had been expelled. Youth who had been both suspended and expelled were coded 2, as were any youth who reported expulsion without suspension.

Dummy variables for living in the central city of an SMSA and for living in other portions of an SMSA were introduced as controls. A measure of poverty status was used to indicate the marginal utility of the youth's own wages.

Multivariate Results: Delinquency

Three models were compared. The first, basic model, uses only the family and background variables plus work history. This model provides a baseline for looking at the relationship between current employment and current delinquency. The second model adds the proportion of weeks worked and the proportion of weeks unemployed, and the final model adds school discipline and police contact variables in an attempt to see if relationships between work and crime are mediated by official processing.[16] Table 8.5 and 8.6 present the results for the final model for each of the delinquency indicators.

Overall, little evidence in the multivariate analysis supports the belief that employment reduces delinquent behavior. The control approach to delinquency, however, is upheld somewhat. In general, the variables associated with illegal activities tend to be measures of family or school ties. Ironically, given the general omission of girls and women from studies of crime and delinquency, many of the sociological factors presumed associated with delinquency are significant only for females: e.g., black women are more violent and report more involvement in property crime than those from other races. For both sexes, Hispanics generally report lower levels of involvement in proscribed activity than any other ethnic group.

Consistent with the hypothesis of lower levels of job commitment among students, the significant relationships with any of the three measures of employment (employment, unemployment or work history) tend to be among the adult population. For high school students, even the fairly weak relationships shown in the first-order correlations (table 8.4) do not hold up when background variables are controlled.

Multivariate Results: Labor
Force Outcomes

Given the lack of relationship between the employment indexes and delinquency, it is hardly surprising that the delinquency indexes do not predict much variance in proportion of weeks employed or unemployed, using standard OLS for proportion of weeks employed and Tobit analysis to compensate for a relatively large number of cases with no weeks unemployed. The reservation wage analysis showed no significant results for either the simple or the augmented models, and so are not presented here. No cases bearing a significant relationship between self-reported offenses and any of the employment measures and no effects for official delinquency or illegal income for high school students appear.

Official responses to behavior and reliance on illegal income for a substantial portion of self-support do show some signs of association with employment for nonenrolled adults. For men, having been dismissed from school is associated with fewer weeks worked and more weeks unemployed, and this finding is net of the effect of dropping out, per se. Having been convicted is associated with fewer weeks worked for both sexes.[17] Most important, illegal income, the most direct measure of the economic benefits of crime, is significantly associated with higher unemployment for both sexes and with fewer weeks worked for men.

Table 8.5
Analysis of Delinquent Behavior and Illegal Income: High School Students

Predictors	Females				Males			
	Violence	Drugs	Property	Illegal income	Violence	Drugs	Property	Illegal income
Age	-.105 (-0.60)	-.261 (-1.17)	-.099 (-0.55)	-.303 (-1.07)	-.079 (-0.70)	-.055 (-0.30)	.009 (.064)	-.010 (-0.06)
School satisfaction	-.036 (-1.08)	-.145** (-3.58)	-.152** (-4.44)	-.088† (-1.79)	-.014 (-0.61)	-.089 (-0.24)	-.082** (-2.89)	-.052 (-1.58)
Work history	-.003 (-0.76)	.004 (0.85)	-.001 (-0.34)	-.003 (-0.53)	.006* (2.28)	-.001 (-0.26)	.0003 (0.10)	-.005 (-1.22)
Run away from home	1.33** (2.84)	1.90** (3.29)	1.52 (3.05)	1.21† (1.90)	.676† (1.89)	.797 (1.37)	1.22** (2.79)	.105 (0.21)
Broken home	-.557* (2.10)	.565† (1.73)	-.143 (-0.52)	.004 (0.01)	-.032 (-0.18)	.309 (1.06)	-.119 (-0.53)	-.193 (-0.74)
Parent education	.495* (2.03)	.013 (0.04)	-.128 (-0.50)	-.131 (-0.35)	-.022 (-0.13)	-.841** (-2.92)	-5.28* (2.45)	.175 (0.69)
Poverty	-.108 (-0.40)	-.817* (-2.36)	-.145 (-0.51)	.508 (1.27)	-.204 (-1.08)	.190 (0.62)	-.585* (-2.51)	.252 (0.93)
Noncity SMSA	.109 (0.35)	.259 (0.64)	.178 (0.54)	.089 (0.18)	-.196 (-0.92)	-.423 (-1.22)	-.269 (-1.03)	.262 (0.87)
Central city SMSA	.337 (1.41)	.762* (2.56)	.544* (2.20)	.569 (1.58)	-.076 (-0.47)	.058 (0.22)	.039 (0.20)	.298 (1.23)
Black	1.19** (4.32)	-.971** (-2.78)	.499† (1.73)	.559 (1.34)	-.095 (-0.49)	-.172 (-0.55)	.100 (0.42)	.240 (0.87)
Hispanic	-.704*	-1.21**	-.265	-.819	-.656**	-.328	.141	-.579†

	(1)	(2)	(3)	(4)	(5)	(6)	(7)	(8)
School discipline	(-2.16)	(-3.03)	(-0.81)	(-1.53)	(-2.85)	(-0.88)	(0.51)	(-1.66)
	1.35**	1.57**	.660*	1.30**	.819**	1.45**	.794**	.939**
	(5.65)	(5.14)	(2.56)	(3.97)	(5.85)	(6.57)	(4.71)	(4.98)
Ever convicted	.742	2.63	-.159	1.09	.704†	1.12†	.744	.623
	(0.52)	(1.50)	(-0.10)	(0.61)	(1.87)	(1.95)	(1.63)	(1.28)
Ever charged	.587	-.006	1.82	-.079	.380	1.29**	.579	1.02**
	(0.48)	(-0.00)	(1.36)	(-0.05)	(1.37)	(3.05)	(1.71)	(2.84)
% weeks worked	.003	.007†	.004	.012*	-.0004	.004	.003	.002
	(0.87)	(1.69)	(1.03)	(2.32)	(-0.20)	(1.15)	(0.88)	(0.62)
% weeks unemployed	.004	.009	.004	.008	.001	.002	.005	-.001
	(0.48)	(0.98)	(0.45)	(0.69)	(0.33)	(0.37)	(1.06)	(-0.14)
Constant	1.58	7.04	4.80	4.08	2.70	2.60	2.70	.242
	(0.52)	(1.81)	(1.53)	(0.84)	(1.34)	(0.79)	(1.10)	(0.08)
N	761	755	753	742	817	804	798	792
L (max)	-997.34	-1013.44	-1039.01	-367.50	-1352.44	-1194.60	-1328.51	-662.58

UNIVERSE: Civilians age 16-23 on interview date who were enrolled in high school.

Table 8.6
Analysis of Delinquent Behavior and Illegal Income: Nonenrolled Adults

Predictors	Females				Males			
	Violence	Drugs	Property	Illegal income	Violence	Drugs	Property	Illegal income
Constant	-.277	3.06	2.81	-1.27	4.87**	1.11	4.89	2.50
	(-0.22)	(2.56)	(2.36)	(-0.76)	(4.89)	(0.86)	(4.26)	(1.90)
Age	-.065	-.136*	-.169**	-.064	-.231**	-.004	-.216**	-.166*
	(-1.00)	(-2.26)	(-2.80)	(-0.75)	(-4.61)	(-0.61)	(-3.75)	(-2.51)
Dropout	.676**	-.007	.261	.055	-.238	-.280	-.439*	.367†
	(3.02)	(-0.35)	(1.22)	(0.79)	(-1.54)	(-1.38)	(-2.42)	(1.84)
More than 12 years education	-.930**	-.104	-.306	-.477	-.132	.443	.220	-.201
	(-3.53)	(-0.46)	(-1.33)	(-1.38)	(-0.61)	(1.62)	(0.91)	(-0.66)
Work history	.002	.002	.006*	-.001	-.002	-.0004	-.003	-.001
	(0.80)	(0.87)	(2.11)	(-0.31)	(-1.02)	(-0.15)	(-1.34)	(-0.33)
Broken home	.072	.182	.057	-.450	-.042	.127	.060	.064
	(0.36)	(0.96)	(0.30)	(-1.68)	(-0.27)	(0.61)	(0.33)	(0.31)
Parent education	-.147	-.413*	-.287†	.005	-.009	-.589**	-.579**	-.103
	(-0.80)	(-2.38)	(-1.66)	(0.02)	(-0.06)	(-3.20)	(-3.55)	(-0.56)
Spouse present	-.604**	-.777**	-.667**	-.360	-.084	-1.08**	-.496†	-.752*
	(-2.82)	(-3.95)	(-3.37)	(-1.28)	(-0.35)	(-3.39)	(-1.77)	(-2.14)
Children present	.213	.125	-.120	-.238	.402	.658†	.273	.182
	(0.94)	(0.59)	(-0.56)	(-0.81)	(1.39)	(1.73)	(0.80)	(0.45)
Poverty status	.129	-.679**	-.201	.170	-.066	-.160	-.362†	-.177
	(0.58)	(-3.18)	(-0.96)	(0.61)	(-0.37)	(-0.68)	(-1.73)	(-0.77)
Noncity SMSA	-.301	.235	.184	.530†	.118	.728**	-.040	-.033
	(-1.20)	(1.00)	(0.79)	(1.67)	(0.61)	(2.90)	(-0.18)	(-0.13)
Central city SMSA	-.225	.291†	-.113	.358	-.054	.396*	.084	-.023
	(-1.17)	(1.66)	(-0.64)	(1.45)	(-0.38)	(2.13)	(0.51)	(-0.12)

Black	.551*	-.880**	-.328	.278	.016	-1.01**	-.231	.274
	(2.42)	(-4.01)	(-1.51)	(0.97)	(0.95)	(-4.52)	(-1.18)	(1.26)
Hispanic	-.546	-.732**	-.815**	-.458	-.551**	-.783**	-.117	-.243
	(-2.10)	(-3.11)	(-3.40)	(-1.33)	(-3.02)	(-3.31)	(-0.57)	(-0.98)
School discipline	.895**	1.10**	.834**	.618**	.746**	.855**	.67**	.611**
	(5.21)	(6.63)	(5.08)	(2.96)	(7.08)	(6.20)	(5.40)	(4.59)
Ever convicted	1.20*	-.556	.058	-.204	.031	.962**	.786**	1.00*
	(2.23)	(-1.03)	(0.11)	(-0.33)	(0.13)	(3.12)	(2.87)	(3.51)
Ever charged	.977**	2.13**	1.59**	1.84**	1.00**	.816**	.968**	.385
	(4.83)	(5.73)	(4.32)	(4.36)	(2.60)	(3.10)	(4.14)	(1.53)
% weeks worked	.002	.004	.008	-.001	.006*	.008*	.005	-.003
	(0.76)	(1.34)	(0.27)	(-0.13)	(2.05)	(2.02)	(1.35)	(-0.88)
% weeks unemployed	.006	.007	.004	.011†	.005	.004	.003	.006
	(1.11)	(1.50)	(0.81)	(1.93)	(1.31)	(0.77)	(0.69)	(1.14)
N	1694	1680	1675	1648	1345	1319	1317	1299
L (max)	-1896.96	-2640.84	-2159.53	-709.35	-2147.01	-2291.37	-2125.71	-1064.09

UNIVERSE: Civilians age 18-23 on interview date who were not enrolled in high school or college.

Three-Wave Path Analysis

While the results of the previous analysis indicate very little mutual or independent effects of crime and employment, it is possible that there are long term consequences for employment based on earlier participation in illegal activities that are not captured when crime and employment are measured simultaneously. While crime was measured at a single point, indicators of labor force participation are present before, during, and after the period covered by the crime measure. The multiple observations of individuals in the panel design of the NLS allow use of the recent developments in path analysis to assess the validity of causal hypotheses.

The theoretical perspectives outlined above were used to construct two path models. In the economic model, the effects of human capital variables on crime operate through their effects on current employment and on expected wage, while in the control model, expected wage is deleted and human capital variables operate directly on crime through their association with commitment to employment. The effects of criminal activity in 1980 can affect employment in 1981 both directly and through effects on 1980 employment.

The analysis is restricted to youth who were out of school in 1980, the year the data on illegal activities were collected. The tradeoff between legal employment and crime should be most clear among those who are free to seek full-time employment. The restriction of the sample to youth who are out of school also means that the analysis is largely of adult crime rather than juvenile delinquency. Evidence suggests that while more juveniles are involved in illegal activities than are adults, crimes committed by adults are, on the whole, more serious than crimes committed by youngsters (Wolfgang 1977; Hindelang and McDermott 1979).

The path analysis strategy, while very useful for decomposing direct and indirect causal influences, does not easily allow inclusion of background variables such as sex, race, and region, which do not fit into the causal structure of the problem, but which may have pervasive effects on the relationships among factors. As before, the model is run separately by sex. Sample size considerations preclude further splitting the sample by race, so the analysis is run for whites only. Other control variables such as region are excluded, since they do not have clearly hypothesized effects on the process to be modeled.

The NLS has no measures of attachment in the sense of direct emotional bonds between respondents and other people. Rather, it provides indicators of social roles, such as marital status and presence of children in the home. These will be termed *commitment* variables, to emphasize that they represent role functions rather than attachments to individuals. Two areas of commitment are defined: commitment to work and commitment to family roles.

There are two indicators of commitment to work. The initial interview of the panel included items on the acceptability of several hypothetical alternatives in the case that the respondent was unable to obtain enough income to support a family. These ranged from obtaining more training in order to find a better job to going on welfare or shoplifting. Responses were combined into an index of commitment to the labor force. While such items have not been directly applied to criminal activity, orientation to alternate sources of income has been found to be associated with labor force participation among low income youth (Goodwin 1979). Another item asked whether the respondent expected to be working in five years. Especially for young women, this variable should tap whether the youth's labor force participation is considered to be temporary or relatively permanent. Commitment to family was proxied by two dichotomous variables indicating whether or not the respondent was living with a spouse or living with offspring.

Standard human capital measures included in the model are prior work experience, measured in weeks, and dummy variables separating youth who were high school dropouts or still students in 1979 from youth who had graduated from high school and not received further education. These human capital indicators were measured as of the 1979 interview.[18]

A key construct in the economic model is the inclusion of expected returns to work, measured by the imputed value of hourly rate of pay.[19] It is hypothesized that, to the extent there is a relationship between human capital variables and crime, the relationship should be mediated through pay.

Employment is measured over three time periods in the models estimated. Prior experience was defined as the number of weeks worked up to the interview date in 1979. Percent of weeks worked between the 1979 interview and the 1980 interview represents approximately the period covered by the criminal activity scales. Employment during this period was specified only in terms of weeks worked both to simplify the model and to avoid collinearity problems. The total of weeks worked during the period between interviews and weeks worked before the first interview, of course, add up to the total work experience prior to the final period.[20] There is some problem of simultaneous causation in the inclusion of weeks worked and criminal activity measures which cover the same time span, since it is possible that some of the youth were incarcerated for a period of time, necessarily limiting the number of weeks available for work. This figure should be quite small, given the infrequency with which an incarceration was reported by the respondents.

Labor force participation in 1981 was defined in terms of the three major labor force statuses: weeks worked, weeks unemployed, and weeks out of the labor force. Since paths to each of these outcomes were estimated in separate equations, the problems of multicollinearity are avoided.

The analysis technique selected is path analysis (Asher 1976). This procedure involves estimating sequentially the hypothesized relationships in a model, using ordinary least squares for each set of estimators. The technique allows decomposition of direct and indirect effects of predictors on outcomes. For example, prior work experience should have a direct effect on weeks worked in 1980. Prior work experience is also a predictor of expected wage, which in turn affects weeks worked, so that prior work experience affects subsequent work indirectly. The total effect of experience on weeks worked in 1980 is the sum of the direct effect and the indirect effect. Further detail on the interpretation of path coefficients is given in the next section of the paper.

Employment is measured over three time periods in the models estimated. Prior experience was defined as the number of weeks worked up to the interview date in 1979. Percent of weeks worked between the 1979 interview and the 1980 interview represents approximately the period covered by the criminal activity scales. Employment during this period was specified only in terms of weeks worked both to simplify the model and to avoid collinearity problems. The total of weeks worked during the period between interviews and weeks worked before the first interview, of course, add up to the total work experience prior to the final period.[20] There is some problem of simultaneous causation in the inclusion of weeks worked and criminal activity measures which cover the same time span, since it is possible that some of the youth were incarcerated for a period of time, necessarily limiting the number of weeks available for work. This figure should be quite small, given the infrequency with which an incarceration was reported by the respondents.

Labor force participation in 1981 was defined in terms of the three major labor force statuses: weeks worked, weeks unemployed, and weeks out of the labor force. Since paths to each of these outcomes were estimated in separate equations, the problems of multicollinearity are avoided.

The analysis technique selected is path analysis (Asher 1976). This procedure involves estimating sequentially the hypothesized relationships in a model, using ordinary least squares for each set of estimators. The technique allows decomposition of direct and indirect effects of predictors on outcomes. For example, prior work experience should have a direct effect on weeks worked in 1980. Prior work experience is also a predictor of expected wage, which in turn affects weeks worked, so that prior work experience affects subsequent work indirectly. The total effect of experience on weeks worked in 1980 is the sum of the direct effect and the indirect effect. Further detail on the interpretation of path coefficients is given in the next section of the paper.

Path Analysis Results

Table 8.7 shows the means for the variables used in the models, separately by sex. Distinct differences appear in the amount of labor force participation reported by young men and women, with men having more prior work experience and a larger proportion of weeks worked in both 1980 and 1981. There is no increase in the percent of weeks worked from 1980 to 1981. Expected wages for women are approximately $.20 per hour less than for young men. Interestingly, there is little difference between males and females in work commitment. Over 90 percent of the young women say that they expect to be working in five years, a figure only slightly lower than the 98 percent of the young men reporting such plans.

The large percentage of young women with work plans is more striking in light of the fact that 27 percent were mothers in 1980 and in 1981 this figure had risen to 35 percent. The rates of marriage and parenthood for young men were substantially lower, although almost a third had started families of their own by 1981. The difference in family commitments no doubt reflects the continuing trend for women to marry and start families at an earlier age than do young men.[21]

Table 8.7
Descriptive Statistics for Variables Used in Path Models

	Females		Males	
	mean	std. dev.	mean	std. dev.
Prior work experience - 1979	55.89	52.88	68.55	59.04
High school dropout - 1979	0.19	0.39	0.22	0.42
Still in school - 1979	0.34	0.47	0.37	0.48
Work commitment - 1979	13.08	1.87	13.14	1.88
Intention to be working in 5 years - 1979	0.91	0.29	0.98	0.13
Expected wage - 1980[a]	5.86	0.32	6.07	0.40
% weeks worked - 1979-1980	62.41	37.37	77.01	29.47
Property crime - 1980[a]	1.82	0.17	1.94	0.27
Drug use - 1980[a]	0.95	0.48	1.11	0.61
Violence - 1980[a]	1.23	0.20	1.39	0.38
Married, spouse present - 1980	0.35	0.48	0.18	0.39
Children present - 1980	0.27	0.44	0.09	0.29
% weeks worked - 1980-1981	63.51	38.77	77.76	30.94
% weeks unemployed - 1980-1981	7.80	18.05	11.77	22.62
%weeks OLF 1980-1981	28.70	37.50	10.47	22.81
Married, spouse present - 1981	0.42	0.49	0.27	0.44
Children present - 1981	0.35	0.48	0.16	0.37
Number of cases	1470		1177	

a. Logarithmic form.

Young men tend to score higher on each crime scale than do young women, but, as with other self-report instruments, the sex difference is much smaller than the sex difference observed in official court records.

Results for young men. Figures 8.1 and 8.2 show the results for young men. The unstandardized coefficients are shown, with standardized coefficients in parentheses. The standardized scores can be used to assess the relative influence on predictors within any one model, while the unstandardized coefficients are more useful in making comparisons across groups.[22] Nonsignificant paths are not shown, in order to make the figures easier to read. The figures allow both direct and indirect effects of predictors to be traced through the model. The information in the figures for the male sample is summarized in table 8.8. The hypothesis that delinquency and work are linked through expected returns to employment is not supported. There is no significant path from expected wage to any of the measures of illegal behavior. However, if the economic model is not supported, neither is the control model, at least in terms of measures of commitment to the labor market. Work commitment and intention to be working in five years are not related to any of the crime scales.

Marital status and the presence of children in the home are related to property crime. As expected, married men are less likely to participate in property offenses. However, the positive association between having a child in the home and property crime is contrary to the commitment hypothesis.

Violent activity is the only one of the crime indexes associated with significantly fewer weeks worked during the period over which the illegal activities were measured. However, both violence and property crimes were significantly associated with labor force participation measured in the following year. That is, young men who report more involvement in violent activities in 1980 tend to report fewer weeks worked and more weeks unemployed in

Figure 8.1
Path Analysis of Economic Model for White Males

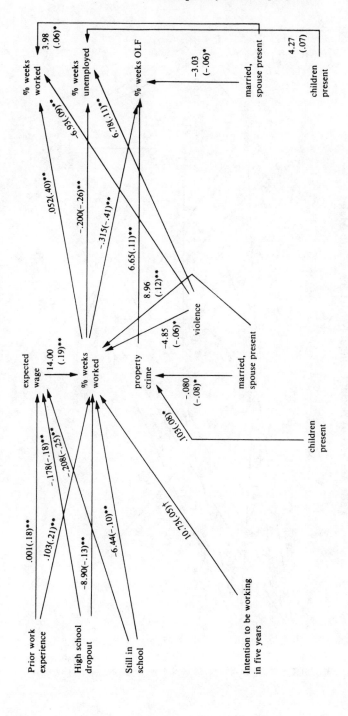

UNIVERSE: Nonenrolled civilians age 18-23 on interview date. N = 1177

Figure 8.2
Path Analysis of Social Control Model for White Males

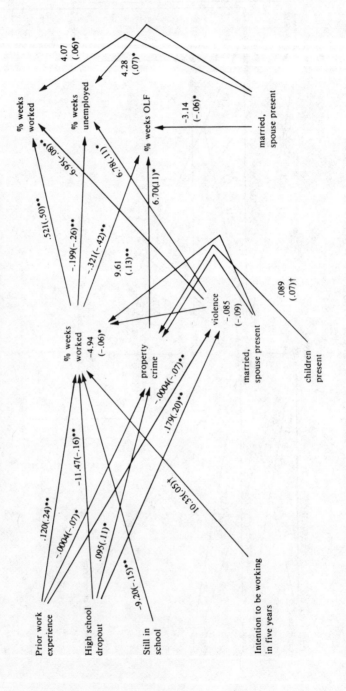

UNIVERSE: Nonenrolled civilians age 18-23 on interview date. N= 1177

the following year than do their more peaceable counterparts, while youths with higher reported levels of property crime spend a larger percentage of their time out of the labor force relative to other young men. There is an additional, indirect effect of violence on labor force participation, since violent men tended to work less in 1980. The lower level of prior experience is associated with fewer weeks worked, more unemployment, and more time out of the labor market in 1981. Since there was no significant relationship between property crime and weeks worked in 1980, there is no significant indirect link between property crime and labor force participation in the following period.

For young men, the magnitude of employment effects of human capital, commitment, and delinquency are further described in table 8.8, which shows the direct, indirect, and total effects of each variable used to predict the labor market outcomes of the model.[23] In the control model, prior experience and school status are linked to employment through the violence scale, but these indirect effects are small. Using the economic model, it appears that a substantial proportion of the effect of the school variables on weeks worked is through their effect on expected wage.

About one-quarter of the total effect of violent behavior on subsequent weeks worked is due to the reduction in weeks worked in 1980. The indirect effects of violence on time unemployed or out of the labor force are relatively small. Since property crime is apparently unrelated to weeks employed, there is no significant indirect effect of property violations on subsequent labor force activities.

Marital status has the predicted effects on employment, reducing time out of the labor force and increasing weeks worked. The presence of children, however, is associated with more time unemployed.

Table 8.8
Direct and Indirect Effects of Predictor Variables on Labor Force Participation, White Males

| | Type of effect | | | | | |
| | Direct | | Indirect | | Total | |
	B	Beta	B	Beta	B	Beta
I. Economic Model						
Percent weeks worked, 1980						
Prior experience	.103	.21	.014	.03	.117	.24
School status						
Dropout	-8.90	-.13	-2.49	-.04	-11.39	-.17
Student	-6.44	-.10	-2.91	-.05	-9.35	-.15
Graduate	–	–	–	–	–	–
Work commitment	ns	ns	ns	ns	ns	ns
Intention to work	10.73	.05	ns	ns	10.73	.05
Expected wages	14.00	.19	–	–	14.00	.19
Criminal activity						
Property	ns	ns	–	–	ns	ns
Drugs	ns	ns	–	–	ns	ns
Violence	-4.85	-.06	–	–	-4.85	-0.06
Married, 1980	8.96	.12	ns	ns	8.96	.12
Parent, 1980	ns	ns	ns	ns	ns	ns
Percent weeks worked, 1981						
Expected wages	ns	ns	.728	.09	.728	.09
Percent weeks worked, 1980	.052	.40	–	–	.052	.40

Illegal activities						
Property	ns	ns	ns	ns	ns	ns
Drugs	ns	ns	ns	ns	ns	ns
Violence	-6.93	-.09	-.252	-.03	-7.18	-.12
Married, 1981	3.98	.06	–	–	3.98	.06
Parent, 1981	ns	ns	ns	ns	ns	ns
Percent weeks unemployed, 1981						
Expected wages	ns	ns	-2.80	-.05	-2.80	-.05
Percent weeks worked, 1980	-.200	-.26	–	–	-.200	-.26
Illegal activities						
Property	ns	ns	ns	ns	ns	ns
Drugs	ns	ns	ns	ns	ns	ns
Violence	6.78	.11	.97	.02	7.75	.13
Married, 1981	ns	ns	–	–	ns	ns
Parent, 1981	4.27	.07	–	–	4.27	.07
Percent weeks out of labor force, 1981						
Expected wages	ns	ns	-4.41	-.07	-4.41	-.07
Percent weeks worked, 1980	-.315	-.41	–	–	-.315	-.41
Illegal activities						
Property	6.65	.11	ns	ns	6.65	.11
Drugs	ns	ns	ns	ns	ns	ns
Violence	ns	ns	1.52	.02	1.52	.02
Married, 1981	-3.03	-.06	–	–	-3.03	-.06
Parent, 1981	ns	ns	ns	ns	ns	ns

(continued)

Table 8.8 (continued)

	Type of effect					
	Direct		Indirect		Total	
	B	Beta	B	Beta	B	Beta
II. Commitment Model						
Percent weeks worked, 1980						
Prior experience	.120	.24	.002	.00	.122	.24
School status						
Dropout	-11.47	-.16	-.884	-.01	-12.35	-.17
Student	-9.20	-.15	ns	ns	-9.20	-.15
Graduate	-	-	-	-	-	-
Work commitment	ns	ns	ns	ns	ns	ns
Intentions to work	10.33	.05	ns	ns	10.33	.05
Illegal activity						
Property	ns	ns	-	-	ns	ns
Drugs	ns	ns	-	-	ns	ns
Violence	-4.94	-.06	-	-	-4.94	-.06
Married, 1980	9.61	.13	ns	ns	9.61	.13
Parent, 1980	ns	ns	ns	ns	ns	ns

Percent weeks worked, 1981						
Weeks worked, 1980	.521	.50	–	–	.521	.50
Illegal activities						
Property	ns	ns	ns	ns	ns	ns
Drugs	ns	ns	ns	ns	ns	ns
Violence	-6.95	-.08	-2.57	-.03	-9.52	-.11
Married, 1981	4.07	.06	–	–	4.07	.06
Parent, 1981	ns	ns	–	–	ns	ns
Percent weeks unemployed, 1981						
Percent weeks worked, 1980	-.199	-.26	–	–	-.199	-.26
Illegal activities						
Property	ns	ns	ns	ns	ns	ns
Drugs	ns	ns	ns	ns	ns	ns
Violence	6.78	.11	.983	.02	7.76	.13
Married, 1981	ns	ns	–	–	ns	ns
Parent, 1981	4.28	.07	–	–	4.28	.07
Percent weeks, OLF, 1981						
Percent weeks worked, 1980	-.321	-.42	–	–	-.321	-.42
Illegal activities						
Property	6.70	.11	ns	ns	6.70	.11
Drugs	ns	ns	ns	ns	ns	ns
Violence	ns	ns	1.59	.03	1.59	.03
Married, 1981	-3.14	-.06	–	–	-3.14	-.06
Parent, 1981	ns	ns	ns	ns	ns	ns

UNIVERSE: White male civilians, not enrolled in school 1981, 18 years old or older, N = 1177.

–: coefficient not calculated as part of model.

ns: coefficient not significant at .10 level.

While expected wage in 1980 has a substantial indirect effect upon subsequent labor force participation, leaving this variable out of the model, as done in the commitment analysis, makes no substantial change in any of the estimated coefficients, so that the second panel of table 8.8, the commitment model, tells essentially the same story as the first panel, the economic model.

Results for young women. For young women, the crime scales are neither predicted by variables in the model nor predictive of other outcomes. Ironically, it is among young women that the commitment variables explain employment, although there are no significant relationships with any of the crime scales. Children exert a very strong dampening effect on employment in both 1980 and 1981, while marriage is significant only in the latter year. The magnitudes of the coefficients linking the human capital variables to employment are somewhat smaller for the young women than for the young men, but all estimates are of the same general order of magnitude.

III. Conclusions

Despite the sensitivity of the subject material, one conclusion from this analysis is an assurance that the measures of delinquent behavior and police involvement seemed to produce reasonable and consistent results both with respect to each other and with respect to previous findings. By any measure, criminal or disruptive behavior is widespread. Marijuana and its derivatives have been used at least once by almost half of the total sample, and use is particularly prevalent among young adults. Fewer than half of the respondents report never having been involved in any of the criminal activities on the index. One-third of the males report some form of police contact.

Sex and enrollment status had strong and consistent relationships with all measures. Enrollment status, which to a large extent reflects self-selection, has a much more consistent relationship with both delinquent behavior and with involvement with social control systems than do unselected demographic categories like race and poverty. The weak and inconsistent relationships of race and poverty with self-reported delinquent behavior, while counter to the popular stereotypes of delinquents or adult criminals, are in line with findings from previous studies using self-report measures (Hirschi 1969; Ageton and Elliott 1978). Middle income and white youth are not much different in their reports of delinquent behavior from poor and minority youth.

The discrepancies between delinquency patterns from self-report and from police contact data have generated much debate in the criminological literature.[24] Gradually, these discrepancies have been reduced. Recent work indicates that the association between social class and official records is weaker than had previously been assumed. Race remains the area of the most serious inconsistencies, with self-reports indicating much lower race ratios than police records. NLS data also show this discrepancy: we find no evidence that the poor or the minority youth engage in more criminal activity, but these groups are progressively more likely to be found at more serious levels of involvement with the criminal justice system, probation and incarceration.

Other processes than bias in the criminal justice system have been advanced to account for the observed patterns. Ageton and Elliott's work suggests that, while similar proportions of whites and blacks report some level of delinquent activity, black youth are more likely than whites to be found among those who commit crimes very frequently. Such highly delinquent youth are properly the focus of more intensive police and judicial attention than are the more casually delinquent.

The results for the analysis of illegal income are consistent with the notion that, while whites may participate in illegal activities as much or more than blacks, blacks are more likely to rely on crime for financial support. This implied difference in motivation for illegal actions, if observed by the courts, could conceivably justify different dispositions. That is, judges may consider that crimes committed as part of a regular pattern of income acquisition are more serious than crimes committed as part of a turbulent adolescence. Also, in determining which youths are to be dealt with by diversion, probation, or incarceration, courts may take into account the resources available to the child's family. Middle class families are more able to afford private counseling, for example, than are the poor.

Thus, when a criminal justice system does not deliberately treat youths from poor or minority homes more harshly than youth from the white middle class, socially disadvantaged youth may be more likely to end up in the correctional system. To the extent that the popular image of delinquent youth continues to exaggerate the relationship between social status and criminal behavior, the associated stigma makes it more difficult for disadvantaged youth to avoid the appearance of being a possible threat to others. The lack of direct relationship between employment and crime does not mean that classes of individuals are not disadvantaged because of social stereotypes. Clearly the social labeling process has the potential for imposing yet another barrier to employment on the poor and on blacks.

The regression results indicate that the economic model of the relationship of crime to employment is at best appropriate only for youths who have left school. For high school students, the important variables tend to be those which measure the quality of the youth's relationships with their families and their schools. If anything, delinquency among high school students is positively associated with participation in the paid labor market. The results for students are consistent if both illegal activity and employment characterize youths who are moving away from dependency on parents, and so least likely to be controlled by their ties to adults.

Role relationships, especially marriage, are also important for adults, with much weaker effects for variables relating to the family of origin. While employment measures tend not to reach traditional levels of significance for the adult population, the signs of the parameters are in the directions consistent with a substitution of illegal for legal earnings. The analysis of illegal income suggests that it may be possible to identify people who use crime as a regular source of earnings, based more on the lucrativeness of crimes committed than on the sheer frequency of offenses. Official responses to behavior, in the form of school dismissals or convictions, also seem to have an independent effect on employment.

It is somewhat ironic that factors such as living in central cities and coming from minority ethnic groups are more likely to be related to deviant activity among young women than among young men. Indeed, demographic characteristics seem generally to explain less of the behaviors under investigation than do measures of individual links with the major sources of social definitions in their lives, namely, schools and families.

The path analysis supplements the regression analysis, showing that there are weak, complex links between crime and employment. Neither the economic nor the control models are supported in detail, although each shows some significant links, at least for males. For females, crime remains largely unexplained by any of the constructs used.

The lack of relationship between the predictor variables and crime among young women may be due to the relative infrequency of illegal activities among females, or to a real sex difference in the etiology of crime, such that traditional theories based on male samples are simply invalid for females. In any case, there is no hint in the data about the causes of crime among women. The data simply replicate the known deterrent effects of young children on maternal employment.

The relationship for young men between crime and employment appears to vary both by type of offense and by the measure of labor market participation. The pattern seems to imply less a substitution of income than a matter of lifestyle.

The interpretation of these patterns may hinge on the relationships between the types of choices involved in defining labor force status. The distinction between being in and out of the labor force is basically one of self-definition: an individual decides to seek work or to pursue other activities. Once having decided to look for work, the individual may or may not find an acceptable job, and may or may not be able to hold a job once one has been found. Presumably, then, the distinction between employed and unemployed is determined both by individual choice and by the availability of jobs in the local labor market. Of course, these distinctions are more heuristic than real. In particular, the lack of suitable job opportunities for youth may lead to giving up on job search, so that the OLF status is not entirely optional.

Violent crime is not associated with weeks OLF, implying that there is no link with the decision to enter the labor market. Apparently, however, violence is associated with difficulty in getting or holding a job, resulting in more time unemployed and less time working. It seems likely that men who are prone to involvement in fights and assaults would not limit their aggressive behavior to off-work times, making them less desirable as employees. If, as has been suggested (Berkowitz 1980), violent behavior is largely impulsive, violent men may also be more likely to quit jobs in response to frustrations than are more controlled, less violent men.

The effect of property crime on being out of the labor force in 1981 demonstrates substitution of crime for employment. No association appears with either time employed or time unemployed, suggesting that the crucial factor is the decision not to participate in the conventional labor market, not merely the lack of a paying job. Since having less work experience and being a high school dropout in 1979 were significant predictors of property crime, there is some encouragement for further exploration.

The presence of children in the home was, as expected, a strong deterrent to employment for young women. However, the effects of parenthood on young men were quite unexpected. Having a child seems to be associated with higher levels of property crime and greater time unemployed and, indirectly, greater time out of the labor force. Currently, there is nothing in either the data or in standard theories of crime to explain this pattern. Relatively few young men have started families at this early age, and it may be that there are general lifestyle differences captured by the parenthood variable for young men which are associated with higher levels of property crime and unemployment.

It is tempting to interpret the overall findings as evidence that the employment-crime link is, for young men, a matter more of lifestyle than of economic rationality. Employment and unemployment among young people are in part due to forces external to the youth—economic conditions, layoffs, inability to find a job. However, being out of the labor force as opposed to in the labor force is more a matter of choice. Men with a tendency to engage in violent behavior do not seem more or less likely than others to choose to be OLF, but they may have difficulty in keeping a job, whether their leaving is through quitting or being fired. Young men who engage in property crimes, however, may be involved in a different lifestyle, characterized by early fertility (presumably indicating early sexual activity) and time spent out of the conventional labor force. These interpretations are highly speculative, but seem to be consistent with the emerging evidence on the etiology of crime.

NOTES

1. I would like to express my appreciation to Dr. Delbert Elliott for his generosity in providing both data and substantive consultation in the development of this instrument. Also freely providing the benefit of their extensive experience in this field were Drs. Lloyd Johnston, Gerald Bachman, and Martin Gold.

2. Details of this development and analysis of the validity of the self-report measures are included in Crowley (1982).

3. The factors emerged clearly only for older males and for the total sample. Possibly because the general level of participation in delinquent activities among females is so low, solutions failed to converge for either female adults, minors, or the full sample of young women.

4. Scores on the delinquency items were calculated by assigning the midpoint of the selected response category, that is, zero, one, two, four, eight, thirty-five, and a score of fifty to those who responded in the "50 or more" category.

5. See: Hirschi (1969); Williams and Gold (1972); Ageton and Elliott (1978); Hindelang, Hirschi, and Weis (1979).

6. The lack of association between race and self-reported delinquency, a fairly consistent result in self-report studies, has led to questions being raised as to the possibility of differential validity of the self-report measure. The single most comprehensive study of validity of survey measures of criminal activity does show that, for black urban males, there may be substantial underreporting, while reporting among females and among white males seems accurate within quite reasonable limits (Hinderlang, Hirschi, and Weis 1981). Thus the apparent lack of dif-

ferentiation by race may be to some extent artifactual. However, the same study indicates that the face to face interview, essentially the technique used in the NLS, produced the lowest level of underreporting of offenses. The reasons for the apparent differences in the way that black males respond to self-report instruments as compared to the responses of other groups cannot be addressed with the available information.

7. Indeed, an entire session of the 1981 annual meeting of the American Society of Criminology was devoted to the link between social class and crime, and concluded that the link was weak at best in any of the data sets investigated.

8. Since the police contact items asked for incidents over the respondent's entire life span, there is an artificial correlation between age and frequency of reported contact. Older youths have had more time to come to the attention of the police than have their younger siblings. For this reason, age will not be used as a descriptor of police contacts.

9. The comparisons of high school dropouts with other enrollment groups is complicated by the difference in age distributions. High school students are, on average, younger than dropouts, while college students and high school graduates are somewhat older. Both high school graduates and dropouts, however, are out of regular school, and presumably face similar problems in entry into adult roles. The relative age of the enrollment groups makes the comparison a conservative one, since the age difference would give the graduates more opportunity to have come in contact with the law.

10. See Brier and Feinberg (1980) for a discussion and critique of some of the econometric approaches to crime. Erlich (1981) provides an elaborate presentation of the economic approach to criminal deterrence.

11. The relationship of youth to the labor market is vastly different depending on the degree to which they have accepted adult roles. Youths still in school are expected to look for much less in terms of long term employment possibilities in their jobs, while youths who have completed their education should have a commitment to the labor market both more immediate and long range. Therefore, the analysis of the link between crime and work is run separately for in-school and out-of-school youth.

12. The lack of relationship may be in part due to the relatively small number of cases. Reservation wage was asked only of those not working as of interview date.

13. The vast majority of other family structures are female headed households. Broken homes have long been a favorite explanation for delinquency, as in Bowlby's classic paper on juvenile thieves (1946). The link has been called into question in more recent work (Wilkinson 1974). Other measures of family social background, notably presence of reading materials in the home and the employment of the mother when the youth was aged 14 were tried in the initial analysis and deleted because they produce negligible coefficients.

14. Much previous research finds that running away is a symptom of disturbed family relationships. See Blood and D'Angelo (1974).

15. Elliott and Voss (1974) actually found that dropping out reduced delinquent activity for individuals who were thereby freed from the pressures of school. Other work supporting this position include Noblit (1976), Mann (1980), and Gold and Mann (1972).

16. A truncation problem appears in the distributions for weeks unemployed and for all the delinquency indexes when used as dependent variables. Responses are constrained to be zero or greater, and there are a large number of cases with zero values—youths who report no weeks unemployed or no offenses. For these dependent variables, Tobit analysis was used as the appropriate analogue to OLS. For reservation wage and for proportion of weeks employed, truncation was not such a problem, so standard OLS techniques were applied. Due to program limitations, multivariate analyses were run on unweighted data.

17. Conceivably, some of the relationship between proportion of weeks worked and convictions could be simply a function of time during which the respondent was not available for work due to incarceration. A more refined test would eliminate convictions between interviews, but this cannot be done reliably from the level of detail available. In any case, relatively few of those convicted are incarcerated, so this factor should not be a serious bias.

18. Indicators of participation in training programs outside of regular school were included in earlier analyses and dropped due to lack of significance.

19. Hourly rate of pay was estimated using one of three figures. For youth who worked at some time in 1979 or 1980, the actual wage at the current or last job was used. If 1979 wage was used, the amount was adjusted to 1980 dollars. If a youth had not worked in either 1979 or 1980, it was assumed that the expected wage was equal to the minimum wage,

or $3.10 per hour. This assumption was made by reasoning that this sample has relatively few youth with advanced education, and that respondents who had not held a job in the past few years would expect to start in minimum or near-minimum wage positions.

Returns to employment include not only pay, but also such intangibles as job satisfaction and on-the-job companionship. However, none of these can be estimated for youth not currently employed. Job satisfaction is a function of the specific job rather than the type of worker, so that estimations based on such factors as race, education, and experience are invalid as instruments (Hills and Crowley 1983).

20. There were other considerations in limiting measurement of labor force participation in 1980 to weeks worked. In predicting the next stage of the model, labor force participation in 1981, the multicollinearity of the various labor force statuses creates problems in estimating effects. Also, an already complicated analysis becomes even more complex, and it was decided to eliminate the measures of weeks unemployed and out of the labor force between the 1979 and 1980 interviews in part to simplify the problem.

21. Note that parenthood and marriage are measured independently, since a number of youth have children prior to marriage. All combinations of the two variables occur with some frequency in the data.

22. Unstandardized coefficients are highly sensitive to the scale of measurement of the variables. Thus, a dichotomous variable such as school status will tend to have a large coefficient, while a continuous variable such as prior work experience will have a very small one. Standardized coefficients put all of the predictors on a scale based on the variance of the sample. Using standardized coefficients, it can be seen, for example, that prior work experience is very strongly linked to weeks worked, despite the small unstandardized coefficient. Since the variance of each predictor is likely to be different across groups, the unstandardized coefficients provide a better comparison across groups of the magnitude of the links between predictors and outcomes.

23. To calculate indirect effects of a variable, first identify the paths from that variable to the outcome of interest through the other variables in the model. For example, prior work experience has a direct effect on weeks worked, as shown by the significant coefficient on the arrow between the two. The indirect effect of prior work experience on weeks worked is described by the path found by following the path from prior experience to expected wage, then following the path from expected wage

to weeks worked. The magnitude of the indirect effect is calculated by multiplying the coefficients on the adjacent paths. Thus, for young white men the indirect effect of prior experience on weeks worked in 1980 is:

$$.001 * 14.00 = .014$$

The total effect is simply the sum of the direct effect and all of the indirect effects linking the predictor variable with the outcome. Roughly speaking, the interpretation of the indirect path goes like this: An increase of ten weeks in the number of prior weeks of experience increases the expected wage by one cent (.001 * 10 = .01). An increase of one cent in the young men's expected wage increases the percent of weeks worked by .14 (.01 * 14.00 = .14). Thus, by increasing the expected wage, increased work experience increases subsequent weeks worked. The analogous calculation could be made using standardized coefficients, in which case the real-world units (dollars and weeks) would be converted into points on the standardized scales.

24. For a comprehensive discussion of the history of measures of individual criminal activity and the controversies mentioned, see Hindelang, Hirschi, and Weis (1981).

REFERENCES

Ageton, S.S. and D.S. Elliott. 1978. "The Incidence of Delinquent Behavior in a National Probability Sample of Adolescents. (Project Report No. 3) *The Dynamics of Delinquent Behavior: A National Survey* MM 27552. Boulder, CO: Behavioral Research Institute.

Asher, H.B. 1976. *Causal Modeling.* Beverly Hills: Sage Publications.

Bachman, J.G. 1978. "Delinquent Behavior Linked to Educational Attainment and Post-High School Experiences." Paper presented to Law Enforcement Assistance Administration Conference on the Correlates of Crime and the Determinants of Criminal Behavior, Rosslyn, Virginia.

Bachman, J.G., P.M. O'Malley and J. Johnston. 1978. "Adolescence to Adulthood-Change and Stability in the Lives of Young Men." *Youth in Transition,* Volume VI. Ann Arbor: Institute for Social Research, University of Michigan.

Berger, R.J., J.E. Crowley, M. Gold and J. Gray. 1975. *Experiment in a Juvenile Court: A Study of a Program of Volunteers Working with Juvenile Probationers.* ISR-4055. Ann Arbor: Institute for Social Research, University of Michigan.

Berkowitz, L. 1980. "Is Criminal Violence Normative Behavior?—Hostile and Instrumental Aggression in Violent Incidents." In E. Bittner and S.L. Messinger, eds., *Criminology Review Yearbook,* Vol. 2. Beverly Hills: Sage Publications.

Blood, L. and R. D'Angelo. 1974. "A Progress Report on Value Issues in Conflict Between Runaways and Their Parents." *Journal of Marriage and the Family* 36: 486-490.

Bowlby, J. 1946. *Forty-four Juvenile Thieves: Their Characters and Home Life.* London, England: Bailliere, Tindall, and Cox.

Brier, S.S. and S.E. Feinberg. 1980. "Recent Econometric Modeling of Crime and Punishment: Support for the Deterrence Hypothesis?" *Evaluation Review* 4: 147-191.

Crowley, J.E. 1982. "Delinquency and Employment: Substitutions or Spurious Association." Paper presented at the Annual meetings of the American Society of Criminology, November 1981, Washington, DC.

_____ . 1982. "Delinquency and Employment: Substitution or Spurious Association." In Michael E. Borus, ed., *Pathways to the Future, Vol. II.* Columbus: Center for Human Resource Research, Ohio State University.

Elliott, D.S. and H.L. Voss. 1974. *Delinquency and Dropout.* Lexington, MA: Lexington Books.

Erlich, I. 1981. "On the Usefulness of Controlling Individuals: An Economic Analysis of Rehabilitation, Incarceration, and Deterrence." *American Economic Review* 71: 307-322.

Farrington, D.P. 1977. "The Effects of Public Labelling." *British Journal of Criminology* 17: 112-125.

_____ . 1982. "Longitudinal Analyses of Criminal Violence." In Marvin E. Wolfgang and Neil A. Weiner, eds., *Criminal Violence.* Beverly Hills: Sage Publications.

Gold, M. and D. Mann. 1972. "Delinquency as Defense." *American Journal of Orthopsychiatry* 42: 463-479.

Goodwin, L. 1979. "The Social Psychology of Poor Youth as Related to Employment." Paper submitted to Vice-President Walter Mondale's Task Force on Youth Employment.

Hills, S. and J.E. Crowley. 1983. "The Quality of Youth Employment." In M.E. Borus, ed., *Pathways to the Future, Vol. III.* Columbus: Center for Human Resource Research, Ohio State University.

Hindelang, M.J. 1973. "Causes of Delinquency: A Partial Replication and Extension." *Social Problems* 20: 471-487.

Hindelang, M.J., T. Hirschi and J.G. Weis. 1981. *Measuring Delinquency.* Beverly Hills: Sage Publications.

Hindelang, M.J., T. Hirschi and J.G. Weis. 1979. "Correlates of Delinquency: The Illusion of Discrepancy Between Self-Report and Official Measures." *American Sociological Review* 44: 995-1014.

Hindelang, M.J. and M.J. McDermott. 1979. *Juvenile Criminal Behavior: An Analysis of Rates and Victim Characteristics.* Analysis of National Crime Victimization Survey Data to Study Serious Delinquent Behavior, Monograph 2, Washington, DC: Office of Juvenile Justice and Delinquency Prevention, U.S. Department of Justice.

Hirschi, T. 1979. *Causes of Delinquency.* Berkeley: University of California Press.

Mann, D.W. 1980. "Disruptive Students or Provocative Schools? School Differences and Student Behavior." Paper presented at the Annual Convention of the American Psychological Association, 1980, Montreal, Quebec.

McNeeley, R.L. and Carl E. Pope. 1981. "Socioeconomic and Racial Issues in the Measurement of Criminal Involvement." *Race, Crime, and Criminal Justice.* Beverly Hills: Sage Publications.

Minor, W.W. 1977. "A Deterrence-Control Theory of Crime." In Robert F. Meier, ed., *Theory in Criminology: Contemporary Views.* Beverly Hills: Sage Publications.

Monahan, J. and D. Klassen. 1982. "Situational Approaches to Understanding and Predicting Individual Violent Behavior." In Marvin E. Wolfgang and Neil A. Weiner, eds., *Criminal Violence.* Beverly Hills: Sage Publications.

Noblit, G.W. 1976. "The Adolescent Experience and Delinquency: School Versus Subcultural Effects." *Youth and Society* 8: 27-44.

Wilkinson, K. 1974. "The Broken Family and Juvenile Delinquency: Scientific Explanation or Ideology?" *Social Problems* 21: 726-739.

Williams, J.R. and M. Gold. 1972. "From Delinquent Behavior to Official Delinquency." *Social Problems* 20: 209-228.

Wolfgang, M.E. 1977. "From Boy to Man—From Delinquency to Crime." Paper presented to the National Symposium on the serious offender, September 1977, at Department of Corrections, Minneapolis, Minnesota.